WRESTLING WITH
THE PROPHETS

WRESTLING
WITH THE
PROPHETS

Essays on Creation Spirituality and Everyday Life

MATTHEW FOX

Jeremy P. Tarcher/Putnam
a member of Penguin Group (USA) Inc.
New York

Most Tarcher/Putnam books are available at special quantity discounts for bulk purchase for sales promotions, premiums, fund-raising, and educational needs. Special books or book excerpts also can be created to fit specific needs. For details, write Penguin Group (USA) Inc. Special Markets, 375 Hudson Street, New York, NY 10014.

Jeremy P. Tarcher/Putnam
a member of
Penguin Group (USA) Inc.
375 Hudson Street
New York, NY 10014
www.penguin.com

First published in 1995 by HarperSanFrancisco

First Jeremy P. Tarcher/Putnam Edition 2003

Library of Congress Cataloging-in-Publication Data

Fox, Matthew, date.
Wrestling with the prophets : essays on creation
spirituality and everyday life / Matthew Fox.—1st
Jeremy P. Tarcher/Putnam ed.
p.   cm.
Originally published: [San Francisco, Calif.]:
HarperSanFrancisco, ©1995.
Includes bibliographicall references.
ISBN 1-58542-235-5 (alk. paper)
1. Creation.   2. Spiritual life—Christianity.
3. Nature—Religious aspects—Christianity.
4. Mysticism.   5. Postmodernism—Religious aspects—
Christianity.   I. Title.

BT695 .F68   2003   2002072149

Printed in the United States of America
10   9   8   7   6   5   4   3   2   1

TO MY STUDENTS AND FACULTY, co-workers all, at ICCS and FCS over the years, in celebration of our common wrestling with prophecy and mysticism.

And to my brother Bill Everson (1912–1994), poet, mystic, and prophet, who never ceased his wrestling with demons, angels, prophets, and mystics.

CONTeNTS

WRESTLING WITH

THE PROPHETS

INTRODUCTION

WHAT DO Karl Marx, Hildegard of Bingen, Meister Eckhart, Julian of Norwich, Thomas Aquinas, Howard Thurman, Teresa of Avila, Mechtild of Magdeburg, Francis of Assisi, M. D. Chenu, and Otto Rank all have in common? They are all prophets wrestling in their times with the demons of inertia and injustice, of closed minds and closed hearts. They each attempted to live and speak a path of awakening and enlivening, a path that interfered (Rabbi Heschel's definition of what prophets do) with the prevailing attitudes and ideologies of their day. Otto Rank calls this the mark of true saintliness or heroism: living beyond the psychology of one's day. He believes that Jesus did this and did it successfully and that the greatness in each of us is manifested when we too live beyond the psychology of our day.

Today we are all being invited to live beyond the psychology of our times, for we are being invited to move from the modern to the postmodern era. No one is exempt from this passage. Thus, the lead essay in this book attempts to demarcate what will characterize the postmodern period. David Ray Griffin, founder of the Center for a Postmodern World, indicates two directions for postmodernity: that of deconstruction and that of reconstruction. Creation Spirituality is a postmodern movement that does deconstruct (for example, by shining a harsh spotlight on the devastating results of Saint Augustine's narrow definitions of sin and church and his overriding patriarchal dualisms) but that nevertheless is also thoroughly committed to reconstruction.

Whether honoring the wisdom of native peoples of Australia, Africa, or the Americas, or inviting the artist to lead us in meditation practices, or hearing the new creation story from science, Creation Spirituality chooses to give birth rather than merely to criticize the shortcomings of the modern worldview. Indeed, the act of giving birth constitutes the primary prayer activity in the Creation Spiritual tradition, as indicated in the essay "Deep Ecumenism, Erojustice, and Art as Meditation."

Creation Spirituality offers an invitation to reconstruct religion itself by moving from an original sin ideology to an original blessing or original grace consciousness as a starting point for spirituality; by moving from anthropocentric attitudes to a cosmological and therefore ecological attitude; and by letting go of the three paths of spirituality that have dominated our naming of the journey (that of purgation, illumination, and union) in favor of the four paths of the Via Positiva (awe and delight), the Via Negativa (darkness, letting go, and suffering), the Via Creativa (creativity), and the Via Transformativa (compassion, celebration, and justice making). This rhythm of deconstructing and reconstructing could so invigorate religion itself that religion would regain its primal meaning, to re-legere—that is, to teach people to reread their lives and stories and nature itself, seeing them now as a home for the sacred.

To address the pressing issues of our time, such as the need for an Environmental Revolution and an ecospiritual consciousness (see essays 2, 3, 4, 5), we need not only to interfere as prophets do but also to celebrate as mystics do. This celebration lies not only in our response to beauty and awe but also in our willingness to go into the dark together, to grieve, let go, forgive, empty, and be emptied—in short, to taste nothingness together and in this sense to celebrate pain. All this—the celebration of the blessing of life and the journeying into the collective dark night of the soul—is a journey the mystics name for us. To be a prophet is to be a mystic. "The prophet is the mystic in action," the American philosopher William Hocking wrote early in this century. Thus, Karl Marx, Hildegard of Bingen, Meister Eckhart, Julian of Norwich, Thomas Aquinas, Howard Thurman, Teresa of Avila, Mechtild of Magdeburg, Francis of Assisi, M. D. Chenu, and Otto Rank are each mystics as well as prophets. We have much to learn from them since we— every citizen on the planet today—called as we are to be spiritual warriors on behalf of the Environmental Revolution, need to be both prophet *and* mystic.

If it is the prophet's task to *act*, what is it the mystic does? The mystic *sees.* The mystic beholds, holds being up for examination and wondering at. The mystic *listens* and beholds being in that way as well. The mystic awakens and is awakened. This is one reason why the mystic and the artist and the prophet are such integral allies in the spiritual journey of awakening *and* struggling.

This life path is not as foreign and strange as the modern era has made it out to be. Mysticism was ridiculed in the modern era but not in the premodern (which is one reason I return to the medieval mystics and to the native peoples so often in these essays and in my own life for refreshment, challenge, and nourishment). When communities form that are grounded in the trust of their experience of the Spirit, then mysticism and prophecy can become common gifts among us once again. Then our wrestling with the prophets becomes also our wrestling with the mystics. And the wrestling is not just with persons who lived in another age or another culture but with our own times, our own demons, our own issues, including AIDS and earth peril and youth despair. It becomes a wrestling with our own souls in order to see them more honestly, more profoundly, to honor

their power and to purify their intentions, to plumb their
depths of forgiveness, compassion, humor, and joy, while
linking up with others on soul journeys to healthy empowerment and justice making.

Spirituality is about power and empowerment. That is
why it interferes with power structures, power ideologies,
and the power toxins residing in the souls of all of us. Spirituality is about a different kind of power than our modern
cultures have been preaching. It is about spirit power, the
power of joy and letting go, of simple living and conscien-
tious giving through healthy work and healing graces.

In the Creation Spiritual tradition, all persons are understood
to be born mystics—we are all here to say yes to life. In addition, all persons have within them the capacity to be
prophets, to stand up and say no to injustice and what inter-
feres with life. These essays serve as reminders of our spiritual depths, our shared spiritual journeys, our shared
struggle. They have been written over a period of sixteen
years. To me, they represent the themes of the movement, in
both theory and praxis, from modern religion to postmodern spirituality. To maintain the integrity of the original
thought in each essay, an occasional concept or short citation
may be retained that is repeated in another essay.

To say that our becoming mystics and prophets again
need not be a foreign task is not to say that it is easy. Wrestling
is not easy. What is easy is denying that our souls and institutions need deep reconstruction. We need to wrestle anew
with the lost, banished, wounded, and ridiculed mystic in
our own souls, in the souls of our religions, and in the souls
of our cultural institutions. We also need to wrestle anew
with the prophet in us and in our ancestral traditions. Becoming a prophet is never an easy task; prophets are seldom
popular in their lifetimes or in their own countries. And so
the theme of *wrestling* seems very appropriate for these essays.

Wrestling is an ancient archetype for the spiritual task, as theologian Arthur Waskow points out in his book, *God-Wrestling*.

> It would be easy if Things-As-They-Might-Be and Things-As-They-Ought-To-Be were utterly separate: if there were two basic principles in the universe, struggling against each other. But to assert that the two are ultimately One! as the Torah asserts. . . . To face a God who teaches that merciful loving kindness is strict justice. . . . With such a God a fully human being must wrestle. . . . To wrestle with God is also to wrestle with human beings—ourselves and others.[1]

To wrestle with the prophets who are also mystics, both inside and outside ourselves, is to wrestle with the Godself, to wrestle with the face of God. Just as Jacob did. And when Jacob arose from his long night of wrestling with God, not only was he wounded and limping, he also had his name changed to *Israel*—that is, "one who wrestles with God." The Godwrestler. We who descend from the spiritual tradition of Israel, whether we name ourselves Jew or Muslim or Christian or have consciously rejected all of these names, we are, all of us, Godwrestlers.

My hope is that these essays may encourage our deep wrestling and our coming out of the closet as mystics and prophets. The suffering of the earth and earth creatures, the despair of our young people, the emptiness of our souls that sets us up for addictions on such an immense scale—all this argues for a spiritual awakening, for a living out of Creation Spirituality in our daily lives.

NOTE

1. Arthur I. Waskow, *God-Wrestling* (New York: Schocken Books, 1978), 10.

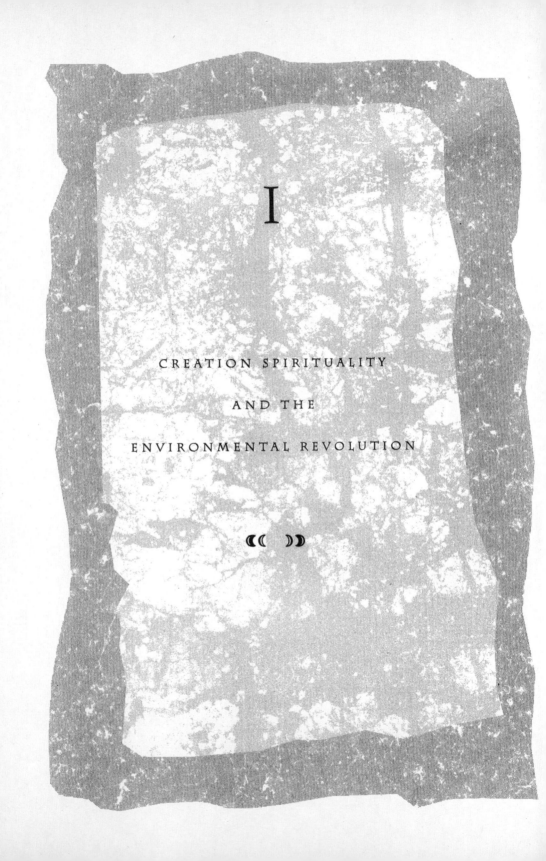

I

CREATION SPIRITUALITY

AND THE

ENVIRONMENTAL REVOLUTION

《《 》》

CHAPTER 1

A Mystical Cosmology:
Toward a Postmodern Spirituality

☾

We are emerging from the modern age into a postmodern one. In this essay I explain how this paradigm shift is affecting spirituality and how Creation Spirituality is in many ways a postmodern spirituality. Geologian Thomas Berry has commented that "ecology is functional cosmology." If this be true, then the ecological crisis is also a crisis in cosmology. Without the return of a mystical cosmology, we will not have the tools or the energy to be instruments of an "Environmental Revolution."

THE MODERN ERA VERSUS SPIRITUALITY

From the point of view of spirituality, the modern era has
been devastating. It has tainted our souls to the point that we
no longer even know what *soul* means; it has cut the most
powerful instrument of humankind—our science—adrift
from conscience, morality, and wisdom; it has trivialized
economics and politics; it has waged war on Mother Earth
and her children with increasing vengeance and success, fulfilling Francis Bacon's command that we "torture mother
earth for her secrets"; it has set our youth adrift without
hope or vision; it has bored people in what ought to be the
great communal celebration known as worship; it has legiti-
mated human holocausts and genocides, from that of the
seventy million native people exterminated in the Americas
between 1492 and 1550 to that of the six million Jews, as
well as many Christians and homosexuals, murdered in German death camps. Lacking a living cosmology, the modern
era has sentimentalized religion and privatized it, locating it
so thoroughly within the feelings of the individual that the
dominant religious force of our civilization is that pseudo-
religion known as fundamentalism.

In this essay I trace some elements of a postmodern spirituality that are possible and emerging already in practice as
well as theory in this country and abroad. For fifteen years I
have been involved in a postmodern spiritual practice and
theory called "Creation Spirituality." Many of my observations will be gathered from my experience of that practice
and theory. Our thinking about spirituality cannot take place
from armchairs or academic towers but must include the
dirtying of the hands, the stretching of the heart, the opening of the mystic inside, the practice of the "unselfconsciousness" (Eckhart's word) of the child or fool, the
awakening of the right brain, the encountering of our greatest mystics of the past and present, the struggle for justice

on many levels of society and its institutions and of our psyches, and the coming together of mystical traditions of East, West, North, and South. This inherently nondualistic methodology of *doing spirituality* is not unlike the call from Liberation Theologians of Latin America and the so-called Third World to combine *praxis* with reflection on that practice. If this is necessary for theology, it is even more necessary for spirituality.

Spirituality is about heart knowledge and about awakening the being in us. We need to learn just to be. I have learned as much from sitting in sweat lodges, attending Sun Dances and powwow dances, and attempting a practice of celibacy or of fasting as I have from reading histories of spirituality. No area of intellectual life suffers more from Cartesian educational one-sidedness—that is, from the modern world's definition of truth as "clear and distinct ideas" (Descartes)—than does spirituality. Experiences are seldom clear and distinct. They demand an exercise of our right brains. Here lies the authentic meaning of the word *asceticism*: to exercise our right brains.

Spirituality is not only about doing and exercising to be and become; it is also about power. During the modern era, there was an almost exclusive emphasis on spirituality as "asceticism"—the term *ascetic theology* was first coined in 1655. Ascetic spirituality came to be understood as self-imposed deprivations that would bring about an altered state. This model of spirituality fit the Cartesian and Newtonian machine model of the universe very neatly and offered the added attraction of feeding the inherent need of an industrial society (society as machine) to be sadistic—that is, in control. Such a society needs masochists on which to run and over which to rule. Appeals to ascetic spirituality played into such needs very conveniently during the modern era. The result was that spirituality was not identified with power but with the relinquishing of power.

True spirituality, however, is about power. It is about developing the powers of creativity, justice, and compassion in all persons. It is about unleashing the divine powers in us all. It is about grounding persons and communities in the powers that will enable them to survive and even flourish in the midst of adversity. Was Gandhi a powerful person? Or Martin Luther King Jr.? Or Dorothy Day? Or Thomas Aquinas? Or Francis of Assisi? Or Hildegard of Bingen? Were Mozart, Marc Chagall, and Gustav Mahler powerful? Is the spirituality of nonviolence not a spirituality of a kind of power that is alternative to the ways of our modern civilization? "The prophet is the mystic in action," as William Hocking used to teach.[1] The mystic has somehow managed to imbibe the powers of the universe, the powers of the cosmos.[2] The power that the spiritual person imbibes is not human-made power; in fact, the mystic contributes to the redefinition of power in a culture—Jesus, for example, found power in compassion rather than in legalism and institutional sadism. He paid the price of a prophet for so doing. Jesus too was a person with power—the power to heal, to awaken, to excite, to transform. Such spiritual leaders are, of course, dangerous. In our day, feminists like Adrienne Rich are helping to redefine power.[3]

Where does the practice and the development of power in spiritual practice ultimately come from? It comes from one's cosmology, from the world in which one lives, from the universe itself. When Immanuel Kant separated the laws of the "starry heavens without" from the "moral law within," he was introducing a dualism into the religious consciousness of the West that would suck all power out of morality and render it passive vis-à-vis the true decision makers of industrial civilization. Kant was, in effect, depriving modern men and women of their cosmic power. He was rendering them sentimentalized, powerless regarding the

powers of the world, leaving them only the power of their
own inner feelings and of buying things. Not only Kant but
the entire modern era did this to spirituality; it emasculated
it and feminized it, in the pejorative use of that term employed by Anne Douglas in *The Feminization of American Culture*.[4]
It rendered spirituality a "womanly thing," in the pejorative,
dualistic, and patriarchal use of the term *womanly*. That is, it
rendered spirituality passive and inert. This was a very useful
thing for a massively patriarchal society to accomplish; it
allowed patriarchy to run wild with its militarism and war
games, with its bloated left-brain definitions of schooling,
with its rape of Mother Earth, with its disregard for youth,
with its replacement of a mystical sexuality with its own
industry of pornography, with its replacement of authentic
worship—which is always a matter of relating microcosm
to macrocosm—with words.[5]

A dualism that haunts spirituality to this day is that between individual and society, or the personal and the communitarian. A living spirituality, one built on experience,
power, and cosmology, would never acquiesce even to the
naming of such a dualism. In fact, spirituality is the naming,
and the living out, and the feeding of the vision of the
people—yes, it must be personally appropriated at a deep
level of commitment; but no, it is never private or capable
of being privatized. I would propose, along with historian
M. D. Chenu, that a society's renaissance is by definition a
spiritual event, a "rebirth based on a spiritual initiative."[6]
Without a growing consensus as to what spiritual values a
community shares and what spiritual practices it engages in,
there can be no renaissance, no rebirth of the community.

I propose, then, that all of these themes—spirituality as
practice, as power, as the basis for a community's rebirth—
represent a shift from the modern to the postmodern era of
spirituality.

STEPS TO A POSTMODERN SPIRITUALITY

I would characterize a postmodern spirituality as occurring in five steps.

1 *The most critical change between the modern and postmodern era in spirituality has to be the emergence of a living cosmology on which to base a living spirituality.* Newton's picture of the universe as a machine; Descartes's dualism between object and subject; Kant's insertion of moral law into our "souls," cutting them off from the universe; Bacon's dualistic ferocity against nature and women, which assumes that we are not nature—all this rendered authentic mysticism impossible during the modern era. What Max Weber called the "disenchantment of the world"—a prime characteristic of the modern era—might also be called the death knell of mysticism. The denial of the mystic has continued right up to our own day and is evident in both cultural pathologies and in seminary classrooms—Catholic, Protestant, and Jewish—where our next generation of presumed spiritual leaders learn next to nothing of their own mystical heritage: where, for example, courses on the Wisdom literature of the Bible, which is the cosmological and mystical literature of the Bible, have been practically nonexistent and where practices in spirituality such as art as meditation are next to invisible. Would-be scientists get academic credit for hours spent in laboratories, but would-be spiritual leaders get no credit for hours spent in art-as-meditation classes where prayer and mysticism are learned, where the right brain is developed and the link between microcosm and macrocosm is experienced. Just as it was scientists and their kept philosophers who got us into this antimystical bias, so, ironically, it is scientists who are leading us out of it. It was Einstein himself who said that "mysticism is the basis of all true science" and that "one who cannot stand rapt in awe is as good as dead."[7] Awe is what mysticism is all about—it begins with awe, as Rabbi Abraham Heschel makes clear ("Awe precedes faith," he writes)[8] and as Meister Eckhart declared in his sermon on "amazement."[9]

Cosmology reawakens our awe at being here. "Truly it is glorious, our being here," declares Rilke.[10] For cosmology gives us a story about how we came to be here—a story in the full context of the universe and its coming to be here—and how we fit into that story. Cosmology is thereby three things: it is the scientific story of our being here and our coming to be here (however one defines "scientific"—ancient peoples all had their scientific story of how we came to be here); it is mysticism, or our psychic response to the awe of our being here; and it is art—that is, the expression of our response to the amazing news that we are here.

Einstein, like Moses of old, has led us from the bondage of Newtonian mechanism to a certain wandering in the desert that may eventually result in a promised land, one flowing with the milk and honey of a living cosmology. In my opinion, it is no accident that Einstein was a Jew and thus had imbibed the Jewish spirituality from Wisdom literature, which taught that the "spirit of the Lord fills the whole universe" (Wis. 1:7). Jewish cosmology teaches that the universe is one and that we are part of it and can know our place in it. It is no secret that premier scientists, such as Nobel Prize winner Ilya Prigogine, Erich Jantsch, Brian Swimme, Fritjof Capra, Loren Eiseley, Alfred North Whitehead, Niels Bohr, and Lewis Thomas, are readmitting the essential mystery of the universe from microcosm (atomic levels) to macrocosm (galactic levels).[11] The fact that the scientific stories being told today are transcultural and that scientists are leading in the telling augurs well for the repollination of the mystical brain of humanity, for a reenchantment of the universe. As more and more scientists come out of the closet as mystics, more and more other persons will be given the courage to do the same, persons from all professions and ways of life—even, eventually, the ordained ones. Mysticism means, etymologically, "to enter the mysteries." Science, with the rediscovery of the mystery of nature that comes with it, is today inviting us all to enter the mysteries of our being here. This invitation represents the rebirth of a civilization, the lighting of the fire of a living cosmology.

2 How this translates theologically can be put in the following manner: *we need to move from the Quest for the Historical Jesus to the Quest for the Cosmic Christ.*

My book, *The Coming of the Cosmic Christ*, goes into considerable depth on this subject, but let me summarize a few salient points.[12] Yale church historian Jaroslav Pelikan, in a recent book, says that the "Enlightenment deposed the Cosmic Christ and made the Quest for the Historical Jesus inevitable."[13] Pelikan's observation stands as a landmark critique of the modern era of biblical scholarship. All the weapons of theological scholarship during the modern era have been amassed around the Quest for the Historical Jesus. While this has not been an altogether fruitless task—the agreement on Jesus' words and on his identity as prophet has been useful—it is a task that is for the most part completed.

Were theology to redirect its immense energies around the Quest for the Cosmic Christ, new treasures would be unearthed that are exactly the mystical treasures that a new cosmology requires—treasures about the role of cosmology in the Gospels as well as the cosmic hymns of the Christian Scriptures; treasures about "deep ecumenism" or the role of the Cosmic Christ in non-Christian spiritual traditions ranging from Israel to Goddess religions to Native American and Eastern religions; treasures about what true worship can and ought to accomplish when it is placed once more in the proper setting for worship—namely, a living cosmology;

treasures about redoing relationships between *puer* and *senex*, between young and old; treasures about the awakening to folk art and about the awakening of eros, that is, of mystical sexuality, which needs to inspire creativity at all levels of culture and religion. (All these are treated in my book.)

Above all, treasures would be unearthed about the holiness of being, the holiness and theophany of Mother Earth and her amazing accomplishments. In the tradition of the Cosmic Christ—the tradition that every atom and every galaxy is a "glittering, glistening mirror" of divinity (Hildegard's words)—we have a regrounding for a spirituality of reverence for all being, for all of Mother Earth. We relearn our own dignity and responsibility in the context of our own divinization. "Every creature is a word of God and a book about God," says Meister Eckhart. In this tradition we have the groundwork for an ecological spirituality that is truly transcultural as well. Who ever heard of a Buddhist ocean, a Lutheran sun, a Roman Catholic rain forest, or an Islamic cornfield? The Cosmic Christ represents a deep archetype almost totally ignored in the modern era—one that can revitalize religion itself and biblical studies in particular. It once again puts scientist and theologian to work on a common—and worthwhile—task.

3 *A third step is the rediscovery of the creation mystics of the Middle Ages.* Thomas Kuhn points out that one of the characteristics of a paradigm shift is that what was previously considered trivial now becomes central.[14] Just as the cosmological texts of the Bible—those of the Wisdom literature—have been considered trivial during the modern era, so too have the mystics of the Middle Ages. But in fact, the period we call the Middle Ages was the last time the West had a living cosmology, and the great mystics of that era therefore have much to teach us today. They all understood the Cosmic Christ theology of which I speak, and they lived it out in prophetic forms of social and institutional renewal. I speak of Hildegard of Bingen, Francis of Assisi, Thomas Aquinas, Mechtild of Magdeburg, Meister Eckhart, Julian of Norwich, and Nicolas of Cusa. The latter has been called by British physicist David Bohm a significant influence on his work. The fact that the seminary training of Protestants and Catholics today ignores the living cosmology of which these mysticprophets boast is a sign of the intellectual decadence bequeathed us by the modern era. Westerners cannot recover our spiritual roots without the gift of these great cosmological mystics of our past and the tradition they represent—a tradition that is thoroughly grounded in Scripture as well as in practice of a personal and a social-justice kind.

4 *A fourth step is a deepening of our images both of God and of our relationship with divinity.* One gift of any viable spirituality is to awaken us to living—and often forgotten—images of divinity. When religion and society become tired, so do their images of God. A spiritual renaissance always involves an awakening to new, although often very ancient, divine images. Following are a few that the modern era managed to bury for three hundred years.

God as Mother

This ancient image, celebrated in our Scriptures in Second Isaiah and the Psalms and deeply developed by the medieval mystics, is essential for a society that wishes to recover the sense of creativity as a divine activity. "What does God do all day long?" Eckhart asks. He answers, "God gives birth. From all eternity God lies on a maternity bed giving birth."[15] And Julian of Norwich writes, "Just as God is truly our Father, so also is God truly our Mother." God "feels great delight to be our Mother," and "God is the true Father and Mother of Nature and all natures that are made to flow out of God to work the divine will."[16]

God as Below, Not Above

The dominant spiritual symbol during the patriarchal era and the modern era has been that of "climbing Jacob's ladder." Such symbolism reinforces hierarchical ladder climbing and escape from the earth. I have criticized this symbolism elsewhere in writing of the need to move from "climbing Jacob's ladder to dancing Sarah's circle."[17] The sky god alone cannot awaken the deep levels of creativity and eros for which the modern era has left humanity starving. When Meister Eckhart says that "God is a great underground river that no one can dam up and no one can stop," he is reimaging divinity for us. Hildegard does the same in painting the divine waters as an "abyss" from which Wisdom arises and the Christ arises and in painting Sophia as a mermaid—that is, as the goddess Ea or the *magna mater*, the great mother of the sea.[18] To relocate divinity in the depths of nature and of the self is to reencourage an entire civilization to listen to its creative powers and to allow those powers to emerge once again. Divinity most emerges from the depths of human creativity. Not surprisingly, this is also the place from which the demonic most readily emerges. When ordinary persons are deprived of their creativity, the creativity of the Pentagon and of wasters of our forests and soil will take over.

Godhead, Not Just God

The tradition of the two sides of divinity—that of God and that of Godhead—has been roundly ignored in mainline theologizing during the modern era for the same reason that mysticism has been ignored. Divinity is not just God; it is also Godhead. What is the difference? Meister Eckhart says that "God acts but the Godhead does not act."[19] Godhead represents the absolute mystery of divinity, our deepest origins from which we came and to which we shall return. The

Godhead is nonjudgmental; "no one missed me where God ceases to become," says Meister Eckhart.[20] In the Godhead there is total unity and utter silence. There, all things are one. God is that side of divinity that engages itself in history and in creation; therefore, God becomes as creatures themselves become and unfold. "Before creatures were, God was not yet 'God.' "[21] Humans are invited to experience and undergo both sides of the Divinity—God in history as well as the Godhead of mystery. It is more than coincidence, I believe, that the words for "God" in Latin and German are masculine (Deus and Gott, respectively), while the words for "Godhead" are feminine (Deitas and Gottheit, respectively). Godhead is a mystical term for divinity, and there is something cosmically maternal about it. "You are hugged by the arms of the mystery of God," declares Hildegard of Bingen.[22] The modern era of spirituality, so committed to patriarchy, lost a sense of the living Godhead.

God as Beauty

The modern era lost the sense of beauty as a theological category and a spiritual experience. Descartes actually developed a philosophy without an aesthetic anywhere to be found in it! Yet during the West's cosmological period, Thomas Aquinas and other creation mystics, such as Francis of Assisi, talked of God as Beauty. "God is the most beautiful thing there is," Aquinas writes. "God is superabundant beauty."[23] Tellingly, Aquinas gets this imaging of divinity from the Eastern church, namely from the sixth-century Syrian, Denis the Areopagite. Eastern Orthodoxy never lost the Cosmic Christ and therefore never discounted the experience of beauty as the experience of divinity or, indeed, the naming of beauty as God and God as beauty.[24] It never succumbed to Saint Augustine's ignoring of cosmology that set the West up for the split between science and mysticism.

A Trinitarian Divinity

For all its call to orthodoxy around such doctrines as the
Trinity, the modern era of spirituality, driven by and almost
obsessed by the Quest for the Historical Jesus, has itself
practically committed a heresy of Christolatry (or better,
Jesusolatry). Where is the theological ink spent on God as
Creator? Does it in any way balance out the emphasis given
"my relationship with Jesus" or our redemption by Jesus?
Traditionally, Christians considered three articles of faith as
summarized by Luther: (1) creation, (2) redemption, and
(3) sanctification (which ought to be understood in the
mystical or Cosmic Christ tradition as our divinization). Yet
the modern era has so zeroed in on the second of these
three that the first and third points are left hanging—and
with them the spiritual experience and theological grounding for a God who is Creator and who is Spirit, Sanctifier or
Divinizer. No one could accuse Western Enlightenment theology of developing a theology of the Holy Spirit—which is
one reason the West is so easily set up for pseudospiritu-
alisms ranging from charismatic flight-from-justice spiritualities to fundamentalist Holy Roller ones. The creation
mystics bring a healthy, dialectical, Trinitarian divinity back
to our images and archetypes.

The Cosmic Christ

Perhaps the archetype that most summarizes the very ancient
and premodern as well as postmodern images of divinity is
that of the Cosmic Christ. The Cosmic hymns celebrate this
Christ as the one "who holds all things in unity" (Col.
1:17), who "sustains the universe by his powerful command" (Heb. 1:3), "in whom all things have their being"
(John 1:3), and whom "all the living things in creation—
everything that lives in the air, and on the ground, and
under the ground, and in the sea" praise (Rev. 5:13). The

tradition of the Cosmic Christ answers Gregory Bateson's question, "What is the pattern that connects?"[25] The Cosmic Christ describes the pattern that connects as just, loving, and essentially friendly toward the universe and all things, humans included. The Cosmic Christ, then, being the divine image in every atom and every galaxy, grounds a global morality in reverence for being. As Teilhard de Chardin put it, "Christ, through his Incarnation, is internal to the world, . . . rooted in the world, even the very heart of the tiniest atom."[26] The tradition of the Cosmic Christ also represents the Goddess and Gaia tradition in the West. The Goddess tradition is about divinity's immanence in all things and in the celebration of creation. So too is the tradition of the Cosmic Christ.[27]

Integral to the tradition of the Cosmic Christ has always been a development of the doctrine of sanctification, not in terms of Augustine's neurotic and egotistical question—"Am I saved?"—but in terms of the tradition of our being Cosmic Christs.[28] Are we divinized, and, if so, what is the evidence for it? Mechtild of Magdeburg and other mystics from the medieval era, when a Cosmic Christ theology thrived in the West, are blunt as to our divinization: it means our being instruments of compassion understood as justice making and celebration. Says Mechtild, "Who is the Holy Spirit? The Holy Spirit is a compassionate outpouring of the Creator and the Son. This is why when we on earth pour out compassion and mercy from the depths of our hearts and give to the poor and dedicate our bodies to the service of the broken, to that very extent do we resemble the Holy Spirit."[29]

Panentheism

The modern era, in its immense dualism and compulsion to control—even God and certainly the Goddess—has left us

with two options by which to envision humanity's relationship to divinity. One of these is by way of theism (of which
Deism is just a logical outcome). Theism teaches that we are
here and God is out there somewhere. (Deists simply put
God farther out.) One problem with this image of our relationship with divinity is that it literally kills the soul, as Jung
warned when he said that one way to kill the soul is to
"worship a God outside you." It also destroys any semblance
of Jesus' teaching—a primary datum of the Quest for the
Historical Jesus movement is that Jesus did indeed preach
and that his primary theme was the "kingdom of God is
among you."

The second option offered up by the modern era for
imaging the human's relation to the divine has been that
era's widely heralded stance of atheism. In many respects, theism asks for atheism and invents it. If the only alternative I
had was theism or atheism, I would be an atheist myself.

A God who has wound things up and does not care
enough to be present at their unfolding invites not only neglect but denial. I am convinced that 99 percent of atheism
in the modern era has in fact been antitheism—which, in
my opinion, represents a wise rejection of the only God
served up by this era.

Other images of our relationship with divinity do exist,
however, if one goes back beyond the modern era. One is
pantheism, which teaches that all is God and God is all. While
at first blush this appears to be a Cosmic Christ doctrine, it
falls short, because it too ends up controlling divinity and
eliminating divine surprises and mystery, which carry us beyond what already is. In short, it denies the transcendence of
the divine. For that reason it has rightly been understood as
heretical; it arrogates just too much to creation as it stands.

Still another image of our relationship to the divine is
that of panentheism. This is, in my opinion, the truly adult,

truly mystical, truly appropriate imaging of the relationship between the divine and nature (remembering—as the modern era did not—that humans *are* nature). I am not alone in this opinion; all my creation-centered mystical brothers and sisters of the Middle Ages concur. Mechtild of Magdeburg declares that "the day of my spiritual awakening was the day I saw and knew I saw all things in God and God in all things."[30] This is a precise naming of panentheism: "all things in God and God in all things." This perfectly orthodox naming of our relationship to divinity is alluded to in the vine-and-the-branch imagery of John 15 as well as in Acts, which says, "God is the one in whom we live, move, and have our being" (Acts 17:28). Meister Eckhart is as strong as I am about the essential need to envision divinity in panentheistic categories. "Ignorant people falsely imagine," he writes, "that God is outside of things. Everything that God does or creates, he does or creates in himself, sees or knows in himself, loves in himself."[31] Hildegard of Bingen actually painted a picture of panentheism—that is, of all creation existing in the belly of divinity—a divinity she called "Love" and a "Lady."[32]

Panentheism is one way of understanding the unfolding of God, for if creatures that exist within divinity are being constantly created and recreated, then divinity is also being affected. As Eckhart puts it, "God becomes where all creatures express God."[33] "What is creative," says Eckhart, "flows out but remains within." Creation is itself this way in relation to divinity.[34] Thus, panentheism, while being deeply curved and maternal in its imagery, also allows for the historical or undeveloped to happen. It combines elements of immanence and transcendence. The latter is understood as the "not yet"—not as what is above. Historical transcendence with spatial immanence, one might call this. Another name for it would be a prophetic mysticism or a mystical prophecy,

where prophecy means a changing of history, a critique of
history, and an interference with history. History and mystery
come together in a panentheistic understanding of our relationship to divinity. Its image is not one of linear "progress"
(a heresy of modernistic thinking), nor is it an image of
repetitive cycle (an image the East offers too blithely). Rather
it is imaged as an ever-expanding spiral.

Panentheism destroys that dualism of dualisms bequeathed to us by the modern era: the dualism of God/
nature and God/us. "Everything that is in God is God," said
Thomas Aquinas, citing a twelfth-century synod.[35] Once
again, the tradition of the Cosmic Christ emerges as a dominant archetype in a postmodern spirituality. Panentheism, by
picturing our creative relationship to the Creator, also en-
courages creativity itself. Images of God do that for a civilization—or they do the opposite. Theism kills creativity as a
spiritual imitation of divinity. Panentheism demands it.

5 *A fifth step to a postmodern spirituality is to name the mystical journey
in Four Paths.* It is curious how beholden the modern era's
naming of the spiritual journey has been to Plotinus and
Proclus, third- and fifth-century individuals who were neither Jewish nor Christian and who named the spiritual journey in the all-too-familiar fashion of the three ways of
purgation, illumination, and union. A postmodern spirituality must consciously reject this naming of the spiritual journey not only because it is utterly nonbiblical but also
because it does not correspond to the depth experience that
mystics of our time are having. Awe, wonder, delight, creativity, and justice are left out. This is a lot to leave out in a
time of an awakened cosmology. Let us consider briefly the
Four Paths of the Creation Mystical Journey, because they—
and not the three ways—will constitute the postmodern
spiritual journey.[36]

Path One: Via Positiva Our first experience of the divine is in
terms of the delight, awe, and wonder of our being here.
"Radical amazement," Rabbi Heschel calls it, and this experience is available to all of us on a daily basis, provided we
are ready to undergo such ecstasies—be they in nature, in
our work, in relationship, in silence, in art, in lovemaking,
even in times of suffering.[37] "Just to be is a blessing, just to
live is holy," says Rabbi Heschel. This intuition that creation
is indeed a blessing, and the response of gratitude for it,
constitute the experience of the Via Positiva. This is what
drives so many scientists, working as they do with the won-
ders of nature, to mysticism, to what Einstein described as
"standing rapt in awe." It is about seeing the Cosmic Christ
in all things, including oneself. As Meister Eckhart put it,
"when I flowed out of the Creator, all creatures stood up and
shouted and said, 'Behold, here is God!' They were
correct."[38]

Path Two: Via Negativa Our second journey into the mystery of
divinity and ourselves is that of experiencing the darkness—
of letting go and letting be. In this movement, we "sink
eternally from letting go to letting go into God," as Meister
Eckhart puts it.[39] The sinking may be through meditation
practices that allow us to let go of sensory input, such as
fasting, Zen sitting, celibacy, or sweat lodges. Such letting go
leads to a return to our source, a return to our origins. A
letting go of words and images is essential to this journey;
it is essential to a postmodern spiritual practice because so
much of the modern era is wordy (part of the price we pay,
no doubt, for an awakening of the left brain and for the fear,
in a patriarchal and "enlightenment" era, of the dark, of
silence, of what cannot be controlled).

Another way we undergo the Via Negativa is by way of
suffering and pain. Letting pain be pain is an essential ingre-

dient in learning from pain and in experiencing the dark. It is also essential for letting go of pain. As Mechtild of Magdeburg put it, "from suffering I have learned this: that whoever is sore wounded by love will never be made whole unless she embrace the very same love which wounded her."[40] The "dark night of the soul," the time when, in Mechtild's words, "the lantern burns out and we are reminded of our nothingness,"[41] can be a bottoming-out experience of profound spiritual depth and a source for new birth. God is not only a God of light (the cataphatic divinity of the Via Positiva) but also "superessential darkness," as Eckhart puts it (the apophatic divinity). In many ways the divinity we experience on Path One is God, while the divinity of Path Two is the Godhead, which is a "mystery within mystery who has no name and will never be given a name."[42]

Path Three: Via Creativa The modern era did not highlight creativity as a moral imperative, as the basic spiritual discipline, or as the most important ingredient of a living cosmology. Yet that is what is required in a postmodern era, one that carries us beyond the notion that the universe is already completed or is a machine in motion. In the creation mystical tradition the center of the spiritual journey is creativity itself. Paths One and Two—our experiences of delight and of darkness—culminate in Path Three, creativity. (And Path Four, as we shall see below, flows out of Path Three.) From the point of view of Christian theology, the incarnation and creation, which constitute Path One, plus the crucifixion and *kenosis* (emptying), which constitute Path Two, culminate in the resurrection—the creative rebirth of Path Three.

Creativity lies at the core of the creation journey because this is what it means to be divinized or sanctified—namely, to be *like God*. But who is God? God is Creator, God is constant birther of the universe, and we are called to be cocreators with God. We birth, for example, the Cosmic Christ who is uniquely us when we birth ourselves. The primary spiritual practice in Creation Spirituality is that of art as meditation, wherein we come to grips with our images: trusting them, birthing them, accepting responsibility for them, and taking the consequences of them.[43] Delight itself is one of the consequences of birthing our images. Meister Eckhart declares that it is good to be a virgin, namely one emptied of images, Via Negativa, but it is better to be a "fruitful wife."[44] For it is "by our fruits that they will know us," as Jesus warns about testing the spirits of mysticism.

When Meister Eckhart celebrates how we are "heirs of the fearful creative power of God,"[45] he is naming the Via Creativa for us. Our creativity is truly fearful, because it can lead to more weapons bent on destroying the earth, on the one hand, or on recreating jobs and society, on the other. Our divine power—creativity—is also our demonic power. Human choice is never of greater consequence than in the journey of the Via Creativa. It is in our creativity that we are called to choose between images. A fascist society would have us always choose their images, those of the ruling elite. But art as meditation grounds persons to listen to and then to choose their own deepest images; it grounds persons to know their treasure—which is hidden in the field of our psyches—and to cherish it, choose it, and put it out there. As Eckhart puts it, "what is true cannot come from the outside in but must come from the inside out and pass through an inner form."[46]

It is no small thing that contemporary science has reestablished creativity and generativity as basic laws of the universe and that, at the same time, we rediscover the creation-centered mystical tradition that insists that our entire spiritual journey culminates in what we give birth to. Here we have a powerful instance of the rebirth of a cosmology: science and mysticism agreeing on the importance of creativity once again.

Path Four: *Via Transformativa* While creativity lies at the heart of the universe and at the heart of the human psyche and spiritual journey, it finds its fullest expression in the transformation of society itself. This transformation is an issue of *compassion*, the response to an interdependent universe in which "all beings love one another" (Eckhart).[47] Because of this fact, celebration and justice making are meant to reign as the basis of all political action and structure. The spiritual journey culminates in compassion, as in Jesus' words, "be you compassionate as your Creator in heaven is compassionate" (Luke 6:36). And compassion means both celebration and healing by way of justice making. Path Four constitutes a theology of the Holy Spirit, because the Holy Spirit is the Spirit who anoints all as prophets to "interfere" with the causes of injustice and its multiple expressions in racism, sexism, militarism, adultism, impersonal capitalism, and impersonal socialism. As the Holy Spirit worked to end the babbling symbolized by the Tower of Babel at the original Pentecost event, when persons of all races and countries and cultures understood the Good News, so too this same Spirit works to bring persons together today around the Good News of humanity's power and responsibility to heal Mother Earth, to celebrate our shared existence, and to revere creation.

Justice making lies so at the core of the creation journey that Meister Eckhart could declare, "The person who understands what I say about justice understands everything I have to say."[48] Justice, after all, is not an anthropocentric invention any more than is interdependence or compassion. Rather, in a living cosmology, justice as well as interdependence are laws of the universe and *therefore* (in contrast to

Kant) laws by which humanity ought to be living. A living cosmology regrounds humankind's politics in the laws of the universe. This is the primary gift that wisdom brings. The modern era has sought knowledge, not wisdom. A post-modern spirituality seeks wisdom along with its knowledge.

The Four Paths of the creation journey never end. They constitute the dynamic of the ever-expanding spiral journey which never ends as long as we are alive. As Eckhart says, "God is delighted to watch your soul enlarge."[49]

TOWARD A POSTMODERN SPIRITUALITY: A SUMMARY

We can summarize the paradigm shift from modern to post-modern spirituality in terms of the following elements:

1 From anthropocentric to cosmological

2 From theistic (and deistic and atheistic) to panentheistic

3 From left brain (analytic) to both left brain *and* right brain (synthetic)

4 From rationalistic to mystical

5 From patriarchal to feminist

6 From the Quest for the Historical Jesus to the Quest for the Cosmic Christ

7 From knowledge to wisdom

8 From the three ways of Plotinus and Proclus to the Four Paths of Creation Spirituality

9 From linear to spiral

10 From modern alone to an inclusion of premodern, modern, and postmodern spiraling

11 From climbing Jacob's ladder to dancing Sarah's circle

12 From obedience as the dominant virtue to creativity in birthing compassion as the dominant societal and personal virtue

13 From the sectarianism and piecemealness of the Newtonian parts mentality to the deep ecumenism of an era of the Cosmic Christ in all world religions

14 From dualism (either/or) to dialectic (both/and)

15 From sentimentalism to a passionate embrace of awe at our existence

16 From a flight from the world to a commitment to social and personal transformation

17 From Eurocentrism to a celebration of the wisdom of ancient and primordial peoples' spiritualities of micro- and macrocosm

18 From worship as words—read, preached, and sung—to worship as a nonelitist celebration of our shared existence

19 From divinity in the sky (theism) to divinity of Mother Earth crucified (the mysticism of the Cosmic Christ theology).

In his last book scientist Gregory Bateson asked the following question: "Is the human race rotting its mind from a slowly deteriorating religion and education?"[50] If our minds are being rotted by religion itself, it is because religion has lost its very core, which is the experience of a mystical cosmology. The same is true of education. Religion needs science and science needs religion, as Einstein insisted. The best hope for our planet is a recovery of a living, mystical cosmology. That can happen, as we let the modern era recede, by incorporating a celebration of the mystical along with a celebration of the analytical. In this way we would be moving toward a postmodern spirituality like the one I have attempted to outline in this essay. And we as a species would experience a rebirth of art, politics, and spirituality that would constitute an authentic global renaissance.[51]

NOTES

1. See William Hocking, *The Meaning of God in Human Experience* (New Haven, Conn.: Yale University Press, 1912), 511.

2. Writes cosmologist-physicist Brian Swimme, "We sometimes fall into the delusion that power is elsewhere, that it belongs to a different group, that we are unable to find access to it. Nothing could be further from the truth. The universe oozes with power, waiting for anyone who wishes to embrace it. But because the powers of cosmic dynamics are invisible, we need to remind ourselves of their universal presence. Who reminds us? The rivers, plains, galaxies, hurricanes, lightning branches, and all our living companions" (*The Universe Is a Green Dragon* [Santa Fe, N.M.: Bear & Co., 1985], 151).

3. See Adrienne Rich, *The Dream of a Common Language* (New York: Norton, 1978).

4. For critical studies of this sentimentalizing of mass culture in the modern era, see Anne Douglas, *The Feminization of American Culture* (New York: Knopf, 1977), and Matthew Fox, "On Desentimentalizing Spirituality," *Spirituality Today* (March 1978): 64–76.

5. On the vital role of worship in connecting micro- and macrocosm, see Otto Rank, *Art and Artist* (New York: Agathon Press, 1932), 113–15.

6. M. D. Chenu says that renaissance "literally involves new birth, new existence in all the changed conditions of times, places, and persons" (*Nature, Man, and Society in the Twelfth Century* [Chicago: University of Chicago Press, 1968], 3).

7. Albert Einstein, *Ideas and Opinions* (New York: Crown Publishers, 1982), 39, 11.

8. Abraham Heschel, *God in Search of Man* (New York: Farrar, Straus, and Cudahy, 1955), 77. See the excellent study of "Wonder and Awe" in Heschel's thought in John C. Merkle, *The Genesis of Faith: The Depth Theology of Abraham Joshua Heschel* (New York: Macmillan, 1985), 153–72.

9. See Meister Eckhart, "Sermon Two," in Matthew Fox, ed., *Breakthrough: Meister Eckhart's Creation Spirituality in a New Translation* (Garden City, N.Y.: Doubleday, 1980), 65–67.

10. Stephen Mitchell, trans., *The Selected Poetry of Rainer Maria Rilke* (New York: Vintage, 1984), 189.

11. Ilya Prigogine and Isabelle Stengers say, "Today the balance is strongly shifting toward a revival of mysticism, be it in the press media or even in science itself, especially among cosmologists" (Ilya Prigogine and Isabelle Stengers, *Order out of Chaos* [New York: Bantam Books, 1984], 34).

12. See Matthew Fox, *The Coming of the Cosmic Christ* (San Francisco: Harper & Row, 1988).

13. Jaroslav Pelikan, *Jesus through the Centuries* (New Haven, Conn.: Yale University Press, 1985), 182.

14. Thomas S. Kuhn, *The Structure of Scientific Revolutions* (Chicago: University of Chicago Press, 1970), 103.

15. Matthew Fox, *Meditations with Meister Eckhart* (Santa Fe, N.M.: Bear & Co., 1982), 88.

16. Brendan Doyle, *Meditations with Julian of Norwich* (Santa Fe, N.M.: Bear & Co., 1983), 71, 75.

17. For a fuller discussion of this basic mystical symbol change, see Matthew Fox, *A Spirituality Named Compassion* (San Francisco: Harper & Row, 1979), 36, 67.

18. See Matthew Fox, *Illuminations of Hildegard of Bingen* (Santa Fe, N.M.; Bear & Co., 1985), 773.

19. See Fox, *Breakthrough*, 78.

20. Ibid., 77.

21. Ibid., 215.

22. Gabrielle Uhlein, *Meditations with Hildegard of Bingen* (Santa Fe, N.M.: Bear & Co., 1982), 90.

23. Thomas Aquinas, *De divinis nominibus, c. IV,* 1.v, nn. 343–56.

24. Nicholas Berdyaev, writing from the Russian Orthodox tradition, declares that "the beauty of a dance, a poem, a symphony, or a picture enters into eternal life. Art is not passive, but active, and in a sense theurgic [that is, a work of cocreation with God]" (*Slavery and Freedom* [New York: Charles Scribner's Sons, 1939], 171–72).

25. See Gregory Bateson, *Mind and Nature: A Necessary Unity* (New York: Bantam Books, 1979), 8–10.

26. See the excellent study by J. A. Lyons, *The Cosmic Christ in Origen and Teilhard de Chardin* (Oxford, England: Oxford University Press, 1982).

27. See Charlene Spretnak, *Lost Goddesses of Early Greece* (Boston: Beacon Press, 1978), 42–47.

28. Krister Stendahl says that Augustine "was the first person in Antiquity or in Christianity to write something so self-centered as his own spiritual autobiography. . . . With Augustine, Western Christianity with its stress on introspective achievements started. . . . The introspective conscience is a Western development and a Western plague" (*Paul among Jews and Gentiles* [Philadelphia: Fortress Press, 1976], 16–17).

29. Sue Woodruff, *Meditations with Mechtild of Magdeburg* (Santa Fe, N.M.: Bear & Co., 1982), 117 (henceforth abbreviated *Mechtild*). Compassion is also the ultimate divine attribute for Meister Eckhart and the culmination of the spiritual journey, because "whatever God does, the first outburst is always compassion" (see Fox, *Breakthrough*, 417–546).

30. Woodruff, *Mechtild*, 42.

31. Fox, *Breakthrough*, 73.

32. Fox, *Illuminations*, 38–41.

33. Fox, *Breakthrough*, 77.

34. Ibid., 65.

35. Thomas Aquinas, *Compendium theologiae*, 37, 41. The synod referred to is the Synod of Rheims, held in 1148.

36. I elaborate at length on the Four Paths and twenty-six themes of Creation Spirituality in *Original Blessing* (Santa Fe, N.M.: Bear & Co., 1983). On Eckhart's outlining of the Four Paths, see my "Meister Eckhart on the Fourfold Path of a Creation-Centered Spiritual Journey," in Matthew Fox, ed., *Western Spirituality: Historical Roots, Ecumenical Routes* (Santa Fe, N.M.: Bear & Co., 1981), 215–48.

37. For a fuller elaboration of natural ecstasies, see Matthew Fox, *Whee! We, wee All the Way Home: A Guide to a Sensual, Prophetic Spirituality* (Santa Fe, N.M.: Bear & Co., 1981), 43–54.

38. Fox, *Breakthrough*, 302.

39. Ibid., 174.

40. Woodruff, *Mechtild*, 69.

41. Ibid., 61.

42. Fox, *Breakthrough*, 175.

43. See Matthew Fox, "The Case for Extrovert Meditation," in *Spirituality Today* Vol. 30 (June 1978): 164–77, and Mary Caroline Richards, *Centering* (Middletown, Conn.: Wesleyan University Press, 1964).

44. Fox, *Breakthrough*, 274.

45. Ibid., 405.

46. Ibid., 399.

47. Matthew Fox, *Meditations with Meister Eckhart*, 26.

48. Ibid., 5.

49. Fox, *Breakthrough*, 146.

50. Bateson, *Mind and Nature*, 109.

51. For more on this global renaissance, see Fox, *The Coming of the Cosmic Christ*.

CHAPTER 2

Religion As If Creation Mattered

☾

This essay was originally a lecture given at the E. F. Schumacher Society in autumn 1992. My talk followed one by Lester Brown of the Worldwatch Institute in which he called for an "Environmental Revolution" within twenty years and said that the number one obstacle to that revolution was human "inertia."

WHAT WOULD AN ecological and sustainable religion look like? Is the universe sacred or not? The universe with its eighteen-billion-year history—the universe with its one trillion galaxies. Can our species recover the sense of the sacred? In the West, humankind has been involved in a gross desacralization of this planet, of the universe, and of our own souls for the last three hundred years, and there lies the origin of our ecological violence. Can we recover the sense of the sacred?

It seems to me that religion's future is not in religion as such. Religion has to learn to let go of religion. As Meister Eckhart said in the fourteenth century, "I pray God to rid me of God" in order to rediscover the spirituality that is at the heart of any living, authentic, and healthy religion. Spirituality is the praxis of the heart, the praxis of our living in this world. It means dealing with our inner selves and not just living on the level of our outer selves.

E. F. Schumacher, in his prophetic way, named for me this very same issue in his epilogue to *Small Is Beautiful* when he said, "Everywhere people ask, 'What can I actually do?' The answer is as simple as it is disconcerting. We can, each of us, work to put our own inner house in order. The guidance we need for this work cannot be found in science or technology, the value of which utterly depends on the ends they serve. But it can still be found in the traditional wisdom of humankind." And as he wisely pointed out in his introduction, wisdom comes from two sources: nature and religious traditions.

Thomas Aquinas in the thirteenth century said that revelation comes in two volumes—the Bible and nature. But theology since the sixteenth century has put so much emphasis on the word—meaning the word in the book called the Bible, the word of the professor and the academician, or the word in the fundamentalist sense, whether from the Vatican or from the Bible—that we have put all our eggs in the basket of the word, the human word. We have forgotten the second source of revelation, that of nature itself.

Meister Eckhart said, "Every creature is a word of God and a book about God." In other words, every creature is a Bible. How do you approach that biblical wisdom, the holy wisdom of creatures? You approach it with silence. You need a silent heart to listen to the wisdom of the wind and the wisdom of the trees and the wisdom of the waters and the soil. We have lost this sense in our obsessively verbal culture, since the printing press was invented in the sixteenth century. Schumacher said we are now far too clever to survive without wisdom.

The British scientist Peter Russell has said: "The root of our environmental crisis is an inner, spiritual aridity. Any truly holistic environmental policy must include this in its approach—we need not only to conduct research in the physical and biological sciences, but to explore the psychological and more sacred sciences." We need to explore our inner houses. When I think of the term *inner house*, I remember that the soul is not in the body. The inner house is not this little thing situated in the pineal gland, which Descartes called the soul. All our great cosmological mystics—Hildegard of Bingen, Thomas Aquinas, and Meister Eckhart—said that the soul is not in the body; the body is in the soul. The body is an instrument of our passions, of what we really care about, of our grief, of our wonder. Exploring the inner house of our soul means listening to the deep self. I would propose that this exploring of the inner house is not just your personal inner house but the inner house of our communities, the inner house of our nations, the inner house of our gender, the inner house of our species. In other words, the inner house is not just part of an individual; rather, our whole way of life contains an inner house. It is because we are violent inside that our environment is dying all around us. We are fouling the nest in which we live.

So this exploration of our inner house has everything to do with the ecological era, if for no other reason than that the word *ecology* means the study of our home. Ecology is not something "out there." We are in nature and nature is in us. The sacred wilderness is not something "out there" in our national parks. There is a sacred wilderness inside every one of us, and it needs our attention. We are out of touch with the sacred wilderness of our passions in the West. That is why we see such devastation all around us.

The paradigm of religion in our time must be the recovery of a mystical tradition. The British monk Bede Griffiths has been living in India for the last fifty-five years, and I have had some encounters with him in the past year. During one of these encounters he said, "If Christianity cannot recover its mystical tradition and teach it, it should simply fold up and go out of business. It has nothing to offer." To that I say amen. The churches are empty and the souls of our young people are being possessed by despair. It does not have to be this way; we can recover our mystical tradition, for there is a mystic in every one of us, yearning to play again in the universe. When you develop mysticism, you are beginning to develop prophets. As the American philosopher William Hocking said, "the prophet is the mystic in action." Carl Jung wrote in this century that "belief is no substitute for experience." The mystic in every one of us trusts his or her experience of the divine—the divine in nature and in the deep journeys of the dark night of the soul, which open our hearts by breaking them. And when our hearts break, the divine comes through in a different form. This trust in our experience is the basis of all mysticism. The psalmist says, "Taste and see that God is good." Mysticism is about tasting. There is no such thing as vicarious mysticism:

the pope can't do it for you, your parish rector can't do it for you, you can't rent a mystic, not even in California! We are moving into an era in which we must all take responsibility for our mystical lives, calling on the wisdom of our ancestors and the wisdom of our communities, including, of course, the wisdom of the non-two-legged community that is constantly feeding us its revelation and truth and teaching us that we can still taste and see that divinity is good. Aquinas in the thirteenth century put it this way: "The experience of God must not be restricted to the old or to the few." We do not need a lot of professional mystics; we all need to wake up to our own mysticism.

I want to speak about the development of our spiritual journeys, that inner life which is the basis of a healthy outer life, of healthy action. Healthy action is based on nonaction, and we in the West must give more attention to the issues of nonaction if we are to create a truly authentic revolution, a real change of history. In *Steps to the Ecology of Mind*, Gregory Bateson says, "The hardest thing in the Gospel is that of Saint Paul addressing the Galatians when he says, 'God is not mocked.' This saying applies to the relationship between humanity and ecology. The processes of ecology are not mocked." In other words, the earth has been keeping a ledger about the ozone layer, the pollution of the atmosphere, the deforestation, and so on, because the earth will not be mocked. As Hildegard of Bingen said in the twelfth century, "there is a web of justice between humanity and all other creatures." She said that if humanity breaks this web of justice, then God permits creation to punish humanity. It is not an avenging God but creation that is already responding with cancer and leukemia. The earth is not mocked. Bateson then analyzes the three main threats to human survival. The first is technological progress, the second is population increase, and the third consists of certain errors in the thinking

and attitudes of Western culture—our values are wrong. This
is where healthy religion comes in. Healthy religion is still in
touch with the masses in three-quarters of the world. In fact,
it is my belief that only Western civilization over the last
three hundred years has added to its vocabulary the word
atheism. We invented atheism in response to our silly theism.
When we put God up in the sky behind the machinelike universe and put in one hand an oilcan that he would use once
in a while to keep the system going, then theism seemed
too silly to comprehend, and a-theism or no-theism was the
result. If we relate to God as an object "out there," we are
setting ourselves up for ecological devastation and for a complete dismissal of the sacred within our lives. Otto Rank said,
"Therapists heal people one to one, artists heal people in
groups, but religious prophets heal the masses."

If we have only twenty years left, as Lester Brown says,
then we have to start awakening the masses, and the ordinary route for awakening the masses, as Otto Rank observed,
is religion, the sacred traditions. Healthy religion would af-
fect our conventional attitudes toward our bodies, toward
health, toward wholeness, toward the sacredness of all creatures in whole new ways. I am talking about a religion as if
creation mattered. It will teach us spirituality, it will teach us
ways to live nonviolently with ourselves and therefore with
others. To retrieve this kind of wisdom, we need to look at
our own spiritual tradition, which have often been condemned within the same religious tradition. The greatest
saint of the creation tradition, Hildegard of Bingen, was
ignored for seven hundred years after her death. Francis of
Assisi was sentimentalized and put in a birdbath! We have to
liberate him from that birdbath. Thomas Aquinas was condemned three times and then made a saint. Meister Eckhart
was condemned and is still on the condemnation list six
hundred years later. Julian of Norwich was ignored. Her

book was not published until three hundred years after her
death. All these creation mystics carry within them some
of the wounds of the minority traditions in the West. The
creation-centered Celtic people of Britain in the seventh century had their nature mysticism smothered at the Council of
Whitby and gradually taken away from them, but it is because the Celts settled all the way down the Rhineland that
we have these great Rhineland mystics like Hildegard of Bingen and Eckhart. These people were steeped in a creation-
centered spirituality, a spirituality that begins with original
blessing instead of original sin, because, to begin with, original sin is radically anthropocentric. Sin is only as old as the
human race—four million years old at the most. The universe is eighteen billion years old! I deny the prominence
that the Western church has given to original sin. It has fed
this anthropocentrism. It is so egoistic to think that religious
experience begins with our sins. I believe that religious experience begins with awe and wonder. That is the first step
in the spiritual journey. Awe is the beginning of wisdom.
There can be no compromise on this truth. The first step
toward spiritual revolution is to recover awe and wonder in
our time, and this is, in fact, a rather easy task, because we
are being given a new creation theory from science itself, a
new cosmology about how our species got here, how this
planet got here, and no one can hear this story without
being filled with awe and wonder.

To hear that all the elements of our bodies were birthed
by a supernova explosion five and a half billion years ago,
which unites us with all the elements in the universe, is
awesome. To hear that in the first seconds of the fireball, decisions were made eighteen billion years ago on our behalf,
that the temperature of the fireball had to be within one degree of what it was for this planet to evolve, is awesome.
And that is how it happened. When you hear these stories

tumbling out of the mouths of scientists, it is no wonder
that they are leading the way to mysticism today. I hear the
echo of Julian of Norwich in the fifteenth century, who said,
"We have been loved from before the beginning."

Unconditional love is the first lesson of the new creation
story, and it is the lesson of all the mystics as well. When
you put science and mysticism together, you have cosmology bubbling up. When the artist gets on board and tells
these stories in song and dance, music and ritual, then
you have a renaissance, then you have a revolution in our
species, a spiritual rebirth based on a new vision. All this
awe is the starting point for a spiritual life. Aquinas put it
this way: "All things have been made in order that they imitate the divine beauty in whatever possible way. Divine
beauty is the cause of all states of rest and motion, whether
of minds or spirits or bodies."

My friends, we have not heard the word *beauty* held up
as a theological category for three hundred years. Descartes,
the father of Western academia and the father of Western
science, built a whole philosophy without any mention of
beauty or aesthetics. Native people cannot believe that
beauty is not a category for the divine in the West. The last
time we had a cosmological spirituality in the West was in
the Middle Ages where there was a celebration of the beauty
of God. Francis of Assisi said, "God is Beauty," and Aquinas
mentioned that all of us share and participate in the divine
beauty. This speaks to us at the most radical level and causes
us all to fall in love again. The first step in the ecological
journey is to fall in love with the beauty of this place, so that
we will defend it and liberate it when injustice threatens it
and abuses it. Rabbi Heschel said, "Just to be is a blessing,
just to live is holy." Heschel explains that there are three
ways in which we humans respond to creation. The first way
is to enjoy it, the second is to exploit it, and the third way is

to accept it with awe. I propose that our Western civilization has never practiced the third way—at least not *as a civilization* in the last few centuries. Awe was taken out of the classroom because Descartes defined truths as ideas, so all our educational systems have been modeled on the left-brain search for truth.

We have become a one-sided, psychically unjust civilization because we have not been nurturing the right side of our brain, where the experience of awe occurs. Our species has to redefine our relationship to nature, including in this sense of awe the wonder of our being here. This is why I dismiss the stewardship model in theology as being totally inadequate for the ecological era and an Environmental Revolution. The stewardship model tells us that God is "out there"; it is theistic. God is an absentee landlord, and we are here to do God's dirty work and steward the earth. Therefore, we have a duty-oriented morality—but you cannot arouse people by duty. You can make them feel guilty, you can pressure them, but the idea of duty morality only goes back to Kant. It is part of the Enlightenment. Let it go.

Aquinas said that you change people by delight, you change people by pleasure. The proper model for theology for an ecological era is not stewardship, which reinforces theism. The proper model is mysticism, the Cosmic Christ and the Garden in the Song of Songs, where we realize that God is the Garden, that God is expressed in the word, and the plants, the trees, the animals, and the soil. And when these are being jeopardized, God is being crucified all over again. When they are splendid and healthy, divinity itself is radiating its *doxa*, its glory. The Cosmic Christ is radiating its glory.

A shift from the duty-oriented stewardship ethic to mysticism and the Cosmic Christ is the basis for an ecological spirituality, because it is more truthful. This is the home, the *ecos* in which we live; it is the divine home. Divinity is everywhere, but our eyes have to learn to see again. Another dimension to ecological spirituality is the very word *environment*. It comes from the French word *environ*, which means "around." The proper theology for our era is not about a God out there somewhere; it is about a God who is around us, or, as Julian of Norwich said, "who is completely enveloping us." It is a very maternal image of God; Hildegard of Bingen said, "You are hugged by the arms of the mystery of God." This is pan-entheism, which is altogether orthodox (if that is important to you), and it teaches us that everything is in God and God is in everything. That is the proper way to name our relationship with the divine today. It is the mystical way, and all mystics experience this. Mechtild of Magdeburg, a social activist and feminist of the thirteenth century, said that "the day of my spiritual awakening was the day I saw, and knew I saw, all things in God and God in all things." That is the day we grow up spiritually, and if we don't have the resources in our culture to assist us in that growing up, if we do not hear the teachings of the mystics, then we have to go out and demand them. Just as we need to take back our bodies from the medical industry, so too do we have to take back our souls from the professional ordained ones who are not doing their job, because they themselves have been wounded in the seminaries and through a reductionist education that has not taught them how to be mystics, even though they probably were as young people. I can tell you of hundreds of priests and rabbis over the last twenty years who have told me they didn't have one class on mysticism, spirituality, or the Cosmic Christ—all the archetypes that are in fact in our tradition but that have been ignored because there is no room for them in a left-brain academic setting.

Lester Brown uses an important word when he speaks of *inertia*. The medievals had a word for this that is very deep. They called it *acedia*, which includes laziness and a refusal to

begin new things. Inertia is one dimension, but acedia includes depression and sadness. I would like to turn now to
how our spiritual tradition can address acedia. Because that is
the issue: how do you awaken the masses? How do we
awaken ourselves? Paul put it this way in his second letter to
the Corinthians: "The sadness of the age is busy with death."
I was so aware of this last January when the American government aroused the people and sent four hundred thousand
human beings halfway around the world with an untold ton-
nage of weapons. They aroused the people, but over what?
Going to war. We have not managed to arouse our people
over the despair in the cities, the treatment of the soil. It is
just as Paul said, the sadness of the age is busy with death.
We only wake up to see death, our entertainment. Death is
now about the only thing that arouses us. Aquinas said, "Despair comes from the loss of belief in our own goodness, and
the loss of awareness of how our goodness relates to the divine goodness." In other words, it is a blessing theology that
is the response to despair and the response to acedia or inertia. It is when you get excited about the goodness of things
that you are prepared to act. Again I will use the phrase *falling
in love*. We have anthropocentrized falling in love—we think it
is something you do to find a mate for the rest of your life—
but I propose that we can fall in love several times a day for
the rest of our lives. You could fall in love with the galaxies—
there are one trillion out there! Every day you could fall in
love with one galaxy and still, on your deathbed, leave many
virgins for the next generation! You could fall in love with
species of wildflowers, of which there are still ten thousand
on this planet; you could fall in love with fish and plants,
trees, animals, and birds, and with people, especially those
who are different from us. This capacity for being in love has
no limit, and it is all about experiencing blessing. Aquinas
said, "To bless is nothing else than to speak the good." We

bless God, and in another way God blesses us. We bless God
by recognizing the divine goodness, so we must take some
time to meditate on the goodness of things, the goodness of
the forests, of healthy clean air and water. God blesses us by
causing goodness in us. We have to take time to meditate on
our own blessing, on how we are uniquely good, because
there has never been another collection of DNA like ours in
the history of the universe, and every single person is a
unique expression of the Cosmic Christ. As the mystics say,
everyone is a unique mirror of God. That is why there is such
a diversity of creation: to delight divinity. That is why all
creatures are here: for the sake of delight.

So we must let go of the original sin ideology that has
us growing up with shame and guilt about being here,
which in turn creates compulsions of perfectionism and
more guilt. The fact is, my friends, all creatures are imper-
fect—let us celebrate that. I think divinity purposefully
matched our imperfections with one another, so we need
one another and must build relationships with one another,
and there is glory and beauty within the imperfection. Every
tree is beautiful, but if you go up close, it has its dead ends,
its knots, and its broken branches. We are all that way too,
and there is no shame in that. The shame is in wallowing in
it and not paying attention to our goodness, which is deeper
because it is so unique. Aquinas said that the sin of acedia,
the sin of inertia, is a sin against the commandment to enjoy
the sabbath, because what the word Sabbath meant in the creation story of the Jewish people is that God spent the Sabbath delighting in creation; we have to recover that delight
in creation. That is how we fill our hearts, which yearn for
awe. When we delight in creation, it is a spiritual praxis.

The second path of the spiritual journey is what the
mystics call the Via Negativa, the negative way. It is the way
of darkness, it is the way of despair, it is the way of grief.

The first path, Via Positiva, is the way of light; the second, the way of grief. Our hearts are daily broken with facts about what humankind is doing to the earth. Despair and grief hit us, but the first thing to do is to pay attention to that grief and to let it be, to journey with the grief, to journey into the darkness. The mystics call it the dark night of the soul. My friends, today our whole species is involved in the dark night of the soul, but that is not necessarily a bad thing. It can be the beginning of radical conversion, the beginning of new life. But first we have to take that journey, not unlike the one Jesus on the cross took into despair, when he said, "My God, my God, why have you forsaken me?" Bede Griffiths says in his book *The River of Compassion*, "It is significant that the experience of despair is a yoga. Despair is often the first step on the path to spiritual life, and many people do not awaken to the reality of God and the experience of transformation in their lives until they go through the experience of emptiness, disillusion, and despair."

As a civilization today, we are going through this emptiness, disillusion, and despair, and we need the mystical tradition to support us, because God is found not only in the light and glory of creation but also in absolute darkness. The mystical naming of the God of the Dark is the Godhead. I am sure very few of us have ever heard one sermon on the Godhead (I had one theological class on it), but that is the tradition of the God of the Dark. The God of the Light is active, cocreating and redeeming, but the Godhead does nothing, the Godhead is pure being. The image I have of the Godhead is a great big cosmic Mama with creation on her lap. Eckhart believed that we were born out of the Godhead: we began in the Godhead, we travel through life in this world, and then we return to the Godhead. He said that when you return, no one will ask you where you have been or what you have done, because in the Godhead there is such total unity that no one will have missed you. Maybe there is no final judgment after all, there is just this return.

Our anger is part of the Via Negativa. Anger and grief always go together. Of course we are angry. If we are not, we have lost touch with our deepest feelings. Aquinas said, "A trustworthy person is one who is angry at the right people, for the right reasons, for the right length of time, and expresses it in the proper manner." Permission to be angry!

I have spoken about the first two paths of the mystical journey, the path of creation and awe and delight, the path of darkness, letting go, and grief. But now we turn to the third path, which is that of creativity, the Via Creativa, the rebirth of creativity that comes from following the first two paths. Artwork is heart work, and after the darkness, the mourning, and the grieving, there always comes creativity. Again you see this in the story of Jesus. After the crucifixion comes the resurrection, the new birth, the surprise. Today we need to give birth in many areas of our civilization, and I want to touch on a few of them.

One of these is the church itself, which needs to be rebirthed with an ancient vision of base communities where we practice our spiritual praxis, where we listen to the mystics in our hearts, read them and dance to them, celebrate them and celebrate ourselves as mystics; where we recover our mystical heritage, not in the head but in the heart and the body. Birthing base communities is one of the most important things that religion can do today.

Traditionally in the West we have political virtues, domestic virtues, and civic virtues. Today we need to hear and teach ecological virtues. For example, vegetarianism or semivegetarianism is an ecological virtue, and there is no longer any excuse for a human being in the so-called First World not to question the amount of his or her consumption of meat. In theory, if North Americans alone were to cut back just 10 percent in their meat consumption, sixty million starving humans would eat today. The amount of land, water, and grain we are using to feed an addictive meat habit is simply unconscionable in our time. I am not a purist who is saying that everyone must convert to full vegetarianism, but certainly we can cut back 10 percent and move on from there. Another ecological virtue is bicycling, car sharing, or walking to work. Recycling itself is an ecological virtue, and it is very exciting to see young people teaching their parents these virtues. In many cases, the youth of today are bringing a new morality into our homes. Learning the sacredness of water or reverence for water is another ecological virtue. There are simple ways to learn reverence. Here is one I learned from a Native American years ago: if you want to learn reverence for water, go without it for three days; then, with that first sip, you will rediscover the sacredness of water. We must recreate our own entertainment at home and in our neighborhoods. The arts of conversation, gardening, drama, music, and tree planting are delights in themselves. We have turned our entertainment over to others, through television and so forth. For a long time I have maintained that if you are going to have a television in a house with children, for every hour that the kids watch television, they should be asked to put on their own show as well. Conviviality—how do we rediscover the arts of feasting together and enjoying one another's company? And study. Study is a spiritual praxis. To study the new creation story, which is wonderful and awesome, then to put it into drama, ritual, and music is a spiritual praxis. To study the crisis of the forests, the abuse of animals, to study one's own history. The Celtic people, for example, have suffered so much; we must pay attention to that suffering if it is going to be redemptive, if the anger and frustration are going to turn into something creative. Political organizing, including civil disobedience when necessary, in order to defend creation against humanity's worst side—this too is an ecological virtue. And I say that this especially is a virtue: to make rituals. To celebrate sacred times and sacred places and the sacred beings with whom we share this planet. This is how you tell the story swiftly (because we only have twenty years left): it is through rituals. Rituals are how people have always passed on their value systems to the young. We need a revolution in ritual today. Church worship is boring! We need to bring our bodies back to ritual—circle dancing works because the universe is curved. Our bodies need to be involved because we pray with our breath and our heart, not with hymnals and prayer books. Prayer is about strengthening the heart. "Courage" comes from the French words for a large heart, and that is what prayer is about. We need people who can lead us through prayers in ancient ways, new ways, and traditional ways, but the test is always whether our hearts are being enlarged or not, because without courage we will not let go, we will not undergo the transformation that is required of us in the next twenty years.

The Netherlands has recently spent a couple of years trying to legislate lifestyle changes. Finally they quit, and one of the legislators made this statement: "You cannot legislate life changes." Only spirituality brings about life changes, and that is why spirituality is at the heart of the healing of our planet, of our children, and of the child inside every one of us.

Another dimension where our creativity needs to be expressed is education. As I mentioned earlier, we have been educating only one side of our brain—and we wonder why we are in trouble! We are not educating for wisdom, we are educating for knowledge. We have enough knowledge; now we must turn to wisdom. The way to educate for wisdom is essentially through art—in our school we call it "art as med-

itation." I founded this school eighteen years ago because
when I did a study of all the spirituality education programs
in North America, I found them all wanting when it came to
issues of feminism, art, justice, and an integration of the
new science. And I realized why they are wanting: you cannot teach spirituality through a Cartesian model of education. So in our school we do a lot of art as meditation, or
massage as meditation, circle dancing, native rituals, sweat
lodges, drumming. Drumming awakens the lower chakras.
Western thought believes spirituality is in our heads, in the
pineal gland where Descartes located the soul. But we have
to recover our chakras. In the first chakra we experience vi-
brations with all the beings of the universe; the music of the
universe is there, and that is what we have to return to.
Drums do that for you—they keep you low.

The second chakra is our sexuality. Oh, my, how the
church has run from that! This is part of spiritual praxis, to
rediscover lovemaking as a mystical experience. This should
be no surprise. Many people tell me the greatest mystical experience of their lives is the birth of their children. The Song
of Songs in the Bible celebrates sexuality as a theophany—as
an experience of the divine. Cosmic Christ making love to
Cosmic Christ—why wouldn't it be? Except that religion has
cleaned up the book, saying that it is about Jesus loving the
soul and God loving the church.

So we come down to the practical issue, the great debate
about overpopulation. I am convinced that humankind cannot deal with this problem because it has not dealt with the
mysticism of sexuality. In those traditions that have, such as
Tantric yoga and Taoist sexual practice, there are ways of
lovemaking in which the male does not ejaculate sperm, yet
there is no loss of pleasure between the couple. This is an
obvious answer to human overpopulation. So it is only by
paying attention to our sexuality and honoring it as one of

the great experiences of mystical invention in the universe that we can rediscover ways to be sexually responsible. Meister Eckhart said, "Become aware of what is in you, announce it, pronounce it, produce it, and give birth to it." This passion for "giving birth" is within each one of us. We all have an artist inside, we all want to give our images back to the community. That is the task in this moment of need for creativity.

Rupert Sheldrake has said that "in the Newtonian universe there is no freedom or spontaneity anywhere in nature. Everything has already been perfectly designed." When I first read that, I thought to myself that it sounded like liturgy, it sounded like Western worship: that there is something that has been designed to which we must fit in. For me, the key to worship is participation, and we need to take responsibility for that kind of creativity and spirituality in our lives now.

A final point about creativity is that of creating good work. There is no question that when the human species does not have work, it begins to hate itself. Work is the way in which we give our blessing back to the community, the way in which we express our creativity. The fact is that there are over 850 million unemployed adults in the world today. The young all over the world are being raised without the promise of work, and this is a primary reason why the young are in such deep despair. Look around the universe: every other creature has work, every action interlinking with the next. It is only we humans who are out of work. We have invented unemployment, especially in the last few hundred years. We are still defining work in the narrow sense of "industry." The fact is that the world needs a very finite number of factories and military bases, but there is infinite work to be done on the inner house of the human being. That is the basic source of employment and good work for our species.

We have to go into that inner house and find the wounded child, and start cradling it and grieving with it and then bringing it to birth so it becomes the healthy, mystic child that it was meant to be. We have to go inside and find the sources of the violence, the racism, the sexism, and the homophobia, the compulsion to control, the refusal to let go. We have to go into our inner houses and do mystical work. For that, we need a lot of artists. Art is the basic, most fun, and the cheapest way (much cheaper than psychiatrists!) to go in and find the wisdom of our hearts. We could be putting our whole species to work today if we honored the artist as a spiritual director, which is what the primary role of the artist is and always has been in native traditions everywhere. I met an Aborigine a couple of years ago—as you probably know, Aborigines have the oldest culture in the world—and she said, "In our culture, everybody works four hours a day, and the rest of the day we make things." What is it they are making? Rituals, conviviality, beautiful costumes, music, and food for the feasts that follow the rituals. It is in ritual that the community heals itself, enlightens itself, brings forth gifts from everyone to celebrate and to let go.

I believe that the addiction to greed lies deep within our civilization; it is built into the very structure of capitalism, but it may well be part of all of our addictions, this quest for more. Aquinas gave a most amazing analysis of this when he said, "The greed for gain knows no limit and tends to infinity." Avarice is not a problem of materialism; it is a soul issue: it is our quest for the infinite, but it has been misplaced. Consumerism cannot satisfy us, and this is why we are always looking for next year's model; there is an infinite progression in the consumer addiction and the economic system that is built on it. What is the answer to avarice? The answer is to put forward in our educational systems, in our religious traditions, in our political and economic arenas, to put forward as absolute priorities those areas of the human quest for the infinite that are authentic and that can be satisfied in this life. Aquinas said, "The spirit in the human person is our quest for the infinite." We don't want to put down the quest for the infinite. It is because our spiritual traditions have failed to teach us the ways into the experience of God that we have been bought out by a consumer industry.

Aquinas named three ways we experience the authentic infinite. The first is the human mind: "One human mind can know all things. It is capable of the universe." And his proof of this is that you can never learn too much. So to feed the mind is to combat avarice. The second way we experience the infinite, said Aquinas, is in our hearts. "We can put no limit on the amount of love that one human heart is capable of, providing the mind is feeding the heart with delectable objects to love." Fundamentalism stops the mind and therefore it chokes the heart. The third way in which we experience the infinite is through the human hands. Connected to the human imagination, the hands can create an infinite variety of artifacts. When I read that, I started meditating on it, and I had this thought that in the whole of the history of the human race, no two musicians have spontaneously written the same song, no two painters have painted the same painting—an infinite capacity for creativity. If we want to remake our civilization, we must remake it around what is the Spirit in us: mind, heart, and creativity.

When authentic spirituality leads, religion will follow. If religion cannot make the paradigm shifts I am talking about, if it cannot let go of religion itself and its dated sociological forms, its value in the West is about on a par with the value of the Communist party in the former Soviet Union. If it cannot relearn its own spiritual and mystical tradition and thereby offer us ways of putting our inner house in order

and of relating our inner house to all the other inner houses
in the universe; if it cannot touch our hearts and our bodies
again so that awe is experienced for what it is—the beginning of wisdom and the presence of the divine; if religion
cannot teach a blessing consciousness in relation to today's
new creation story from science; if it cannot teach us ways
to journey into our shared grief and anger and darkness
where our souls and hearts are broken; if it cannot teach the
ecological virtues we need to survive; if it cannot offer us renewed forms of worship, forms that free us to be childlike
and erotic mystics, cosmic lambs playing in the universe and
thereby good shepherds to our lambs; if it cannot put an
end to the cycle of greed and reinvent education; if it cannot
teach us about sins of the spirit like acedia, inertia, and
avarice with as much enthusiasm as it has taught us about
sins of the flesh in the past; if it cannot apologize for its own
sins toward native peoples and toward the earth and toward
women; if it cannot lead the way in bringing forth the wisdom of all the world religions—then, my friends, the young
will grow old very quickly, and when that happens, a species
dies. Given the responsibility of our species today, if we die
we will bring down many other species. However, if religion
can do these things, we will have a renaissance, a rebirth of
civilization, a reinvention of our species based on a spiritual
vision.

CHAPTER 3

Creation Mysticism and the Return of a Trinitarian Christianity: Theology in Ecological Perspective

☾

This talk was originally delivered at the Catholic College Teachers Association in New Orleans in the summer of 1990. It caused quite a stir among certain parties who seemed particularly hostile to Creation Spirituality, but in it I took the theme of the conference, "Ecology in Theological Perspective," and turned it around to be less anthropocentric—hence "Theology in Ecological Perspective." I learned from the heated response to this talk that theologians are not my prime audience. The members of the Schumacher Society seemed more eager for my message than did many (though not all) of the audience at the CCTA. After the talk, two young men in the audience invited me to lead circle dancing in downtown New Orleans the next evening, and I was torn as to whether to accept or to attend more of the convention. Trying to practice what I preached, I chose the dancing, and the fifty to sixty people who showed up seemed to enjoy themselves as much as I did. I never regretted my choice.

FIRST, I SHOULD confess where I get the dual title for my presentation. This past January I was doing a series of conferences and lectures in New Zealand and Australia. At my last stop, that of the University of Western Australia in Perth, I had a particularly energetic experience with an overflow crowd of eager learners who had heard the renowned British physicist Paul Davies speak on the New Cosmology the previous evening.[1] My talk on "Creation Theology and Western Religion" was followed by a discussion period, and in the midst of an exciting dialogue on environment and Creation Spirituality, one person asked the following somewhat familiar question: "But are you a Christian? Do you believe Jesus is the Son of God?" I paused for a moment and replied, "I do not deny the divinity of Jesus, but I am a Trinitarian Christian. To focus on Jesus alone is heretical."

I repeat this story because it pertains profoundly to the theme of this conference, "Ecology in Theological Perspective." As long as we Western Christians[2] succumb to this fundamentalist "Jesusolatry," which appears in so many religious guises, we shall continue to commit gross sins of omission that result in sins of oppression toward the earth and therefore toward the peoples of the earth and toward our children, who are destined to inherit our debts of degradation and sickliness. As poet-farmer Wendell Berry put it recently in an interview, "rural America is a bona fide part of the Third World. It's a colony."[3]

We cannot create an ecological theology on the basis of "Jesusolatry." A Trinitarian Christianity is one that honors cosmology and therefore the Creator and the cocreative process of the universe, one that honors Jesus as prophet and liberator as well as a unique bearer of the Cosmic Christ or Sophia tradition,[4] and one that honors the ongoing Spirit who makes "all things new" and is found "pervading and permeating all things" (Wis. 7:24). Such a Trinitarian theology is necessary for an ecological theology. The second part of my title is "Theology in Ecological Perspective." I have chosen to reverse the words in the title of this conference because it is the universe that gives birth to theology and theologians and not the other way around. Theology and theologians have been invented by the universe and the earth over about eighteen billion years of history. It is not the other way around. The earth begets theology and theologians; theologians do not beget the earth. "Every creature is a word of God and a book about God," Eckhart declared six centuries ago.[5] Every creature was already a revelation about God, billions of years before holy Scripture came to be in books.

There are many challenges that the ecological peril and an ecological mind-set or consciousness puts to theology in praxis and theory today. It might be summarized as the challenge to let go of anthropocentrism. I think that there is a hidden anthropocentrism in the title "Ecology in Theological Perspective" that needs to be corrected. Ecology is judging theology, not vice versa.

In this essay I hope to offer some reflections on how the ecological issues challenge theology itself to renewal. Thus my title "Theology in Ecological Perspective." I detect at least nine ways in which theologians are being asked by the ecological crisis of our time to undergo what theologian Leonardo Boff calls a "different way of doing theology and being a theologian."[6] I suspect that it is less seminary professors than a group like college theology teachers who will provide the leadership for altering theology according to the demands of ecology, for we are more on the front lines with the young and with the laypersons who always hold the future for church renewal in a time of great cultural upheaval and potential renaissance, as Père Chenu pointed out.[7] Clearly, the future for theological exploration lies outside of theological seminary establishments.

1. Cosmology as the Basis for Theology—instead of anthropology or psychology or any other expression of anthropocentrism. "Eco" in the word *ecology* means, of course, "home." Economics is about managing our home, and ecology is about studying our home. What is our home? It is not just Western culture, not just educational apparatuses, most of which were invented during the Cartesian era when Descartes declared, "We shall be masters and owners of nature."[8] Our home is the universe itself, which in turn has given us this amazing planet that we call earth, with its stunning four-and-a-half-billion-year history. This needs to be the context for grasping both ecology and theology.

In the twelfth century, Adelard of Bath warned us of the danger of neglecting to study this home: "Were we to neglect coming to know the admirable rational beauty of the universe in which we live, we would deserve to be cast out from it like guests incapable of appreciating a home in which hospitality is offered to them."[9]

In the same century—the last one in which the West truly woke up to a cosmology and therefore birthed a renaissance—Hildegard of Bingen also warned of what happens when humans neglect their home: if humanity breaks the "web of justice" that is creation, then "God's justice permits creation to punish humanity."[10] As humans scurry about looking for places to dump our nuclear waste and our other trash, Hildegard's prophetic insight seems to be coming closer and closer to home. Thomas Berry alerts us to the contemporary price we are paying for neglecting our home when he warns that we are involved in a "supreme pathology" as we go about "closing down the major life systems of the planet."

> We are upsetting the entire earth system that has, over some billions of years and through an endless sequence of experiments, produced such a magnificent array of living forms, forms capable of seasonal self-renewal over an indefinite period of time.[11]

And anthropologist Loren Eiseley comments on our attitudes toward creation today:

> We have reentered nature, not like a Greek shepherd on a hillside hearing joyfully the returning pipes of Pan, but rather as an evil and precocious animal who slinks home in the night with a few stolen powers. The serenity of the gods is not disturbed. They know on whose head the final lightning will fall.[12]

All ecological theology must begin with cosmology— the story of how the universe got here, what it is doing today, and where "here" is; the story of time and space and how together they have birthed and been birthed in a universe of at least one trillion galaxies.[13]

2. Mysticism as Awe and Awe as Blessing. An awakened cosmology results in an awakened mysticism. Thomas Aquinas, who devoted his life to integrating cosmology and theology, offered a one-word exegesis of the psalmist's prayer, "They shall be drunk with the plenty of thy house" (Ps. 35:8) when he wrote, "*i.e., the universe.*"[14] The universe and the ecosystems are not just our home; they are sources of delight and of awe, of wonder and intoxication. Therefore, they are the matrix for a renewed mysticism, for to enter these *mysteries*, as cosmologists are now naming them, is a mystical experience. There is awe to be experienced in all of our relationships with creation. Instead of the sacred as "wholly Other"—a designation that can easily reinforce theistic relationships to divinity and subject-object relationships with nature—we need to recover the sense of the sacred as the sense of the *awesome*. Heschel indicates that there are three ways we can respond to creation: "We may exploit it, we may enjoy it, we may accept it with awe."[15] Awe for Heschel is the beginning of wisdom, the basis of biblical mysticism and of our "radical amazement." Awe is a "categorical imperative." Without it, everything becomes an object of consumerism. "Forfeit your sense of awe, let your conceit diminish your ability to revere, and the universe becomes a market place for you," Heschel tells us.[16] He also points out, in what may be an understatement for graduates of an anthropocentric educational and ecclesial system, "We are shocked by the inadequacy of our awe, at the weakness of our shock."[17] Awe is about an increased sense of the sacred in things—and beyond them. Thanks to the new cosmic story, we are learning how sacred our home is.

There are those who feel that an ecological theology can be addressed from the perspective of the concept of "stewardship." I disagree. Stewardship still denotes a dualistic relationship between humans and creation (as if we humans are not totally interdependent with all other created things). Because this concept is not consistent with the cosmic law of interdependence,[18] it flies in the face of any true cosmology; it remains anthropocentric and subtly sadomasochistic. It is still one species taking upon itself the right to manage another. The word *steward* means "a person who manages another's property, or who administers anything as the agent of another." Joseph Meeker observes that "stewardship of the earth" is a "vision of benevolent, nonviolent management, enlightened by science, and intended to create a gardenlike earth where all creatures will thrive in peace." Are we here to be benevolent managers of the entire planet? Meeker comments on the fallacy of stewardship theology—a theology that was present in the Jewish, Christian, and Islamic texts of the Assisi Declaration derived from the Conference of World Religions held at Assisi in 1986.

> However green and compassionate may be the language of these three religions, their concepts of stewardship emphasize the power and dominance of humanity. These stewards are kings, managers, pilots, and executive officers who serve as benevolent bosses of the natural world for its absentee landlord. All specific references to nature in their statements are to domesticated plants and animals and to habitats used for human benefit. Wilderness has no place in their thinking, and there is no intrinsic value in the nature they speak of.[19]

Stewardship theology offers a moral model but it lacks mysticism, for it is not about relationships among equals. It reinforces images of God as distant from nature: God is viewed as an absentee landlord, and we are God's serfs or managers. It will not serve us as an ecological theology.

Meeker finds a true ecological spirituality in the two Eastern religions represented at Assisi. The Vedas of Hinduism "celebrate 'all objects of the universe, living or nonliving, as being pervaded by the same spiritual power.' " The Buddhist section of the Assisi declaration states that "Spirit is everywhere, 'in the rivers, mountains, lakes, and trees,' and it must be revered as fully as human spirit."[20]

Yet the West boasts an alternative to the stewardship model as well. The Wisdom tradition and the Cosmic Christ tradition are deeply mystical. In the Book of Wisdom we learn that wisdom "permeates all things," and Hildegard of Bingen said, "No creature lacks a spiritual life."[21] Eckhart taught that "isness is God" and that there exists an "equality of being" among all creatures.[22] A reawakening to a theology of the Spirit is essential for a truly ecological theology. The struggle for ecological justice cannot be waged without

mysticism, because ecology is about our relationship to
things and to the divine, the Spirit, permeating all things.
Indeed, it is an awakening to what scientists today are calling
the "mind" in all things—an idea very close indeed to that
of the biblical Sophia.[23] Ecology is not one more item for
our political agendas; it is a nonnegotiable reality. Creation
cannot be destroyed without the destruction of the Spirit
itself.

Only an awakened mysticism can usher in an era of deep
ecology. The dominance implied in a stewardship model,
however benign it is, needs to give way to the *participation*
that is implicit in all mystical experience. To make this paradigm shift, we have to heed the warning of biblical scholar
Claus Westermann to reimmerse ourselves in a theology of
blessing, for to concentrate solely on salvation as deliverance
constitutes a "serious distortion of the biblical data."

> From the beginning to the end of the biblical story, God's
> two ways of dealing with mankind [sic]—deliverance and
> blessing—are found together. . . . Here lies the error that
> led Western theology to a number of further misinterpre-
> tations of and deviations from the message of the Bible. . . .
> In the primeval history (Gen. 1–11) blessing is found in
> the context of creation and extends to all living creatures.[24]

In other words, blessing is cosmological. Blessing and awe
go together, for awe can be said to be our response of blessing for blessing.

3. Images of God. The very images of the divinity to whom
we relate must undergo change. Today, under the impetus of
the paradigm shift from an anthropocentric and patriarchal
theological model to a more curved and maternal one, there
is occurring simultaneously a veritable explosion of images
of God. New names for the Divine One, which are often ancient ones, are emerging from many places. For example,
Godhead; Goddess; Isness; the Beloved; God as Mother; God

as Caring Father, not Theistic Father; Great Spirit; Holy
Spirit; Sophia; Cosmic Christ; Cosmic Wisdom; the Sacred;
the Face behind the Face; Compassion; the "I am" in every
creature; Beauty; Justice; Underground River; Life—all these
invite us to rediscover the divine all about us and within us.
We encounter God's face whenever we encounter being itself—if we are prepared for it. Altering our images of God
or, if you will, allowing new ones to bubble up from our
collective memories and traditions is a significant move on
the part of believers. Eckhart gives us a clue to the reason for
this when he says that "all the names which the soul gives
God, it receives from the knowledge of itself."[25] In other
words, to change our images of God is to allow ourselves to
undergo change as well. It is little wonder, then, that a time
of paradigm shift would be a time of rich renaming of divinity, a time for letting God be God in all new—and ancient—forms.
It is a time for doing what Eckhart dared to do: "I pray God
to rid me of God," he declared.[26] That is, we need to give
ourselves permission to let go of clinging to images of God
that are not serving us or the earth or divinity as well as they
should, in order to allow new images to emerge.

4. Images of Our Relationship to God. "Awe awakens," poet
William Everson observes. Part of the awakening that occurs
in a creation mysticism is the developing of new images of
our relationship to divinity. The environmental imperative
challenges us to reconsider the ways we image our relationship to divinity. In particular, it challenges us to move from
theism to panentheism, with all the implications of this
move. It is reminding us that the word environment derives
from the French word environ, meaning "around." We see a
more rounded, a more encompassing imagery for our relationship to divinity. Creation mystics offer us such rounded,
circular images that derive from panentheism—the awareness of God in us and us in God, when the "us" does not

refer to humans alone but to all of creation and all created things. Here are some examples:

> The reign of God is among you. (Luke 17:21)
>
> Make your home in me, as I make mine in you. . . . Whoever remains in me, with me in him or her, bears fruit in plenty. (John 15:4–5)
>
> God is the one in whom we live, move, and have our being. (Acts 17:28)
>
> God hugs you. You are encircled by the arms of the mystery of God. (Hildegard of Bingen)
>
> God is a wheel, a circle. (Hildegard of Bingen)[27]
>
> The day of my spiritual awakening was the day I saw and knew I saw all things in God and God in all things. (Mechtild of Magdeburg)
>
> God speaks: "When your Easter comes I shall be all around you, I shall be through and through you." (Mechtild of Magdeburg)[28]
>
> God is roundabout us completely enveloping us. (Meister Eckhart)
>
> God created all things in such a way that they are not outside the Godself, as ignorant people falsely imagine. (Eckhart)[29]
>
> We have all been enclosed within God. (Julian of Norwich)
>
> We are in God, and God, whom we do not see, is in us. (Julian)
>
> God is our clothing that wraps, clasps, and encloses us so as never to leave us. (Julian)
>
> The deep Wisdom of the Trinity is our Mother. In her we are all enclosed. (Julian)[30]

Panentheism is basic to a true environmental spirituality because it celebrates the sacred presence of the divine—the Cosmic Christ or the Goddess—in all things. Is it surprising that so many of the citations I offer come from feminists?

Not really. Theism gives us the imagery of Jacob's ladder; panentheism, on the other hand, is better imaged as "Sarah's Circle."[31] Theism supports a flight upward away from earth, matter, and the mother principle; panentheism keeps us grounded in eye-to-eye contact with the Divine One in us all.

5. Renewal of Worship. It is rare to find people today—Protestant or Catholic—who feel nourished by the forms of worship offered them, and yet there is a renewed passion for rituals that heal, that tell the new creation story, that allow us to tell our stories of interaction with the Spirit in nonverbal ways, that bind young and old, that teach letting go, that involve the body, that cause us to breathe deeply again (hence *ruah* or spirit), that delight. This should not surprise us, for a time of cosmology is a time of renewed worship, a time when we discard forms that are ineffective and integrate other forms—often more ancient ones—into our traditions. We live in such a time. As Joseph Campbell put it, "the first function of mythology—myths and mystical rituals, sacred songs and ceremonial dances—is to waken in the individual a sense of awe, wonder, and participation in the inscrutable mystery of being."[32]

The ecological imperative requires rituals that get the new cosmological story into our bodies and imaginations, whence they will give birth to a renewal of politics, economics, and education. Rituals that involve curves, play, unselfconsciousness, the body, circle dancing, that mirror the sense of our curved universe—all these are required by the new ecological era. Artists are being called on to tell the story in drama, dance, song, poetry, and ritual and to elicit it from the people—thus, liturgy as "*the work of the people.*" Aboriginal peoples with their ancient ways of sweat lodges and circle dances, of animal totems and drumming,[33] will be bearers of wisdom in this regard.

Thomas Kuhn points out that at a time of paradigm shift "the scientist's perception of his environment must be re-educated. . . . He must learn to see a new gestalt." A dimension of worship we often neglect is that of education. Yet worship holds the potential to teach us to see a new gestalt, a new picture of the way things truly are.[34] Education in the cosmological-ecological worldview is sorely lacking when we rely on prayer as reading from books instead of prayer as the opening of the heart.[35] Worship is the most basic of all art forms; when we renew it, we are renewing our relationships to the earth and to all creatures, including ourselves, and to God—"all our relations," as the Lakota people pray in their prayer ceremonies. Ritual is too important to leave to committees and bureaucracies. New forms are emerging, and will continue to emerge, at the level of grassroots praxis. Scientist Rupert Sheldrake points out that in the previous paradigm of a mechanistic universe, "there was no freedom or spontaneity anywhere in nature. Everything had already been perfectly designed."[36] Often our ritual life imitates such a paradigm today. We need to develop rituals that mirror the facts of our universe, including the reality of its deep, deep creativity.

6. An Awakened Eros, Earthiness, and Passion. Compassion simply means "passion with," to be in solidarity of feeling with the joy and pain of another. An awakened passion can lead to a renewal of compassion, a fuller, deeper living out of our interdependence with all creation. As Hildegard put it, "O human, why do you live without a heart and without blood?"[37] Erotic justice flows from moral indignation, from the passion of moral outrage. Yet, as Heschel observes, "we are a generation that has lost the capacity for outrage."[38] If this was true in the seventies, how much more true it is after the sleepy eighties. Our country is engaged in a war against the poor—a war being carried out in Central America for ten years and in our own country as well. And through it all the middle class—who are in fact also becoming poorer—are asleep. Our passion has been muted.

Consider the following statistics about income distribution in recent years in our country:

- Between 1980 and 1984, the richest 20 percent of American families gained $25 billion in income, and the poorest 20 percent lost $6 billion.

- In 1968, the poorest 20 percent of American families had an estimated 91 percent of the income they needed for basic requirements; by 1983, they had only 60 percent.

- In 1985, the top 20 percent of American families took in 43 percent of all family income, a postwar high. The bottom 20 percent got only 4.7 percent—their lowest share in twenty-five years. And those in the middle dropped from 46 percent to 39 percent.

- Since 1977, the pretax income of the lower 60 percent of American taxpayers, adjusted for inflation, has declined 14 percent. Yet taxes on this group have increased by $19 billion. In the same period, the income of the top 1 percent of all Americans, with inflation adjustments, has soared 86 percent to an average of $549,000.

- Since 1977, tax changes for the poorest 90 percent of Americans have resulted in $25.6 billion less tax. For the richest 10 percent, they have meant a savings of $93.1 billion.

- The richest 1 percent of Americans are paying an average of $82,000 less in taxes today than they would have under the tax system before changes in 1978. The lower 90 percent are all paying higher taxes. Thus, Barbara Ehrenreich comments that "a massive upward redistribution of wealth" occurred during the Reagan years and our society "had succeeded in reducing large numbers of the American poor to the condition of their Third World counterparts—beggars, vagrants, and dwellers in makeshift shelters."[39]

When people learn of the ways in which our society is abusing the earth—its waters, forests, land, air—we can also ignite passion. After conducting workshops recently in eastern Europe, Joanna Macy reports that it was the ecological disasters that motivated people to demand their democratic rights in the streets. They decided they would "rather die of bullets than of choking."

7. New Images of Justice and Compassion. Hildegard of Bingen said that whenever people are asleep, they are asleep to injustice. As we learn to deanthropocentrize justice and place it within a larger, more cosmological setting, we experience new images. Cosmic laws of interdependence and celebration, of interdependence and justice, are being laid out today in the new cosmic story. Justice is not just a moral category for humans—it is a cosmic law, a cosmic "habit," as scientist Rupert Sheldrake would say,[40] into which humans can also fit. The quest for balance and equilibrium is built into our bodies, into our minds (dreams come to bring balance back when we are out of balance), and into the earth body. Scientists call this cosmic habit "homeostasis." Cosmos, after all, is the opposite of chaos. Injustice unravels the ropes of order in the universe, while justice brings them together again.[41]

Ecological facts lay bare issues of justice and responsibility between "First" and "Third" World people—or rather, "one-third" and "two-thirds" world. One North American family does twenty to one hundred times more damage to the planet than one family in the "Third" World. One rich American causes a thousand times more destruction due to our gas-guzzling luxury cars, air-conditioning, and what scientist Paul Ehrlich calls our "high-intensity-the-hell-with-tomorrow agriculture." The average Swede, on the other hand, while still maintaining a quality lifestyle, has learned to use 60 percent less energy than the average American.[42]

8. People of Color and People of the Land. These groups, including aboriginal people and family farmers, will increasingly emerge as sources of nonelitist wisdom. Wisdom in the Bible, after all, "walks in the streets" and offers an everyday encounter. She is not elitist. James Cowan, in his excellent book on the spirituality of the Aboriginal people of Australia—the oldest tribe of humans in the world—summarizes his study in the following manner: "As long as there is no wish to recognize the divinity in all things, then Aboriginal belief will always be regarded as a suspect philosophy grounded in superstition and strange ritual practices."[43] In other words, if our religions and theologies lack a deep awareness of the Cosmic Christ—which is our tradition of "the divinity in all things"—then our racism will continue. African-American theologian Howard Thurman, who studied Meister Eckhart with Quaker Rufus Jones as a young man in college and knew Eckhart's creation mysticism so well, tells us about his cosmic mysticism as a black person in America:

> As a child, the boundaries of my life spilled over into the mystery of the ocean and the wonder of the dark nights and the wooing of the wind until the breath of nature and my own breath seemed to be one—it was resonant to the tonality of God. This was a part of my cosmic religious experience as I grew up.[44]

Elaborating on this "cosmic religious experience," he says, "There is magic all around us—in the rocks, the trees, and the minds of men [sic]. . . . There can be no thing that does not have within it the signature of God."[45] Thurman's theology was a significant influence on that of Dr. Martin Luther King Jr. Another example of the deep cosmological spirituality of African Americans would be that of Alice Walker.

A cosmological mysticism opens the doors to deep ecumenism and new relations among the people of the earth. It honors the wisdom of people of color.[46]

9. Youth and Renewed Education. Youth the world over are in despair, and with good reason. They sense the peril of the planet—the future home for their children and grandchildren—the diminished beauty and health of the earth that they will inherit from the adult world, along with massive debts, unemployment, useless but dangerous weaponry, nuclear wastes, garbage, and overpopulation. Adultism reigns from church to school to government to workplace, and the young are the victims of this sin. But an awakened cosmological-ecological mysticism can assist the young in several significant ways. First, by calling for the awakening of the mystic in every adult, who is the divine child or puer/puella in each adult. A mystical awakening gets to the heart of the oppression of the young, which is, I believe, a reflection of the repression of the mystic or child in the adult. When this child is allowed to "play in the universe" again, there is less need to oppress the young out of a kind of violent envy and projection.

In addition, when education is regrounded in cosmology, the young are empowered, for they learn that they are desired by the universe over an eighteen-billion-year history and that their lives count for something significant. Hildegard of Bingen said that when humans do good work, they make "the cosmic wheel go around." Now there lies a challenge to adventure for the young! By redefining work beyond the narrow, man-made definition of the Industrial

Revolution to include the arts, with their power to evoke healing—the art of gardening, the art of creating rituals and teaching adults to play again and be mystical again—a cosmic mysticism can create *good work* for the masses of unemployed youth in the world. Many youth today, acknowledging that they simply are not wanted in an adultist, capitalist economic system, are being called by history to *create their own culture* with its own work, its own economic system based on bartering, its own entertainment, ritual, and lifestyles. A cosmology assists this important project—a project not unlike that of Benedict sixteen centuries ago or of the Celtic monasteries, which were also places of lay leadership and youthful imagination.

By insisting that education train body *and* mind, heart *and* head, intuition *and* intellect, a creation-centered spiritual education *honors* the youth by emphasizing process and self-discovery in the context of cosmological discovery. Education and spirituality can be renewed simultaneously. A team of scientists, artists, and mystics as teachers in search of a common cosmology will not bore the young but will challenge them to self-discipline. Art as meditation will prove to be a powerful tool for both self-discipline and learning to relate to the universe. We must remember, when we speak of education and the young, the vast and increasing numbers of incarcerated persons in our society who are young. They too deserve to be reached with these new models of education and with the Good News of their empowerment by way of cosmological education and art as meditation.

THESE NINE POINTS indicate some directions that theology might take when we move from an excessive emphasis on Jesus alone to a Trinitarian Christianity, and from an excessive emphasis on a single article of faith (redemption) to all three articles, thus including *creation* and *sanctification* or, in the

Eastern tradition, divinization. All this can happen when we understand faith in the context of the glimmering light of a cosmological-ecological awakening—an awakening that requires but also effects a "greening" of the Trinity and each of its Persons. Hildegard celebrated this *viriditas* or "greening power" as the "vitality to bear fruit," and she credited Christ, who is "the green figure itself," with bringing "lush greenness" to "shriveled and wilted" people and their institutions.[47] Perhaps theology and education themselves might be rendered green and lush by the ecological imperative in our time and thus contribute to a much-needed renaissance in our species.

NOTES

1. See Paul Davies, "Cosmogenesis," *Creation* Vol. 6, No. 3 (May–June 1990): 10–13.

2. Eastern Christians are less tempted to do this since they reject Augustine's introspective conscience in favor of a more cosmic Trinitarian spirituality. See Krister Stendahl, "The Apostle Paul and the Introspective Conscience of the West," in *Paul among Jews and Gentiles* (Philadelphia: Fortress Press, 1976), 78–96.

3. Carol Polsgrove and Scott Sanders, "An Interview with Wendell Berry," *The Progressive* (May 1990), 35.

4. See Susan Cady, Marian Roran, and Hal Taussig, *Sophia: The Future of Feminist Spirituality* (San Francisco: Harper & Row, 1986) and Kathleen M. O'Connor, *The Wisdom Literature* (Wilmington, Del.: Michael Glazier, 1988). Cosmic wisdom is also the Cosmic Christ tradition. See Matthew Fox, *The Coming of the Cosmic Christ* (San Francisco: Harper & Row, 1988).

5. See Matthew Fox, *Meditations with Meister Eckhart* (Santa Fe, N.M.: Bear & Co., 1982), 14.

6. Leonardo Boff and Clodovis Boff, *Introducing Liberation Theology* (Maryknoll, N.Y.: Orbis, 1988), 22–23.

7. M. D. Chenu, *Nature, Man, and Society in the Twelfth Century* (Chicago: University of Chicago Press, 1968), 219–20.

8. René Descartes, *Discours de la Méthode*, 6.

9. Cited in Chenu, *Nature, Man, and Society*, 13.

10. See Matthew Fox, *Illuminations of Hildegard of Bingen* (Santa Fe, N.M.: Bear & Co., 1985), 45.

11. Thomas Berry, *The Dream of the Earth* (San Francisco: Sierra Club Books, 1988), 206.

12. Cited in Berry, *The Dream of the Earth*, 204.

13. For fine summaries of this story, see Brian Swimme, *The Universe Is a Green Dragon* (Santa Fe, N.M.: Bear & Co., 1985) and Thomas Berry and Brian Swimme, *The Universe Story* (San Francisco: HarperSanFrancisco, 1992). For a beautiful commentary from the perspective of a Central American spiritual writer, see Ernesto Cardenal, *Cántico cósmico* (Managua, Nicaragua: Editorial Nueva Nicaragua, 1989).

14. Thomas Aquinas, II *Contra gentes* 2, trans. Thomas Gilby, in *Saint Thomas Aquinas: Philosophic Texts* (Durham, N.C.: Labyrinth Press, 1982), 128.

15. Cited in John C. Merkle, ed., *Abraham Joshua Heschel: Exploring His Life and Thought* (New York: Macmillan, 1985), 126.

16. Cited in John C. Merkle, *The Genesis of Faith: The Depth Theology of Abraham Joshua Heschel* (New York: Macmillan, 1985), 169.

17. Cited in Merkle, ed., *Abraham Joshua Heschel*, 115.

18. See Erich Jantsch, *The Self-Organizing Universe* (New York: Pergamon Press, 1980) and Rupert Sheldrake, *The Presence of the Past* (New York: Timesbooks, 1988).

19. Joseph W. Meeker, "The Assisi Connection," *Wilderness* (spring 1988): 62.

20. Ibid., 62–63.

21. Fox, *Illuminations*, 53.

22. Matthew Fox, *Breakthrough: Meister Eckhart's Creation Spirituality in a New Translation* (Garden City, N.Y.: Doubleday, 1980), 91–101.

23. See Jantsch, *Self-Organizing Universe*, 308–10.

24. Claus Westermann, *Blessing in the Bible and the Life of the Church* (Philadelphia: Fortress Press, 1978), 4.

25. Fox, *Breakthrough*, 175.

26. Ibid., 221.

27. Fox, *Illuminations*, 24.

28. Sue Woodruff, *Meditations with Mechtild of Magdeburg* (Santa Fe, N.M.: Bear & Co., 1982), 42, 95.

29. Fox, Breakthrough, 73.

30. Brendan Doyle, Meditations with Julian of Norwich (Santa Fe, N.M.: Bear & Co., 1983), 24, 27, 89, 90.

31. See Matthew Fox, A Spirituality Named Compassion (San Francisco: Harper & Row, 1990 ed.), Chap. 2.

32. See John M. Maher and Dennie Briggs, eds., An Open Life: Joseph Campbell in Conversation with Michael Toms (Burdett, N.Y.: Larson Publications, 1988), 17.

33. For a discussion on bringing the drum back to Western worship, see Jim Roberts, "Creating Ritual," Creation Vol. 6, No. 3 (May–June 1990): 39–40.

34. Thomas Kuhn, The Structure of Scientific Revolutions (Chicago: University of Chicago Press, 1970), 112.

35. For an analysis of how cosmology can and needs to alter worship, see Fox, Cosmic Christ, 211–27.

36. Sheldrake, Presence of the Past, 51.

37. Fox, Illuminations, 83.

38. Cited in Merkle, ed., Abraham Joshua Heschel, 136.

39. Barbara Ehrenreich, Fear of Falling (New York: Pantheon Books, 1989), 190, 202.

40. Rupert Sheldrake, The Rebirth of Nature (New York: Bantam, 1991), 125–30.

41. Hildegard of Bingen said that the Holy Spirit and wisdom "tie" things together so that "there would be no bundle if it weren't tied together—everything would fall apart." See Fox, Illuminations, 23–24.

42. See Paul R. Ehrlich and Anne H. Ehrlich, Healing the Planet (Reading, Mass.: Addison-Wesley, 1991).

43. James Cowan, Mysteries of the Dreaming (Dorset, England: Prism, 1989), 125.

44. Howard Thurman, With Head and Heart: The Autobiography of Howard Thurman (New York: Harcourt Brace Jovanovich, 1979), 177.

45. Thurman, With Head and Heart: The Autobiography of Howard Thurman, 268.

46. See the work of Alice Walker—for example, as in Alice Walker, Living by the Word (New York: Harcourt Brace Jovanovich, 1989).

47. Fox, Illuminations, 30–33.

II

CREATION SPIRITUALITY

AND THE

PREMODERNS

《　》

Creation-Centered Spirituality from Hildegard to Julian: Three Hundred Years of an Ecological Spirituality in the West

☾

Creation Spirituality is very ancient in the West. It is the oldest tradition in the Hebrew Bible, the tradition that Jesus knew, the tradition of Celtic Christianity and of our greatest medieval mystics. In this essay, which articulates some rich concepts from their Green theologies, I draw on the mystics of medieval Christianity, but it is important to remember how steeped they were in the biblical and Celtic traditions as well.

THERE CAN BE no respect for our place in the environment and the environment's place in us without a spirituality that teaches us reverence for the cosmos in which we find ourselves. The reigning spirituality of patriarchal culture of the West has not been friendly to the environment, nor has it taught persons to be gentle to themselves, their bodies, their enemies, their imaginations. Subject-object dualisms have characterized the mainstream of spirituality in the West from Saint Augustine to Jerry Falwell and points in between. Science historian Michael Polyani has caught the antienvironmental bias of those who preach a fall-redemption religion when he said that Saint Augustine "destroyed interest in science all over Europe for a thousand years."[1] An ideology that considers all of nature helplessly fallen does not look kindly on those who spend their lives studying nature—namely, scientists. To probe the universe is not a salvific act in such a spirituality or religion.

But there is another tradition of spirituality in the West. That tradition, the creation-centered one, considers the environment itself to be a divine womb, holy, worthy of reverence and respect. We are in divinity and the divinity is in us according to this tradition—and by "we" I do not mean merely the two-legged ones but the entire universe: atoms and galaxies, rain and whales, trees and fish, dogs and rabbits, and humans too. While little has been heard from this tradition in religious and theological circles in centuries, the fact is that this tradition was alive and well in medieval Europe for a lively period of three hundred years. This was the period that gave us Chartres Cathedral, Hildegard's amazing music and mandalas, Francis of Assisi's empassioned and Sufi-like lifestyle, Aquinas's *Summa*, Mechtild of Magdeburg's journal and political involvement, Eckhart's mystical-prophetic genius, the rich theology of the *Theologica Germanica*, and Julian of Norwich's metaphysics of goodness. The twelfth-century renaissance in Europe was in great measure an awakening to the creation-centered tradition, which meant first and foremost an awakening to nature itself.[2] It also welcomed those scientists and mystics who took nature seriously and considered it a source of divine revelation.

In this essay I would like to present a survey of four neglected figures and some key concepts that they cherished and developed during this three-hundred-year span. In particular I will invoke the following champions of an ecological spiritual consciousness: Hildegard of Bingen (1098–1179), Mechtild of Magdeburg (1210–1280), Meister Eckhart (c. 1260–1327), and Julian of Norwich (1342–c. 1415). It is evident that I am omitting the two best known creation-centered mystics of this period in the West—Francis of Assisi (1181–1226)[3] and Thomas Aquinas (1225–1274).[4] I am doing so for lack of space but also because these two persons have received considerable attention. The four persons I deal with have been neglected, repressed, forgotten, condemned, misinterpreted, dualistically translated (if at all), and otherwise pushed out of the mainstream of Western Christianity's worldview. This is the principal reason why the ecological and creation-centered tradition they so richly represent has been all but nonexistent in most Christian theologies in the West (though not the East).

These four persons can rightly be called "Rhineland mystics." Two of them, Hildegard and Eckhart, lived and preached on the Rhine, where Bingen is located in Hildegard's case, or in Strasbourg and Cologne in the case of the Dominican Meister Eckhart. Mechtild's writings were circulated heavily among the Beguines, who were especially numerous on the Rhine and to which movement Mechtild herself belonged.[5] Her Dominican spiritual director, Heinrich of Halle, saw to it that her book was translated immediately into Latin in order to ensure its swift dissemination. By

1344 it had been translated into the High German that was
spoken on the upper Rhine in the thirteenth and fourteenth
centuries. From a literal point of view, I am stretching it a
bit to call Julian a "Rhineland mystic" since she was a her-
mitess who once walled up in her cell in about 1393, never
left it to reenter Norwich, much less the continent. However, from a theological point of view, Julian deserves to be
called a "Rhineland mystic," for her tradition is radically and
richly that of Hildegard and Eckhart, as we shall see. She develops the creation-centered theology deeply, for she is a
theologian of the first order. Furthermore, we know that
Eckhart's works were taken into England, often under the
cover of John Tauler's sermons by Dominicans and others.
Dominicans were quite visible in Norwich in Julian's day
and in fact occupied a priory right down the street from
Julian's cell in a city that sparkled at that time with mystical
movements. It is inconceivable that she did not hear Dominicans preach in her church or converse with them and
very likely employed them as spiritual directors at the same
time that she directed them. Furthermore, Julian's apparent
Benedictine roots link her to Hildegard and the rich creation
spirituality of the Benedictine tradition.

The six themes that I wish to touch on as basic to an
ecological consciousness are the following:

1 The goodness (blessing) of creation.

2 The goodness and blessing that the earth itself is (including human earthiness or bodiliness).

3 Cosmic awareness, cosmic consciousness, and a psychology of microcosm, macrocosm.

4 A theology of panentheism as most properly naming
our relationship to God.

5 The motherhood of God and the human vocation to
co-create the cosmos.

6 Compassion understood as interdependence and justice making.

In dealing with these rich themes that are so essential to an ecological spirituality I will weave and interweave the thought of each of the mystics I have named above. Three sources that these mystics draw on extensively need to be named. First is the Jewish and Christian Scriptures—as I have indicated elsewhere,[6] the creation tradition is the oldest tradition in the scriptures dating back to the ninth century B.C., the Yahwist (J) source of the Hebrew Bible. It is the tradition of wisdom literature, of the prophets in great measure and of Jesus Christ. The gospel writers and Paul knew this tradition intimately. A second source that is often neglected or misunderstood is that of the Celts who settled in the Rhineland area as Christians in the seventh century.[7] John the Scot was the first to translate Eastern Christianity's mystical works into Latin, and the Celts depended for their theology on the Eastern traditions—which never forsook creation theology—rather than on Jerome and Augustine in the West (who did indeed forsake creation theology). A keen understanding of the Celtic contribution to Western culture is evidenced by Paul Lang when he writes:

> Ireland and Scotland had never experienced antique civilization as a reality. The Celts came into contact with Rome, the colonizer, much as the East Indians made the acquaintance of modern England. Consequently they did not face the grave conflict between ancient learning and Christian faith which caused a sharp reaction in the countries within the orbit of classical civilization. They were thus eminently suited to bring about a reconciliation of the two philosophies and outlooks on life, and communicated their ideas not only to their neighbors the Anglo-Saxons, but through their monastic settlements in the Frankish Empire and northern Italy, to the whole of Christian Europe.[8]

It was the Celts who most inspired Francis of Assisi's spirituality, as Edward Armstrong has demonstrated.[9]

A third source of the mystics we are treating that needs to be acknowledged is women's experience. Three of these most neglected mystics are women and the fourth, Meister Eckhart, was spiritual director to the Beguines or women's movement of his day. His preeminent contribution to creation theology only serves to underscore how feminism is not a male/female dividing point but is rather a way of seeing the world that both women and men are capable of. Feminist thinkers like Rosemary Ruether and Susan Griffin and Mary Daly and Wendell Berry and Robert Bly in our time have rightly pointed out that the abusive treatment of nature and the abusive treatment of women most often go together in our society. The issue in patriarchy that is most basic is that of dualism.[10] Creation-centered spirituality names dualism as original sin and offers, as we shall see, a wonderful alternative. For it defines salvation as holism, as making whole, making one, and therefore making healthy, holy, and happy.

With this brief introduction we can now begin our exploration of ecological themes in the creation-centered mystics of the Middle Ages.

ECOLOGICAL THEMES IN THE CREATION-CENTERED MYSTICS

The first theme that this line of creation-centered mystics celebrates that is essential for an ecological spiritual consciousness is that of the goodness of creation. Hildegard of Bingen writes: "God is the good. And all things that proceed from God are good."[11] Julian of Norwich, three centuries later, follows up on the same theme. "I know well that heaven and earth and all creation are great, generous and

beautiful and good. . . . God's goodness fills all his creatures
and all his blessed works full, and endlessly overflows in
them." But Julian goes even further. Meister Eckhart's tran-
scendental metaphysics had declared that "isness is God";
Julian borrows from this metaphysics to establish a metaphysics of goodness. She writes, "God is everything which is
good, as I see it, and the goodness which everything has is
God."[12] To say that "goodness is God" is to reestablish the
nondualistic relationship of Creator and creation. More than
that, it is to reestablish a veritable theology of blessing. For
blessing is the theological word for the goodness that creation
is. As Professor Sigmund Mowinckel puts it in his major
study on blessing in Israeli theology, "first and foremost,
blessing is life, health, and fertility for the people, their cat-
tle, their fields. . . . Blessing is the basic power of life itself."[13] For Julian the blessing that our lives are goes back a
very long way. "I saw that God never *began* to love us. For just
as we will be in everlasting joy (all God's creation is destined
for this), so also we have *always* been in God's foreknowl-
edge, known and loved from without beginning."[14] Julian is
celebrating the original blessing that our existences are. Science today can vouch for the accuracy of Julian's theology:
had the stars not exploded six billion years ago, had the
earth not maintained a certain temperature so that water
would flow and life emerge, had the ozone not processed
out certain levels of radiation, we humans would not exist.
Thus we were indeed loved by the cosmos "from before the
beginning."

One reason that a theology of the goodness of creation
is so essential for an ecological consciousness is that without
it the human race remains greedy and unsatisfied. By truly
trusting in the goodness of existence, we open ourselves up
to more goodness and to less and less elitist understanding
of what the good for humankind is and can be. In short, we
let go of the sense that more must be better; we learn some-

thing of necessities and needs. Hildegard of Bingen sees this
clearly when she writes, "God gives, such that nothing that
is necessary for life is lacking." And again, "God has gifted
creation with everything that is necessary."[15] If humanity
can believe that "everything that is necessary" has been
given us, then the compulsion for more will give way to a
celebration of what is—"isness is God" (Eckhart)—and out
of what is, humanity will forge what must be for the earth's
survival. Here indeed lies a theology for sustainability, for
humanity will not choose to sustain instead of hoard or
master until it is at peace with its condition.

Not only is creation radically good and an original blessing, not only is everything that is necessary already here, but
also creation for these mystics is itself a source of divine
pleasure and divine revelation. Creation radiates delight and
beauty and pleasure. Hildegard writes, "There is no creation
that does not have a radiance. Be it greenness or seed, blos-
som or beauty, it could not be creation without it."[16] God
is erotically involved, one might say in love, with creation.
"Creation, of course, was fashioned to be adorned, to be
showered, to be gifted with the love of the Creator. The entire
world has been embraced by this kiss."[17] Meister Eckhart
teaches that the source of all creation's pleasure is God and
that "God finds joy and rapture" in human creation. Furthermore, creation discharges truth as well as pleasure. It is
a source of revelation, a Bible in itself. "Every creature is a
word of God and a book about God," Eckhart declares.[18]
Billions of years before humanity invented books and religions put their teaching into holy writings, God was re-
vealed in the divine and ongoing book that creation is. "If
I spent enough time with a caterpillar," Eckhart vows, "I
would never have to prepare a sermon because one caterpillar is so full of God."[19] All of creation is full of the divine—
provided we have the eyes and ears to perceive it and the
open heart to receive such revelation.

THE GOODNESS OF THE EARTH

A second theme that is essential for a theology of ecology is that of the goodness and blessing that the earth itself is. The creation-centered mystics celebrate not only creation in general but the earth in particular. Hildegard writes, "Holy persons draw to themselves all that is earthly."[20] We are a long distance indeed from the dominant symbol of patriarchal spirituality, which was that of "climbing Jacob's ladder" precisely to escape the earth! And mother. And matter.[21] Hildegard not only brings together holiness and earthiness but she also relates this embracing of the earth with our celebrating of earth as holy mother. "The earth is at the same time mother, she is mother of all that is natural, mother of all that is human. She is the mother of all, for contained in her are the seeds of all."[22] The earth "is the fleshly material of people, nourishing them with its sap as a mother nurses her sons or daughters."[23] For Hildegard the earth is holy because it is the "source" of humanity. It demands on humanity's part "a right and holy utilization of the earth."[24] Our bodies are "supported in every way through the earth," she declares. And the earth "glorifies the power of God."[25] There is no human chauvinism in Hildegard's appreciation of the earth and humanity's relationship to it. Hildegard celebrates the earth as a living organism, for she sees the air as its soul. "The air is the soul of the earth, moistening it, greening it."[26] Earth is holy and fruitful, a source of blessing, because "all creation comes from it." Yet earth is also divinized a second time because the human body of God's Son was fashioned from it. Earth "forms not only the basic raw material for humankind, but also the substance of the incarnation of God's Son."[27]

Meister Eckhart, by imaging God as "a great underground river that no one can dam up, no one can stop," is celebrating images of holy Mother Earth, of the divine power of the earth, of divinity from below and not exclusively from above. If God is an underground river, then the earth is the mediator—the "priest," one might say—between humanity and divinity. It behooves us to embrace and to explore the earth for divinity's sake. Like Hildegard, Eckhart and the other creation-centered mystics celebrate the microcosm or psychic dimension of earthiness. One might call their psychology a geopsychology. Here is where the awful dualism of body versus soul, championed by patriarchy, is healed. Augustine, for example, declared that "the soul makes war with the body." Eckhart, in contrast, says, "The soul loves the body" and consequently "asceticism is of no great importance."[28] Mechtild of Magdeburg composed a poem to the body that celebrates how gently we can and ought to relate to the physical. She places our relationship to body in the context of realized eschatology:

> Do not disdain your body. For the soul is just as safe in
> its body as in the kingdom of heaven—though not so certain.
> It is just as daring—but not so strong.
> Just as powerful—but not so constant.
> Just as loving—but not so joyful.
> Just as gentle—but not so rich.
> Just as holy—but not yet so sinless.
> Just as content—but not so complete.[29]

A key to healing the patriarchal body-soul split is to let go of the idea that the body is "out there"—which is itself a dualistic mind-set—and to begin embracing the body, the earthiness, "in here." Such an earthiness is everywhere at once. This mind-set is itself nondualistic. It is healing or salvific because it celebrates the psychic embracing of earthiness, redeeming earthiness from being an enemy, the dark and repressed shadow of spirituality. Earth too is divine blessing and grace.

Perhaps no one has celebrated the reunion of body and soul, the holiness of matter and earthiness, so richly as has Julian of Norwich. She too sees the issue as one of relationship, as an issue of psychology making room for geology, when she talks about "our sensuality" and God's presence in it. "I understand that our sensuality is grounded in Nature, in Compassion, and in grace. I saw that God is in our sensuality. For God is never out of the soul."[30] Sensuality and human earthiness is not something to be feared in this spirituality but something to be embraced, since divinity itself operates there. "God is the ground in which our soul stands and God is the means whereby our Substance and our Sensuality are kept together so as to never be apart."[31] What incarnation means to Julian is the "oneing" of divinity and sensuality, of God and us. If God is the glue or means that keeps substance and sensuality together, then to explore either pole of our makeup is to explore God. In a wonderful poem about both literal and psychic farming, Julian celebrates the struggle that gardening is all about.

> There is a treasure in the earth that is a food tasty and pleasing to the Lord.
> Be a gardener. Dig and ditch, toil and sweat.
> Turn the earth upside down and seek the deepness and water the plants in time.
> Continue this labor and make sweet floods to run and noble and abundant fruits to spring.
> Take this food and drink and carry it to God as your true worship.[32]

Here we have a psychic geology, a healing of matter and spirit, of external and internal farming, a reverence for the holiness and divinity of earth and our origins. Interestingly, Hildegard also offers an image of psychic geology when she writes that people should "look into the field of their soul in

order to root out the useless weeds and thorns and briars"
that grow there.[33]

Lest we be tempted to sublimate the true implications of
her theology on sensuality and sentimentalize it, Julian
praises explicitly how going to the bathroom is holy.

> Food is shut in within our bodies as in a well-made purse.
> When the time of our necessity comes, the purse is opened
> and shut again in the most fitting way. And it is God who
> does this, for I was shown that the Goodness of God per-
> meates us even in our humblest needs.[34]

The earthiness and the bodily cycles that channel this
earthiness are godly. Eckhart on many occasions celebrates
humility as earthiness, the word coming as it does from the
Latin word *humus* or earth. He images the human soul as the
"soil" in which the divine seed and divine word are planted.
From this sensual grounding, God grows. "The seed of God
is in us. If the seed had a good, wise, and industrious culti-
vator, it would thrive all the more and grow up to God
whose seed it is, and the fruit would be equal to the nature
of God. Now the seed of a pear tree grows into a pear tree, a
hazel seed into a hazel tree, the seed of God into God."[35] As
with Hildegard and Julian, so with Eckhart: our earthiness is
not an obstacle to divine energy but the very setting for it.
Here lies a truly incarnational theology, one that celebrates
the divinizing of the earth. It is one out of which Teilhard de
Chardin drew deep political implications, writing that "the
age of nations has passed. Now, unless we wish to perish we
must shake off our old prejudices and build the earth."[36]

COSMIC CONSCIOUSNESS

A third theme that is richly developed in the creation-centered mystics is that of cosmic awareness, cosmic conscious-

ness. The oldest hymns of the Christian liturgy, those found in the epistles to the Ephesians (1:3–23), to the Colossians (1:15–20), and to the Philippians (2:6–11), celebrate the Cosmic Christ who "fills the whole creation" and "reconciles all things in heaven and all things on earth." Yet Saint Augustine, whose patriarchal spirituality has dominated Western religion, has no Cosmic Christ, as scholars have pointed out.[37] The creation-centered mystics we are speaking of boast a rich sense of cosmic awareness and of its psychological implications. Hildegard of Bingen writes, for example, "I welcome every creature of the world with grace." Hers is not a two-legged chauvinism but an awareness that, as she puts it, "God has arranged all things in the world in consideration of everything else."[38] The patriarchal religious tradition that begins theology with sin is committing an act of immense anthropocentrism. For sin is a human invention in the cosmos and is therefore a latecomer to the universe—as late as humanity itself. To begin religion with sin, instead of with the blessing that the cosmos is, trivializes religion. In fact, the sins that humanity is capable of today are quite cosmic in their scope, as we play with military toys that can put an end to twenty billion years of the universe's birthing of this home we call earth.

Mechtild of Magdeburg also celebrates a cosmic awareness and its political-mystical overtones when she writes, "The truly wise person kneels at the feet of all creatures."[39] Like the rich theology of the Wisdom literature of the Hebrew Bible, Mechtild deliberately connects cosmic awareness with wisdom itself. "The spirit of the Lord indeed fills the whole world," sings the author of the book of Wisdom (1:7). Hildegard urges us to meditate on the beauties of the universe about us and not to become preoccupied with our introspective selves. "Glance at the sun. See the moon and stars. Gaze at the beauty of earth's greenings. Now think what delight God gives to humankind with all these things. Who gives all these shining, wonderful gifts if not God?"[40] It is because the creation tradition celebrates cosmic awareness that it cares deeply not just about knowledge or information but about wisdom. Wisdom and cosmos are corelative terms, as the French philosopher Gabriel Marcel indicates. "The true function of the sage is surely the function of linking together, of bringing into harmony. . . . The sage is truly linked with the universe."[41] Mechtild points out the political implications of a worldview that considers the cosmos as essential. After saying that "the truly wise person kneels at the feet of all creatures," she adds, "And is not afraid to endure the mockery of others."[42] A cosmic consciousness in a patriarchal and introverted society or religion is sure to bring "the mockery of others" down upon it. An ego-logical and an ecological consciousness cannot coexist precisely because we are talking about consciousness—that is to say, the human psyche. Cosmos is itself an element of psyche. If it is left out, then quite literally our psyches are damaged and one-sided. Paul Ricoeur writes of this when he says, "To manifest the 'sacred' on the 'cosmos' and to manifest it in the 'psyche' are the same thing. . . . Cosmos and psyche are the two poles of the same 'expressivity'; I express myself in expressing the world; I explore my own sacrality in deciphering that of the world."[43] Like Mechtild, Marcel also notes the political and moral implications of recovering wisdom and cosmos in our thinking and decision making.

> The important thing—and I think it is hardly possible to insist on it too much—is that in this outlook the true aim of knowledge and of life is to be integrated in the universal order, and not at all to transform the world by bringing it into subjection to the human will, to man's [sic] needs or his desires.[44]

The psychology of microcosm and macrocosm that these medieval mystics offer us is itself radically healing. Hildegard is explicit about the human as a microcosm of the cosmos: "Now God has built the human form into the world structure, indeed even into the cosmos, just as the artist would use a particular pattern in her work."[45] Meister Eckhart too holds a psychology of microcosm/macrocosm. He develops his idea of the "equality of being" in which all creatures are equal at the level of the supreme gift, which is that of existence itself or isness. He says, "God loves all creatures equally and fills them with his being. And we should lovingly meet all creatures in the same way."[46] Like Hildegard, Mechtild, and Marcel, he draws ethical conclusions from his alertness to cosmic awareness. Eckhart believes that "the first intention" of nature "is the preservation of the universe." Eckhart insists that creation is thoroughly ongoing and the cosmos is being birthed not "out there" but very much within the enlargement of the human psyche. He writes:

> I have often said that God is creating the entire cosmos fully and totally in this present now. Everything God created six thousand years ago—and even previous to that as he made the world—God creates now all at once. Now consider this: God is in everything, but God is nowhere as much as he is in the soul. There, where time never enters, where no image shines in, in the innermost and deepest aspect of the soul God creates the whole cosmos. Everything which God created millions of years ago and everything which will be created by God after millions of years —if the world endures until then—God is creating all that in the innermost and deepest realms of the soul.[47]

It is little wonder that one Eckhartian scholar writes that "Eckhart actually abolishes the methodological distinction between theology, anthropology, and cosmology."[48]

Julian of Norwich also celebrates the kingdom of God as the cosmos and in the process stretches one's image of soul or psyche. She writes that she saw "the soul so large as if it were an endless world and a joyful kingdom" with God sitting in the center.[49] Julian offers a meditation on the Cosmic Christ when she speaks of Jesus' crucifixion as affecting all of nature. "All creatures of God's creation that can suffer pain suffered with him. The sky and the earth failed at the time of Christ's dying because he too was part of nature."[50] Like the other persons we have considered, Julian draws ethical implications from a deepened cosmic consciousness. "Those who have universal love for all their fellow Christians in God have love toward everything that exists."[51]

To consider cosmic awareness and cosmic responsibil- ity as essential to spiritual growth is also to welcome the scientist. For who is the scientist if not an explorer of the truths—and hopefully the wisdom—of our universe? There is simply no anti-intellectualism and no fear of science in the creation-centered mystics. Hildegard, for example, sees science as a road to wisdom. "The more one learns about that which one knows nothing of, the more one gains in wisdom. One has, therefore, through science, eyes with which it behooves us to pay attention."[52] She praises the human soul for its "regal rationality,"[53] and she calls the human mind "the best treasure, a living intellect."[54] She leaned heavily in her work on the finest scientist of her day, Bernard Sylvester. Hildegard was no mean synthesizer of sci- ence in her own right. Her scheme of microcosm/macro- cosm, says one scholar, "though complex and difficult, is neither incoherent nor insane, as at first sight it may seem. It is, in fact, a highly systematic and skillful presentment of a cosmic theory which for centuries dominated scientific thought."[55] It has been pointed out that Hildegard herself made scientific contributions with regard to the need for purification of water, the discovery of healing medicines, and the anticipation of the discovery of vitamins.[56]

A THEOLOGY OF PANENTHEISM

A fourth ingredient essential to an ecological spirituality is a nondualistic imaging of God's presence. The creation-centered tradition understands this to be a theology of panentheism. For theism is by definition dualistic, implying as it does a person "here" and a God "out there." Carl Jung says there are two ways to lose your soul, and one is to worship "a God out there." In the panentheistic theology, it is understood that we are in God and God is in us. And by "we" is meant all of creation, all that is—or, as Paul puts it (Acts 17:28), God is the one "in whom we live, move, and have our being." Mechtild of Magdeburg images God as panentheistic when she writes, "I who am divine am truly in you . . . and you are in Me." Indeed, Mechtild dates her awakening to spiritual maturity to the moment she moved from a theistic to a panentheistic spiritual consciousness. She writes, "The day of my spiritual awakening was the day I saw and I knew I saw all things in God and God in all things."[57] Panentheism, as Mechtild speaks of it, includes a conviction—"I saw and knew I saw"—of the truth of imaging God in a way that is no longer subject-object.

Julian of Norwich images our relationship to God in a panentheistic manner as well when she writes that "we have all been enclosed within God." And again, "We are in God and God, whom we do not see, is in us."[58] Hildegard of Bingen, in addition to speaking of the God in us and the Holy Spirit flowing like fire through us, also images God in the following manner: "God hugs you. You are encircled by the arms of the mystery of God."[59] These are panentheistic images of us-in-God as well as God-in-us.

Meister Eckhart has developed a mature spirituality of panentheism at great length. He writes that "God created all things in such a way that they are not outside himself, as ignorant people falsely imagine. Everything that God creates or does, he does or creates in himself, sees or knows in himself, loves in himself." Since "God is a being that has in itself all being," it follows that divinity is "roundabout us, completely enveloping us."[60] Not only are all things in God but "God is in all things. The more he is in things, the more he is outside of things."[61] Inside and outside are not separate. They meld together in a panentheistic theology.

Moving from a theistic ("God out there" or even "God in here") to a panentheistic theology ("all is in God and God is in all") is a requisite for growing up spiritually. Yet because the creation-centered mystics have been so repressed in the West, it is rare indeed to find anyone—whether theologian or scientist—who has heard of panentheism. Without panentheism there is no authentic ecological consciousness for there is no true sense of the interdependence of all things, of the flowing out and the flowing back that characterizes all authentic living and dying. Justice gets reduced to a good deed, and compassion is sentimentalized as feeling sorry for others. The divine Dabhar, that permeating energy that pulsates and quickens all life, is not tapped as the source of divine energy that it is for all peoples and creatures. A theistic imaging of God is essentially adolescent, for it is based on an egoistic mind-set, a zeroing in on how we are separate from God. How many religious believers—and so-called unbelievers!—who may be very adult in their specialized professions have remained adolescents in their imaging of the relationship to God! And how seldom the churches have known enough of their creation-centered mystical traditions of panentheism to instruct people to move beyond this ego stage of development to a mystical stage of adult panentheism.[62]

THE MOTHERHOOD OF GOD

A fifth theme that deserves attention in an ecological spirituality and which the creation-centered mystics develop is that of the motherhood of God. We have already seen how Hildegard praises "Mother Earth" and how Eckhart celebrates God as "a great underground river" that bubbles up from this hallowed ground. Mechtild of Magdeburg says candidly, "God is not only fatherly. God is also mother who lifts her loved child from the ground to her knee."[63] Mechtild sees the connection between panentheism and maternal images of embracing and surrounding when she writes, "The Trinity is like a mother's cloak wherein the child finds a home and lays its head on the maternal breast."[64] Like Mechtild, Hildegard celebrates the roundness of God— an image that is both panentheistic and suggestive of the maternal in God. She writes of being "surrounded with the roundness of divine compassion."[65] For Hildegard, "divinity is . . . like a wheel, a circle, a whole, that can neither be understood, nor divided, nor begun, nor ended."[66]

Meister Eckhart frequently images God as mother: he says, "From all eternity God lies on a maternal bed giving birth" and again, "What does God do all day long? God gives birth."[67] For Eckhart a theology of the motherhood of God is so essential because it celebrates all persons' capacities to give birth. Without this side of God being acknowledged, creativity itself is repressed and stifled. Indeed, in patriarchal spiritualities, creativity has not even been a theological category.[68] Whereas in the creation tradition, the *imago Dei*, or image of God in every person, is precisely the imagination or the capacity of each person for creativity. So true is this for Eckhart that he actually declares that "we are meant to be mothers of God." In other words, every time we birth beauty or justice or truth or compassion, we are cocreators with God birthing divinity itself.

Hildegard also celebrates human creativity and the call for humans to cocreate with a creative God. "Humankind alone is called to assist God. Humankind is called to co-create," she says.[69] "Divinity is aimed at humanity," she declares, for "God created humankind so that humans might cultivate the earthly and thereby create the heavenly."[70] "God gave to humankind the talent to create with all the world" and for this reason God can say, "I have exalted humankind with the vocation of creation."[71] When Hildegard, as we saw earlier in this study, alludes to how humanity has been given everything that is necessary, she does not mean it is all just there for the taking. She is sensitive to how much making must also take place if the necessities are to be won and justly distributed. In other words, creativity, human imagination, and ingenuity are themselves essential ingredients in reestablishing need instead of greed as the basis for an economic and political compassion. A creative person is an orchard, Hildegard insists. "This is how a person becomes a flowering orchard. The person who does good works is indeed this orchard bearing good fruit. And this is just like the earth with its ornamentation of stone and blossoming trees."[72]

No theologian in the West has more thoroughly developed the rich theme of the motherhood of God than has Julian of Norwich. "Just as God is truly our Father," she writes, "so also is God truly our Mother."[73] For her the recovery of God as mother is also the recovery of divine wisdom—a theme we saw earlier when treating of cosmic consciousness. For "the deep Wisdom of the Trinity is our Mother. In her we are all enclosed."[74] She connects divine motherhood with panentheism in an explicit way once again when she says that God is "our true Mother in whom we are endlessly carried and out of whom we will never come."[75] Here we have an image of the cosmos as God's womb. Being enclosed is, as we have seen, an essential image of the maternal side of God. Julian says, "As the body is clothed in

cloth and the muscles in the skin and the bones in the muscles and the heart in the chest, so are we, body and soul,
clothed and enclosed in the Goodness of God."[76] She relates
the motherhood of God to a deepening awareness of God as
Creator and lover of all of nature. "God is the true Father
and Mother of Nature, and all natures that are made to flow
out of God to work the divine will will be restored and
brought again into God."[77] The motherhood of God is a
welcome thing on God's part, Julian assures us. Divinity
does not consider motherhood a burden to bear. "God feels
great delight to be our Mother."[78] Finally, to recover the
motherhood of God is to recover compassion as the operative divine energy. Compassion is more powerful than judgment or law or righteousness. For compassion is grace.
"Compassion is a kind and gentle property that belongs to a
Motherhood in tender love. Compassion protects, increases
our sensitivity, gives life, and heals."[79]

Thus we see that the recovery of the theme of the motherhood of God flows naturally from other themes of cosmos, earthiness, blessing or goodness, and panentheism.
A motherhood-of-God theology is no mere trifling kudo
handed out to keep feminists content. It confronts the basic
issue of letting go of the one-sided God of patriarchy and
learning more about the God whose image we are. Therefore it is also about learning more about ourselves and about
our power for birthing and creativity. Today it is especially
urgent that men learn deeply how all persons are motherly
as well as fatherly.

COMPASSION AS
INTERDEPENDENCE AND JUSTICE MAKING

The sixth and final theme we will consider that is basic to an
ecological spirituality is that of compassion understood as

interdependence and justice making. Compassion as feeling
sorry for others is explicitly rejected in creation theology
precisely because in a panentheistic worldview there is no
other. God is not other, and we are not other to one another.
Surely this is Jesus' lesson when he told his disciples that to
clothe the naked is to clothe him and to feed the hungry is
to feed him. Panentheistic thinking requires a consciousness
of interdependence. Such a consciousness is a consciousness
of compassion. Meister Eckhart captures this sense of interdependence when he says, "Whatever happens to another,
whether it be a joy or a sorrow, happens to me." And again
he says, "All creatures are interdependent."[80] Hildegard also
underscores the interdependence of creation when she
writes, "Everything that is in the heavens, on the earth, and
under the earth is penetrated with connectedness, penetrated with relatedness."[81] Eckhart builds on this notion of
relatedness everywhere when he says that relation is the
essence of everything that exists[82]—not substance, not
thingness, but relation. Compassion is about struggling to
right relationships. Hildegard believes that "creation blooms
and flourishes when it remains in right relationship and
keeps to its assigned tasks."[83]

If compassion is first of all an awareness of the intercon-
nectedness of all things, then it is also about the struggle for
justice or for seeing the balance of things restored when it is
lost. Meister Eckhart says simply, "Compassion means justice."[84] And Mechtild of Magdeburg also links compassion
to justice in an explicit fashion:

> If you love the justice of Jesus Christ more than you fear
> human judgment then you will seek to do compassion.
> Compassion means that if I see my friend and my enemy
> in equal need, I shall help both equally. Justice demands
> that we seek and find the stranger, the broken, the prisoner
> and comfort them and offer them our help. Here lies the
> holy compassion of God.[85]

For all of these creation mystics, compassion is the work of the Holy Spirit, for as Eckhart puts it, "the first outburst of whatever God does is always compassion."[86] Compassion then is our origin and our destiny. It is the Holy Spirit at work, as Mechtild says:

> Who is the Holy Spirit? The Holy Spirit is a compassionate outpouring of the Creator and the Son. This is why when we on earth pour out compassion and mercy from the depths of our hearts and give to the poor and dedicate our bodies to the service of the broken, to that extent do we resemble the Holy Spirit.[87]

Hildegard also praises the Holy Spirit as "the hope of oneness for that which is separate," the power that empowers all life. "Holy Spirit, you make life alive, you move in all things, you are the root of all created being. . . . You awaken and reawaken every thing that is."[88] The Holy Spirit, Hildegard says, is "the life of the life of all creatures."[89] Eckhart also connects the Holy Spirit and justice making when he says that the Spirit is the spirit of transformation, the "Transformer."[90]

Compassion and justice making in the creation tradition can in no way be restricted to relations among the two-legged ones. The creation mystics are speaking of cosmic relations and cosmic healings. In this tradition, sin is laid bare as ecological and not trivial. Hildegard envisions the elements of the earth suffering from the sins of humankind toward the earth. "I heard a mighty voice crying from the elements of the world: 'We cannot move and complete our accustomed rounds as we should do according to the precepts of our Creator. For humankind, because of its corruptions, spins us about like the sails of a windmill. And so now we stink from pestilence and from hunger after justice.' "[91] She cries out that "the earth should not be injured! The earth must not be destroyed!"[92] And she warns humanity that human misery generated at Love Canal or Times Beach is not an invention of the two-legged ones but a law of cosmic balance and beauty. "As often as the elements of the world are violated by ill treatment," she warns, "God will cleanse them through the sufferings and hardships of humankind. . . . All of creation God gives to humankind to use. But if this privilege is misused, God's justice permits creation to punish humanity."[93] Thus we see that the creation mystics define the deepest spiritual energy of which humanity is capable in this way: it is the consciousness and work for harmony, justice, or compassion.

CONCLUSION

It should be evident from this study that each of the six themes presented interweaves through the others. The spiral—not the ladder—is the basic image of spiritual journeying in the creation tradition. The goodness of creation bursts into the blessing that earthiness is, which in turn opens one to the whole universe in cosmic awareness, which in turn celebrates the divine grace that all of existence is, bathed in the panentheistic presence of God. The mothering embrace of this same divinity urges us on to our creativity as images of God who are called to return blessing for blessing to the cosmos. (Otto Rank defines the artist as "one who wants to leave behind a gift.") Compassionate healing by way of justice making is the greatest of the gifts we return to creation and the Creator. (In Hebrew, the words for compassion and for womb come from the same root.)

It is evident too from this study that we are indeed dealing with a tradition when we speak of creation-centered spirituality. From the first author in the Bible to Hildegard and from Hildegard to Teilhard de Chardin, we are speaking of a deeply felt and richly developed theology. This essay has concentrated on only four figures whose lives spanned three

centuries of medieval spirituality.[94] I wish to say a word to
Protestant Christians as much as to Catholic ones. There was
no Protestant-Catholic split then; indeed, there was plenty of
protest and prophetic religion in the medieval church and
surely among the four mystics I have presented in this study.
In fact, their protesting spirit and their battling for church
reform are reasons why they are not well known in the
church today. Furthermore, the radical Protestant movement
is a direct descendant of Meister Eckhart's creation theology.[95] And Martin Luther himself, in the first written work
he ever published (his preface to the very Eckhartian mystical work, *Theologica Germanica*), expresses amazingly high
praise for this kind of theology. He writes that "next to the
Bible and Saint Augustine no other book has come to my attention from which I have learned—and desired to learn—
more concerning God, Christ, man [sic], and what all things
are."[96] Luther thus confesses that three influences were key
to his theology: the Scriptures, Augustine, and the
Rhineland mystics. Yet where is the Protestant seminary
today where the study of the Rhineland mystics is given an
equal footing with the study of Augustine and the Bible?
Luther praises the "solid tradition" from which the *Theologica
Germanica* emanates.[97] It is time that the Western churches,
Protestant and Catholic alike, embraced Hildegard and
Mechtild, Eckhart and Julian, and the tradition they represent with at least as much fervor as Augustine has been embraced. Then our culture might benefit from an ecological
consciousness imbued with a power that only spirituality
and a spiritual awakening can effect—and only a religious
renewal can sustain.[98]

NOTES

1. Michael Polanyi, *Personal Knowledge* (Chicago: University of Chicago
   Press, 1962), 141.

2. See M. D. Chenu, *Nature, Man, and Society in the Twelfth Century* (Chicago: University of Chicago Press, 1968), Chap. 1.

3. There is a fine article redeeming Francis from his number one enemy, sentimental hagiography, in Paul Weigand's "Escape from the Birdbath: A Reinterpretation of Saint Francis of Assisi as a Model of the Ecological Movement," in Philip N. Joranson and Ken Butigan, *Cry of the Environment* (Santa Fe, N.M.: Bear & Co., 1984), 148–60. See also the concluding essay in this book, "On Desentimentalizing Spirituality."

4. True lovers of the spirit of Saint Thomas, such as M. D. Chenu and Josef Pieper, have done superb work in showing us the way to this person's creation theology. See M. D. Chenu, "Body and Soul Politic in the Creation Spirituality of Thomas Aquinas," in Matthew Fox, ed., *Western Spirituality: Historical Roots, Ecumenical Routes* (Santa Fe, N.M.: Bear & Co., 1981), 193–214; and Josef Pieper, *Guide to Thomas Aquinas* (New York: Pantheon Books, 1962). Also deserving of mention for his creation approach to Aquinas is G. K. Chesterton, *Saint Thomas Aquinas: The Dumb Ox* (Garden City, N.Y.: Doubleday, 1956). Of course, Dante and Chaucer also deserve to be studied for their Creation Spirituality, but limits of space preclude that happening in this essay. These thinkers and others inspired my recent book, *Sheer Joy: Conversations with Thomas Aquinas on Creation Spirituality* (San Francisco: HarperSanFrancisco, 1993).

5. See Ernest W. McDonnell, *The Beguines and Beghards in Medieval Culture* (New Brunswick, N.J.: Rutgers University Press, 1954).

6. Matthew Fox, *Original Blessing: A Primer in Creation Spirituality* (Santa Fe, N.M.: Bear & Co., 1983).

7. See Matthew Fox, *Breakthrough: Meister Eckhart's Creation Spirituality in New Translation* (Garden City, N.Y.: Doubleday, 1980), 30–35.

8. Paul Henry Lang, *Music in Western Civilization* (New York: Norton, 1941), 70.

9. Edward A. Armstrong, *Saint Francis: Nature Mystic* (Berkeley: University of California Press, 1973), 36ff., 52ff., 206ff., passim.

10. See Rosemary Ruether, "Women's Liberation in Historical and Theological Perspective," in Sarah Benteley Doely, ed., *Women's Liberation and the Church* (New York: Association Press, 1970), 26–36.

11. Cited in Fox, *Original Blessing*, 42.

12. Brendan Doyle, *Meditations with Julian of Norwich* (Santa Fe, N.M.: Bear & Co., 1983), 32. This translation is based on Edmund Colledge and James Walsh, *A Book of Showings to the Anchoress Julian of Norwich* (Toronto: Pontifical Institute of Medieval Studies, 1978), Parts 1 and 2.

13. Cited in Claus Westermann, *Blessing in the Bible and the Life of the Church* (Philadelphia: Fortress Press, 1978), 20.

14. Doyle, *Julian*, 88.

15. Gabriele Uhlein, *Meditations with Hildegard of Bingen* (Santa Fe, N.M.: Bear and Co., 1982), 50–51.

16. Ibid., 24.

17. Ibid., 51.

18. Matthew Fox, *Meditations with Meister Eckhart* (Santa Fe, N.M.: Bear and Co., 1982), 14, 18.

19. Fox, *Breakthrough*, 79.

20. Uhlein, *Hildegard*, 64.

21. See my developed discussion of this key symbol in mysticism in "Sexuality and Compassion: From Climbing Jacob's Ladder to Dancing Sarah's Circle," Chap. 2 in *A Spirituality Named Compassion* (San Francisco: HarperSanFrancisco, 1990 ed.), 36–67.

22. Cited in Fox, *Original Blessing*, 57.

23. Adelgundis FührKötter, ed., *Hildegardis: Scivias* (Turnholti: Brepols, 1978), vol. 1, 116. This and subsequent translations are mine.

24. Uhlein, *Hildegard*, 197.

25. Ibid., 50.

26. Ibid., 61.

27. Ibid., 58.

28. Fox, *Eckhart*, 58; Fox, *Breakthrough*, 122.

29. Sue Woodruff, *Meditations with Mechtild of Magdeburg* (Santa Fe, N.M.: Bear & Co., 1982), p. 43.

30. Doyle, *Julian*, 92.

31. Ibid., 95.

32. Ibid., 84.

33. Hildegard, *Scivias*, vol. 2, 551.

34. Doyle, *Julian*, 28.

35. Fox, *Breakthrough*, 118.

36. Teilhard de Chardin, *Human Energy* (New York: Harvest/HBJ, 1969), 37.

37. Leo Scheffczyk, *Creation and Providence* (New York: Herder, 1970), 100.

38. Uhlein, *Hildegard*, 65.

39. Woodruff, *Mechtild*, 39.

40. Ibid., 45.

41. Gabriel Marcel, *The Decline of Wisdom* (New York: Philosophical Library, 1955), 42.

42. Woodruff, *Mechtild*, 39.

43. Paul Ricoeur, *The Symbolism of Evil*, trans. Emerson Buchanan (Boston: Beacon, 1969), 12–13.

44. Marcel, *Decline of Wisdom*, 42.

45. Uhlein, *Hildegard*, 105.

46. Fox, *Breakthrough*, 100.

47. Fox, *Eckhart*, 24–25.

48. Reiner Schurmann, *Meister Eckhart: Mystic and Philosopher* (Bloomington: Indiana University Press, 1978), 89.

49. Doyle, *Julian*, 114.

50. Ibid., 44.

51. Ibid., 33.

52. Uhlein, *Hildegard*, 66.

53. Hildegard, *Scivias*, vol. 1, 171.

54. Ibid., vol. 2, 557.

55. Charles Joseph Singer, *From Magic to Science: Essays on the Scientific Twilight* (New York: Dover, 1958), 215.

56. See Sister Ethelburg Leuschen, O.S.B., "Hildegard: Saint and Scientist," *Benedictine Review* (summer 1958): 48–53. See Hildegard's books, Naturkunde—"*Physica*" (Salzburg: Otto Müller, 1959) and Heilkunde—"*Causae et Curae*" (Salzburg: Otto Müller, 1957).

57. Woodruff, *Mechtild*, 46, 42.

58. Doyle, *Julian*, 27, 89.

59. Uhlein, *Hildegard*, 90.

60. Fox, *Breakthrough*, 73.

61. Ibid.

62. So essential is panentheism to the creation-centered mystical tradition that I have found myself writing about it and developing the concept in all my books on spirituality and culture including *On Becoming a Musical, Mystical Bear* (New York: Harper & Row, 1972); *Whee! We, Wee All the Way Home* (Santa Fe, N.M.: Bear and Co., 1982); *A Spirituality Named Compassion*; *Breakthrough*; *Western Spirituality: Historical Roots, Ecumenical Routes*; and *Original Blessing*.

63. Woodruff, *Mechtild*, 109.

64. Ibid.

65. Hildegard, *Scivias*, vol. 2, 565.

66. Uhlein, *Hildegard*, 21.

67. Fox, *Eckhart*, 88. See all of Path Three in *Eckhart*, 65–88, and *Break-through*, 293–416, for Eckhart's immensely rich development of the human as mother, birther, and *imago Dei*.

68. For example, in his book, *The Spiritual Life: A Treatise on Ascetical and Mystical Theology* (Westminster, Md.: Newman Press, 1930), the very influential Father Adolphe Tanquerey never touches on the topic of creativity in all 750 pages. Asceticism locks creativity out of one's spirituality. The same is true of Jordan Aumann and Antonio Royo's *The Theology of Christian Perfection* (Dubuque, Iowa: Priory Press, 1962). In its 692 pages, there is no mention of creativity as a spiritual experience, much less as a form of meditation and centering. Perfectionism also locks creativity out, as does patriarchy in all its forms.

69. Uhlein, *Hildegard*, 106.

70. Ibid., 89, 88.

71. Ibid., 125, 110.

72. Ibid., 54.

73. Doyle, *Julian*, 103.

74. Ibid., 90.

75. Ibid., 99. Eckhart offers a similar image when he says that all of creation "flows out of God but remains within him/her" (Fox, *Breakthrough*, 65).

76. Doyle, *Julian*, 29.

77. Ibid., 106.

78. Ibid., 85.

79. Ibid., 81. Space does not allow us to consider how Julian also develops the theme of Jesus as mother based on the Gospel passage in Matthew 23:37 and the tradition of Jesus as wisdom incarnate. See Doyle, *Julian*, 99, 101, 104–5, 110, 132. Hildegard also alludes to this tradition in Hildegard, *Scivias*, vol. 1, 127.

80. Fox, *Eckhart*, 113.

81. Uhlein, *Hildegard*, 41. Consider also her statement: "God has arranged all things in the world in consideration of everything else" (65).

82. Fox, *Breakthrough*, 198.

83. Uhlein, *Hildegard*, 67.

84. Fox, *Breakthrough*, 435. See Eckhart's entire sermon, "Be Compassionate as Your Creator in Heaven Is Compassionate," and my commentary in *Breakthrough*, 417–39.

85. Woodruff, *Mechtild*, 116.

86. Fox, *Breakthrough*, 441.

87. Woodruff, *Mechtild*, 117.

88. Uhlein, *Hildegard*, 41; Hildegard von Bingen, "De Spiritu Sancto," song no. 15, in *Lieder* (Salzburg: Otto Müller, 1969), 228.

89. Uhlein, *Hildegard*, 37.

90. Fox, *Breakthrough*, 369.

91. Hildegard of Bingen, *Liber Vitae Meritorum*, III, II, "Querela Elementorum," in Heinrich Schipperges, trans., *Hildegard von Bingen, Der Mensch in der Verantwortung* (Salzburg: Otto Müller, 1972), 133.

92. Uhlein, *Hildegard*, 78.

93. Ibid., 79–80.

94. For more members of this tradition, see Fox, "Appendix A: Toward a Family Tree of Creation-Centered Spirituality," in *Original Blessing*, 307–15. Special mention should be made of the great Nicolas of Cusa (1401–1464), who was scientist and mathematician, church reformer and advocate of church ecumenism, mystic and philosopher, befriender of artist and prophets.

95. Consider Hans Hut, Hans Denck, and Sebastian Franck and their Eckhartian-like "word-of-God theology" wherein word means all creatures and the "Gospel of All Creatures." See Steven E. Ozment, *Mysticism and Dissent* (New Haven, Conn.: Yale University Press, 1973), 148–49, 105.

96. Martin Luther, "Preface," *The Theologica Germanica of Martin Luther*, trans. Bengt Hoffman (New York: Paulist Press, 1980), 54.

97. Luther also says that in Eckhart's disciple, John Tauler, he found "more solid and pure theology than among all the Scholastics." Cited in Bengt Hoffman, *Luther and the Mystics* (Minneapolis: Augsburg, 1976), 154. Hoffman credits Tauler with teaching Luther about realized eschatology (124).

98. See Robert Bellah, *The Broken Covenant* (New York: Seabury, 1975), 162: "No one has changed a great nation without appealing to its soul. . . . Culture is the key to revolution; religion is the key to culture."

CHAPTER 5

Thomas Aquinas: Mystic
and Prophet of the Environment

☾

In the modern era, we have been taught to think about Thomas Aquinas as a rationalist thinker. Though his intellectual gifts were immense, what makes him so amazing is that he was a mystic as well. His contribution to a cosmological-ecological mysticism has yet to be felt.

WHEN ONE THINKS of a patron saint for the ecological movement, one usually thinks of Francis of Assisi, or perhaps Hildegard of Bingen or Meister Eckhart. But I would like to propose still another thinker from the great cosmological awakening of the Middle Ages—Thomas Aquinas—as mystic and prophet of an Environmental Revolution.

At first blush this may sound hardly possible, much less probable, for those who are familiar with Aquinas at all have been instructed to see him as a rationalist thinker. But that is because most Thomistic interpreters of Aquinas during the modern era have been far more anthropocentric than he was and far less concerned about justice issues than he was. Texts of Thomas that are most familiar to us, such as the *Summa Theologica*, have been translated ad infinitum, but Aquinas's more mystical and cosmological works, such as his *Commentary on Denys the Areopagite* and his biblical commentaries, have rarely been available to English-speakers. In translating these and other works for my book *Sheer Joy: Conversations with Thomas Aquinas on Creation Spirituality*, I have found both a mystical and a prophetic passion in Aquinas's work that we could use in our spirituality and science today. Without going into detail about his life story, which in itself is the parable of a prophet, I think it will suffice here to recall his condemnation three times before his canonization, his shortened life (he died at forty-nine), his mental breakdown at the end of his life (he was rendered mute for the last year before he died), and his strident battles against Christian fundamentalists on the one hand and secularized atheists on the other. All this drama was brought about because of his commitment to a *scientist*—namely, Aristotle, considered the best scientist in Aquinas's day, who was brought into the West by way of Islam.

Not only did Aquinas teach that faith and science cannot contradict each other; he also insisted that you cannot do theology without science. "A mistake in our thinking about nature results in a mistake in our thinking about God,"[1] he declared. And again, "The opinion is false of those who assert that it makes no difference to the truth of the faith what anyone holds about creatures, so long as one thinks rightly about God. For error about creatures spills over into false opinion about God, and takes people's minds away from God, to whom faith seeks to lead them." Aquinas says that Scripture "threatens punishment to those who err about creatures (Ps. 28:5)" and that meditation on creatures leads us to behold the wisdom of God.

But Aristotle, to whose star Aquinas attached himself from his university days in Naples to his death in a monastery in Fossanuova thirty years later, was not only a scientist but a *pagan scientist*. Indeed, Aquinas's attitude toward pagans was far more ecumenical than that of many a churchman today when he said, for example, "All truth—whoever utters it comes from the Holy Spirit" and "revelation has been given to many pagans" and "the old pagan virtues were from God."

Why was Aquinas so at home with Aristotle and other pagans? One reason is that his sense of revelation was not anthropocentric—he didn't see revelation as simply what is in the Bible. He wrote, "Revelation comes in two volumes: the Bible and nature." He took nature seriously as a source of the experience of the divine and of divine truth. To take nature seriously is to want to study it, and to do this, one turns to scientists whose task it is to uncover the revelation of God in nature. "All creatures confess that they are made by God"— we study them because they lead us to the divine wisdom. "All natural things were produced by the divine art, and so may be called 'God's works of art.' " Every single creature leads us to the "Source without a source" who is God. "In the making of the very least creature there is manifested the infinite power, wisdom, and goodness of God because every single creature leads to the knowledge of the first and highest One, which is infinite in every perfection." True to the Cosmic Christ tradition in Creation Spirituality, Aquinas sees creatures as a "mirror" of God or an image of God. "Every creature is for us like a certain mirror. Because from the order, goodness, and magnitude which are caused by God in things, we come to a knowledge of the divine wisdom and goodness and eminence. And this knowledge we call a vision in a mirror."

Truth for Aquinas is not a Cartesian abstraction but a matter of the heart. Indeed, he pictures the heart as "the organ of the intellect" and says that "the objects of the heart are truth and justice." One studies nature in order to love more deeply. "The lover is not satisfied with a superficial apprehension of the beloved, but strives to gain an intimate knowledge of everything pertaining to the beloved, so as to penetrate into the very soul."

This penetrating love leads to an increase of the sense of beauty and the awareness of beauty. For Aquinas, unlike the theologians of the modern period, beauty is a significant theological category. "God is a fountain of total beauty," he writes. "All beauty, through which a thing is able to be, is a kind of participation in the divine brightness." In fact, "God is beauty itself, beautifying all things." Every creature contains a "sheen" to it, a kind of divine radiance—this is not unlike the German physicist Papp's finding of light waves in every atom in the universe. It is also the tradition of the Cosmic Christ—the light of the divine image in every being in the universe. "God puts into creatures, along with a kind of 'sheen,' a reflection of God's own luminous 'ray,' which is the fountain of all light," Aquinas observes.

Indeed, for Aquinas it is our passionate response to beauty that leads to prophetic zeal. "Love and also zeal are caused in us from beauty and goodness, for a thing is not beautiful because we love it, but we love it because it is beautiful and good. . . . God is called zealous because through God things become objects of zeal, that is, intensely loveable." Waking up to the "intense lovability" of things has everything to do with an Environmental Revolution, for surely our sense of the beauty of the earth and all its species urges us to ground our struggle for earth justice. This passion gives us the energy with which to carry on the struggle. In this manner we experience what philosopher William Hocking teaches—namely, that the "prophet is the mystic in action." Through reimmersing ourselves in the beauty of the earth and its systems of blessing (mysticism), we are moved to defend it from forces that will destroy it (prophecy). Zeal is the opposite of what Lester Brown has called the number one obstacle to an Environmental Revolution: inertia. This awakening of eros and passion is a result of faith; inertia is not. For faith, as Aquinas says, "does not quench desire. It enflames it."

A theology of blessing is at the very heart of Aquinas's worldview. God, who is "sheer goodness," has shared the divine goodness with all beings. Aquinas reminds us that a theology of blessing is a theology of the goodness of things. "To bless is nothing else than to speak the good. In one way we bless God and in another way God blesses us. We bless God by recognizing the divine goodness. And God blesses us by causing goodness in us." Aquinas is challenging us in this passage to meditate on the goodness of things—including ourselves. Time and again Aquinas praises the deep-down goodness of things: "Every being as being is good." "All things are good because they flow from the fount of goodness. We can praise God through all things!" For "the infinite goodness is bestowed on each creature according to its unique capacity." Not only is the universe good—it is *very* good. Aquinas teaches the original blessing that creation is when he comments on the Genesis creation story, "In the Book of Genesis it says, 'God saw all the things that God had made, and they were very good, each one of them having been previously said to be good. For each thing in its nature is good, but all things together are very good, by reason of the order of the universe, which is the ultimate and noblest perfection in things."

Aquinas believes that our task is to preserve the blessing or goodness of things. Indeed, his very definition of salvation is as follows: "Salvation means primarily and fundamentally the preserving of things in the good." In other words, the very meaning of redemption is to defend the blessing of creation—preserving things in the good. Thus a redemptive theology finds its deepest application in Aquinas's thought in terms of the struggle for ecological justice. Aquinas does not contrast grace to nature; he contrasts grace to sin.

Aquinas also marvels at the fact that God has bestowed on every creature of the universe "the dignity of causality." I love this phrase! Think of the dignity of causality of a single blade of grass, which can cause other grasses to exist, which can blanket the earth in inviting green colors, which can provide food for the cow that in turn causes milk, which can offer a soft blanket on which to rest one's body, which can feed a horse so it blossoms into its own beauty and dignity, and so on. Yes, the whole idea that every creature shares in the "dignity of causality" is enough to awaken reverence and respect, which in turn will usher in the era of an Environmental Revolution.

Aquinas is awed by the home that our universe is. In commenting on the psalmist's statement that "you shall be drunk on the plenty of thy house," he writes simply, "I.e., the universe." How fittingly this goes with the etymological meaning of the word ecology, a study of our home. Because

Aquinas is a student of nature, he is a student of cosmology; his entire theology is set in a cosmological—not an anthropological—context, as when he says that "nature in its most usual sense includes the relationship of the whole cosmos to God." The fundamental law of the cosmos for him is relationship and interdependence—as it is for contemporary science. "That all things are related to each other is evident from the fact that all are interconnected together to one end." In fact, "the perfection of any one thing considered in isolation is an imperfection, for one thing is merely one part of the entire integrity of the universe arising from the assembling together of many singular perfections." Clearly Aquinas is a *communitarian* thinker, but the primary community for him is not humans but our full home, the universe itself. Moreover, "all things are connected in a common bond of friendship with all nature." All things in the universe "seek God and desire God" with whom they share a common "friendship."

Aquinas recommends meditating on the truth of the interconnectivity of things in the universe, for to Aquinas it is a joy that "we are able to contemplate the marvelous connection of things." He proposes as material for our meditation everything from the sun to plants and animals, mussels and horses. All lead us to the divine wisdom. Because Aquinas is so cosmological a thinker, he is a deep ecologist. That ecological justice is a theological matter is taken for granted by Aquinas because God is the lover of creation with all its creatures. To offend the creation is to offend God. He says, "All artists love what they give birth to—parents love their children; poets love their poems; craftspeople love their handiwork. How then could God hate a single thing since God is the artist of everything?"

Of course the word *environment* comes from the word *environ* or "around." An environmental era is one in which we find the divine not up but *around*. In other words, it is not a time for more theism (which in turn creates atheism) but for *panentheism*, the understanding that God is in things and things are in God and that we experience the divine "in the round." Clearly Thomas Aquinas was a panentheist. For example, he writes that "the Godhead contains all things. God contains every place. God does not rest in some thing but all things rest in God. All things are in God." In a panentheistic worldview the sacred is everywhere. Not only are all things in God but as Aquinas says on numerous occasions, "God is in all things and most intimately so." Indeed, "one can say that God is more closely united to each thing than the thing is to itself." For "just as the soul is whole in every part of the body, so is God whole in all things and in each one." Aquinas spells out the intimacy of the presence of the divine in things when he writes, "God is in all things by the divine power, inasmuch as all things are subject to divine power; God is in all things by the divine presence, inasmuch as all things are bare and open to God's eyes; and God is in all things by the divine essence, inasmuch as God is present to all as the cause of their being."

Yet Aquinas is adamant about defending the autonomy of creatures, each of whom cocreates with God. "God works in things in such a manner that things have their proper operation," for to minimize the power of creatures themselves "derogates from the order of the universe, which is made up of the order and connection of causes. For the First Cause, by the preeminence of its goodness, gives other beings not only their existence but also their existence as causes." It follows that "there is no contradiction between secondary causes and Providence—secondary causes in fact bring about the accomplishment of Providence."

From this sample of citations from the rich creation theology of Thomas Aquinas, we can begin to see how we have in him a substantive ally in the struggle for what Lester

Brown calls the "Environmental Revolution." The fact that
Aquinas emerged from the same poverty movement as
Francis of Assisi means that Francis was less a solitary figure
than we might have been led to believe. Hildegard, Francis,
Aquinas, Eckhart all invite us to a Creation Spirituality that
teaches us to see the world as a blessing worthy of defense.
Herein lies nourishment and courage for our dire times.

NOTE

1. All references to Aquinas can be found in Matthew Fox, *Sheer Joy:
   Conversations with Thomas Aquinas on Creation Spirituality* (San Francisco:
   HarperSanFrancisco, 1993).

CHAPTER 6

Native Teachings:
Spirituality with Power

☾

The great gift of the Americas and the reason why the Creation
Spiritual tradition has been rediscovered here is that in spite of
five hundred years of oppression and colonialism, we are still
graced with the wisdom of the native peoples of this land. This
brief essay recalls a small bit of that wisdom.

THE WEST HAS been amply reminded of the Holocaust of the Jewish people under Hitler. Six million persons—most of them Jews but also others, including dedicated and resisting Christians, clergy, and homosexuals—were exterminated for racial and ideological reasons. How important it is, as Elie Wiesel insists, that our race never forget this genocide. In memory there lies redemption and the possibility that humanity will not repeat its worst crimes.

But there is another holocaust in our Western history that also needs to be remembered. It is even vaster than that of the Jewish people, if one dare speak that way. I speak of the genocide of the native peoples of the Americas. In the 1500s, when Europeans arrived, there were eighty million inhabitants of the Americas. Fifty years later there were only ten million. In Mexico alone the population dropped from twenty-five million to one million. The West needs to meditate deeply on these facts. From the suffering and injustice they represent, from the blood of the martyrs on these lands of the Americas, there is emerging today those liberation movements in South and North America that are truly post-European in their scope and promise. The former we know as Liberation Theology; the latter as creation-centered spirituality. Because they reach back to ancient times, they are pre-European as well.

It is well known that the pride and population of the native peoples of the Americas is beginning to rise again. With this resurrection comes an invitation to the conqueror to be transformed. I can honestly say that I have learned more from Native Americans about prayer directly and indirectly (through dreams) in the past fifteen years than I have from any other source save for the feminist movement, which in many ways is so similar. A journey into the spirituality of the anawim, the ones without a voice, is not mere therapy for a guilty conscience. It is, as Jesus taught, a theological locus, a place for learning wisdom. The question needs to be asked: in killing an ancient civilization, what parts of its own soul did the West also kill? I will enumerate below six areas of spirituality to which Native Americans have awakened me over the years.

THE NEED FOR A SPIRITUALITY WITH POWER

Power is not a dirty word to Native Americans. Power objects and experiences of power in prayer and spirituality are presumed to be part of the journey. I was speaking to a Native American who told me how he took his teenage sons to their first Sun Dance and how a medicine man walked around with hot coals in his mouth breathing the smoke on the young men about to do the dance. When the coals got cooler, he spit them out and put hot ones into his mouth again. "What bishop can do that?" the Native American asked me with gusto. The question has remained with me. Not because I expect every bishop to have the power to hold hot coals in his or her mouth, but because the question behind the question is not only important but essential: is there any power left in Western religion's declared spiritual leadership? If there is no real power, then religion will be reduced to erecting man-made power games that smack of all the worst secular power trips. Otto Rank comments that the "main failure of Western civilization has been its inability to translate supernatural concepts of power into realistic expression."[1]

Where, we might ask, is the power in liturgy? In the sacraments? In the Good News of the Gospel? "By their fruits you will know them," Jesus warned. And the fruits of spirituality include power—the power of divine grace and healing, not the power of coercion or control. Guilt and shame are no substitutes for power. And neither are demands for obedience.

COSMOLOGY

The Native Americans I have known are incapable of living cut off from nature, or oblivious to nature, or in arrogant relationships over nature. They know they are nature and are in nature and from nature. Anthropocentrism does not hold sway over their imaginations or their ethics or their prayer. I remember being at a gathering of fifteen hundred native peoples under the auspices of the Catholic church, and the weeklong event began with a Catholic mass in a large chapel. I was bored by the mass, frankly. I had feelings throughout that this was not the Native American way of praying. When it ended, I stayed in my pew to be quiet, and a Native American came up to me. I asked him how he liked the mass. He said, "This is not our church. Our church is outdoors. We should have prayed outdoors." I was reminded of Francis of Assisi, quizzed one day on where his cloister was. "There," he said, pointing to the fields of Umbrian flowers and grains, "behold my cloister."

A cosmology is such a deep and wonderful and profound way of belonging to the world that I suspect that the greatest evil the white world has perpetrated on native peoples has been the effort to strip them of their cosmology. I wonder if that loss is not the ultimate sadness and cosmic loneliness that eats at the hearts of Native American youth, who so often fall into despair and drink, drugs and suicide. And this happens just at the age of emerging adulthood, the call to be a citizen of the cosmos, an agent of the universe, a giver of one's gift back to the community, back to the universe. I believe that alcohol is a liquid cosmology, and drugs, a quick-fix cosmology. Neither works. Both do devastating damage to body, psyche, spirit—these wonderful gifts of the universe.

AT-ONENESS WITH BODY

Native peoples, because they acknowledge the grace of the universe and its giftedness to us, do not regret being body. There is an at-oneness with one's naturehood and animality. Indeed, there is an at-oneness with animals who carry spirit messages and spirit power. I remember the time I spent in a kiva with a Hopi elder who told me his experience of praying with a rattlesnake for three days and three nights at a time. "Of course he was nervous at first," he explained, "but when I sang to him he recognized the warmth of my body and calmed down. We made good prayer together." European civilization's suspicion of nature has resulted in suspicion of nature's amazing gift: our bodies. The native peoples have no guilty conscience over being body. The silliness into which Saint Augustine's descendants have fallen over issues of sexuality or dance, for example, are simply unbelievable to a Native American. As Jose Hobday once explained to me, "We Indians dance before we walk. At the powwows we are carried in our parents' arms or on their backs for the dance. We never forget that." Yet I have met American Indians who were raised by Christians on reservations who forbade them to dance at all.

The natural processes of puberty and sexual maturation are not tidied up, covered up, or whispered about among native peoples. Rituals for young men and young women coming of age are celebrated as being, once again, part of the cosmological gift of our existence.

RITUAL THAT WORKS

A ritual that works or is effective is one that holds power for transformation—one that effects change. Every time I have had the privilege of worshiping with native peoples, I have experienced the power of their prayer. Their powwow dances, their sweat lodges, their Sun Dances, their fastings, their chants, their drumming all have power. They work. They bring us down to places of depth and silence and darkness and healing. And they demand deep bodily responses. Everyone participates in the great dance. No one just mouths words from the head up. Everyone sweats in the sweat lodge. Everyone gives what they have to give. And it comes from deeper places than mere words usually come from.

I ASK MYSELF why I learn so much more about worship from native peoples than I do from European-educated Ph.D.s in theology and liturgy, and I realize the answer to this question is found in the preceding four points. First of all, native liturgies have power and are about releasing power—power from within, within the individual and within the community. And the community of worshipers consists not just of the two-legged ones. Second, native rituals celebrate a cosmology—that is their principal function, to make the psyche cosmic and the cosmos alive in the psyche. They are dances in microcosm/macrocosm. As Otto Rank put it, an "identity with the universe" is part of the "general human feeling" that characterizes a microcosmic/macrocosmic structure or reenactment in ritual. "Cultural development has advanced by way of the cosmic. . . . Certain celestial processes had to be imitated in cult form on earth in order that man's [sic] cosmic identity, and with it his immortality, might be assured." Third, there is bodiliness in native rituals. No dualism haunts their prayer. Dancing to the drumbeat of Mother Earth's heartbeat, which is also our mother's heartbeat in the womb, is healing for that reason. Fasting is undertaken not out of guilt or moral fears of sinful gluttony but out of a search for real power. As Bill Wahpepah says, "if you want to know the power of water, go without all water for three days. Then, drink water." In that instant you will know how holy water is and what a blessing it is.

EVERYONE AN ARTIST

It is taken for granted among native peoples that creativity and the making of things are everyone's task and are not primarily a matter of economics but of cosmology. Weaving a basket is making a basket, but it is also a means of entering into one of the cosmic processes of the universe, which weaves interdependent strands of creation. When I sat down at a table with fourteen Inuit people at an American Indian conference and we began our conversation, it turned out that all of them (ages ranging from teenagers to seventy-year-olds) made things—their clothes, bracelets, moccasins, and so on. Only one was a "professional" artist who sold a soap sculpture that paid for the other thirteen to fly down to the conference with him. Native peoples give more than lip service to the ancient tradition of the image of the Creator God in all of us. The creative acts that weave a culture—acts of making food and gathering it, making clothes and repairing them, making fun and laughter—are integral to their spiritual outlook. And speaking of making, I learned recently that the Eskimo word for making love means to make laughter together. One more instance of no shame over being body and of celebrating the artist within.

THE MEANING OF AMERICAN

Finally, I am beginning to learn from native peoples what it means to be an American. To be an American does not mean that I wrap myself in the red, white, and blue and acquiesce to the shibboleths and paranoia that so characterize the last days of empire building in the West. Rather, to be American means that I listen with my heart to the history of this land and its peoples who for tens of thousands of years have lived and celebrated on this earth. It means that I make common song and dance, common prayer and worship with those who preceded me to this holy temple we call Mother Earth. It does not mean that I merely return to a precivilized state. Life is not that simple. Rather, it means that I and others take responsibility for the artist inside us in order to create and recreate, to give birth and to recycle. From the pain and suffering, the genius and the silence, of Western and Native American spiritualities, there will be forged finally a vision worth living for our descendants seven generations from now. Mother Earth will not survive without this kind of bonding and mutual interaction. The Native American soul in each of us must be called forth once again. In spite of genocide, it still lives. The wisdom of the native peoples will not go away. And that is good news, indeed![2]

NOTES

1. Otto Rank, *Beyond Psychology* (New York: Dover, 1958), 58.
2. My thanks go to the native peoples who have been my teachers: Jose Hobday, Ed Savilla, Bill Wahpepah, Robert Boissiere, Chuck Leute, and Buck Ghosthorse. May there be more!

CHAPTER 7

Creation Spirituality
and the Dreamtime

☾

The *Aborigines of Australia* are perhaps the oldest tribe of humans in the world. One of their richest concepts is that of the "Dreamtime," and the riches of this tradition speak wisdom to a modern and postmodern civilization. This talk was delivered at a five-day Creation Spirituality program in Melbourne, Australia, in January 1990. At that program two Aborigines taught a seminar, and at the end one of them told me, through tears of joy, that "this was the first time white people have ever asked us to teach them." Honoring another people is as simple as asking them to teach us. We grow and they grow in the process.

THE BEAUTY THAT is the Dreamtime is everywhere. The question is do we have the eyes to see it and the ears to hear it.

I feel it is pure nostalgia to think that only people in the wilderness, in the bush, can experience Dreamtime. It is part of our nature and our histories.

On the other hand, the fact that there is so much wilderness in Australia and that the Australian Aborigines have lived so long and invested so much spirit in this land does invite people here to a special experience of the wilderness Dreamtime as well. And there is a challenge to bring the two together: how does the outback relate to the urban?

What we need is a biculturalism. By this I mean that we need to live both in Dreamtime and in clock time. I am really convinced that we have to find this balance in our civilization. We are so unbalanced. You cannot be a mystic twenty-four hours a day. You would blow all your tubes! You need the dialectic, the dance, the balance.

Is that balance evident in our education system? I know of some cases where it is, some schools that make definite efforts to provide meditation time, gardening time, and art-as-meditation time for the young. But I don't know of many of this type. In our general education system, it is my experience that in adolescence, at the crucial time of puberty, for example, we take away the crayons, the song and dance, the theater, and we get "serious"—precisely when we should be bringing the young people more fully into cosmology, introducing them into the Dreamtime of the stars, into the story of the universe. In fact, this process can begin much sooner now. Some teachers in the United States are giving the creation story to children at a very young age and having them tell the stories about the birth of the stars and the sun. In other words, they are creating rituals with the children.

Ritual is the ultimate way to learn, and the implications for growth when these children become teenagers are great. It is creating Dreamtime; the new cosmic story is Dreamtime.

I am convinced that by their nature children live in Dreamtime. Most parents are given children as their spiritual directors. They come as messengers from another place to teach us all the things our parents didn't teach us! Children are mystical beings. But we have to ask, What does our education system do to kill this natural mysticism?

The overemphasis in our society on comfort makes it difficult for mysticism, for spirituality, to manifest itself. In North America our churches are comfort stations, with padded kneelers, padded seats, air-conditioning, the perfect temperature in winter. (I'm told that this is not the case in Australia!) Our attitude toward worship is too comfort-oriented. We need to learn from native peoples in this regard.

One aspect of this comfort orientation has to do with time. We run our worship by the clock, knowing exactly when it will begin, exactly when it will end, and how long it will take to empty the parking lot! Whereas when you worship with native peoples, you find it is a cosmic process. You get in and you wait until everyone is there. At first you're impatient. Most of the time, for most of us, waiting is an uncomfortable thing to do. But then you settle down and begin to realize that waiting is a deep part of the whole spiritual process.

Still on the topic of comfort, a Native American sweat lodge is radically uncomfortable. In a sweat lodge you face death. During my first twenty minutes in one, I really thought I was going to die—I was looking for the fire exit! Not finding it, at the end of the twenty minutes, I realized I *was* going to die. It was then that I entered into the consciousness breakthrough that the sweat lodge is all about. I just let go of the fear of death and entered into it instead. That's the whole point: real prayer takes one to the brink of things. It takes you to your own transformation.

There's an African-American theologian who says he's convinced that 95 percent of all white worship is dead. I asked him, "How do you define 'dead worship'?" His reply was "Dead worship is when you walk out the same as when you went in—no transformation took place."

There is a need, therefore, to challenge ourselves, to get out of our comfort orientation. In the Western tradition we confuse asceticism with penance for our sins or hatred of our bodies. But the basic meaning of asceticism relates to being an athlete. An athlete pushes herself or himself. There is a point in running or exercising where you go beyond what you thought you could do, where it hurts a little. At this point, ecstasy usually begins. The West moralizes about this process, holding that the hurt is to keep the body down, to punish oneself for being a sexual being or a sinner. All that has destroyed the real meaning of sacrifice and of being a spiritual athlete.

An example regarding true asceticism would be to go without water for a couple of days, to go without food for a while—to fast, in other words, but not in penance for your sins. Let your sins go! Fast in order to reexperience your own health. The fact is that all religious traditions of any antiquity have fasting periods. Why? Because it is good for our health. Our digestive system is kept working twenty-four hours a day, seven days a week. Give it a break! We all should fast for that reason alone, a few times a year. This is holism, for in the process of allowing our physical body to be regenerated, our senses do get cleansed, and we do see the world with greater reverence, greater awe, greater gratefulness.

The Western spiritual tradition distorts the whole language of asceticism. Creation mystics are overlooked. We need to redo our theology.

I have been asked what steps should be taken to plant Creation Spirituality in Australia. I would begin with a seminar exploring creation theology with art-as-meditation gatherings included—and, of course, we would create rituals together. Then the follow-up would be very important. Australians must define Australian theology, Australian spirituality, in the light of the creation tradition and in the light of your Aboriginal roots, as well as the issues of injustice in Australia and your unique experiences of joy and mysticism.

Without doubt, this can be done. Any human group can do it. It is built into us to be able to bring about justice and celebration. That is why we are a gift to the universe and not a curse.

Knowledge of "the heart" is not alone sufficient. The concepts must be grasped, which requires study. There may be toxic concepts to be undone first of all, for we have been fed dualistic categories through religion, education, and culture for centuries. They have to be let go of. We have some cleansing to do of our minds, left brain as well as right brain. The right brain, however, does not need much cleansing; it just needs waking up and exercise.

It is important, then, to gather together in groups; to do rituals together; to read the mystics together with the right brain, with the heart, putting all this through the body; to read our greatest Western mystics—Hildegard and Eckhart, Julian, Mechtild—and don't forget Jesus and the Wisdom literature of the Bible (see the book *Wisdom's Feast* by S. Cady, for the latter); to study together; to apply this to the Australian situation; to make contact with Australian Aboriginal people. The latter effort will, of course, be clumsy at first. Why wouldn't it be, with all the pain on both sides?

Victor Lewis, who gives excellent workshops on racism and, as a young African-American, has been through so much of it, says that white people are in deep grief about racism. Sometimes we hear the anger and suffering from people of color and we get overwhelmed with guilt. But the real issue is our grief. We have to deal with that sadness.

White Australians have to make themselves vulnerable to the Aboriginal people—whatever that may mean.

Australian Aboriginals must be encouraged to give talks, to go into parishes and speak about their experiences, to make contacts. If Hildegard of Bingen and Meister Eckhart are shared with them, they will become excited!

I'll never forget the first time we translated Hildegard, and I shared her with a class of students. There was a fellow in the class who spoke up after I had read just a few lines. "I've just returned," he said, "from living eighteen years with the Lakota people [Native Americans] in South Dakota. Hildegard sounds exactly like the medicine man who was my spiritual teacher for the last ten years!" All kinds of energy can flow when native peoples experience the creation tradition.

As Elizabeth Cain has pointed out, spirituality must begin with the land. This is basic to the entire Aboriginal consciousness. It is also basic to the environmental survival not just of our species but of all the species with whom we share this planet. So obviously this whole issue of land—I prefer the word wilderness—is at the heart of things.

It is not easy growing up, letting go, separating oneself from . . . I believe this is the moment in history when Australians are really doing this. You are realizing you are not just transplanted Europeans. We Americans are only beginning to realize that we have to evolve our own theology, not just translate European books and write their footnotes! We have our own experience, from our own land! For the land is where the spirits are.

You need to get in touch with your Australian poets, writers, and artists, both black and white, on this land. They are the ones who are naming the journeys for you. I get very excited when I look at the writers in my land like Walt Whitman or Annie Dillard, Alice Walker, Ralph Waldo Emerson, Barry Lopez, and many others. The spirit of the land is speaking through these people. There is this tradition of Creation Spirituality in my land. And that is a deep part of my spiritual roots. It will be of yours too. Find these treasures—the musicians, poets, painters, photographers, novelists, and all the writers who can feed your soul *here* because they have lived here.

There is a special link, I think, between the Australian experience and the North American experience. There is much we hold in common. First of all, I would like to cite a criticism, one that raises our consciousness, from a document in Central America. This document was put together in 1988 by one hundred Christian pastors, lay leaders, and theologians of Central America. It is called the Kairos Document, and it images the struggle of the poor there against what it calls "the idols of the Empire."

We have the tradition—Australians have it even more than Americans—of piously nodding our heads whenever we hear the word empire. I'll never forget the first time I went into Saint Paul's Cathedral in London with my eyes open—I was a student at the time. In that cathedral there are all these huge statues to military men, and underneath them are inscriptions to the effect that so-and-so killed one thousand Indians in such and such a battle, and another killed twenty thousand in some other battle. You realize that the marriage of church and empire must be critiqued. If we don't do it, someone will do it for us. The Kairos Document is a good example.

The British Empire is admittedly a kind of harmless pussycat at the present time, but the toxin from it is probably still in your consciousness. Today, of course, what is at issue is the American Empire. And the statement from Central America about the latter empire reads, "In the process of maturing in their historical consciousness with the help of their faith, Central America's poor came to find out that the God of Western Christian society was not the God of Jesus but rather an idol of the empire." Now this is strong language. You might substitute the term *Australian Aborigine* for "Central American."

"The Central American poor at this time," continues the document, "are serving as witnesses and martyrs for the God of Jesus, the God of the poor. They are a living prophecy that invites the Christian churches to abandon the empire's gods and become converted to the true God." Again, that is strong language. I think we have to wrestle with it, put it into our prayers and our discussions. But it's also very traditional language, it's biblical. The idols of the empire are false gods—imperialism, colonialism, slavery, racism, sexism—false gods that must be dealt with openly.

Barry Lopez's book *Of Wolves and Men* really moves me. Here is a man who went to live with wolves in Canada for a whole year or two. He lived with them and then wrote this marvelous book, which, on reading it, accomplishes a wonderful cleansing of the soul. We have a lot of mythology about how evil wolves are and how they are out to get us. There is a projection of the "bogeyman" onto wolves. Lopez brings out the beauty of the wolf, as well as, of course, the terror that is intrinsically associated with all wild animals (including the human!—just look at our history).

Father Bartholomé de Las Casas was a Dominican priest who strongly defended the Indians in Latin America against the Spanish. He underwent a conversion, for he himself was Spanish. In fighting very hard for the rights of the Indians, he made the point that to justify their killing the Indians, the Spanish used the excuse that the Indians practiced human sacrifice. This was true: part of Indian ritual was to sacrifice a young man or woman once a year or thereabouts. But, argued Bartholomé, all the sacrifices that the Indians performed as ritual over the years did not come close to the number of killings for which the Spanish were responsible. He further declared that the Indian civilization was superior to the Spanish.

De Las Casas's final point was that if in the history of the world there has ever been cause for a just war, "these native people have the right to make war against the white Europeans until Judgment Day."

Columbus landed in America in 1492. We are quite close to the commemoration of that event. I purposely do not use the word *celebration*. There will be a lot of people celebrating it, but that is not how Native Americans see it. Five hundred years ago, when Columbus landed, there were eighty million native people in America. Fifty years later, there were only ten million! Seventy million native people died after the Europeans landed—some by disease, yes, but a great many by genocide.

I have read statistics about Australia and New Zealand, and it must be admitted that this same story is repeated everywhere. It is time now for acknowledgment and grief.

There is a fine book on this topic by Frederick Turner called *Beyond Geography*. It is a history of America beginning with Columbus, from the point of view of the native people. Turner calls it an essay in spirituality, in the history of spirituality, for he feels that the reason, the *fundamental* reason for the genocide was European spirituality.

It is his belief that Europeans had repressed the sensual, the sexual, and the darker side; so when they came to America, all this surfaced and was projected onto the native peoples whom they called "savages." The killing of this "enemy" (which was really themselves) was thus justified and legitimized.

I am always asking, What does a homophobic society lose in its soul when it offends a sexual minority? Likewise, what has white Christianity lost in its soul in lashing out at other civilizations? This is not an altruistic question. It is a matter of self-interest: what have we lost in our souls?

In listening to what Australian Aborigines have to say to us, I experience a sense of complementarity. The gifts of Christianity do bring something to the native people of Australia, and the gifts of the Aborigines do give something to Christianity. This is the challenge: to work out that complementarity.

I am convinced that one sign of hope for the world today is that the wisdom of the native peoples is still around. But it won't be for long unless we change our white ways.

In one of his essays, *The Passing Wisdom of Birds*, Barry Lopez has a wonderful passage with an incredible message. It relates to the conquest by Cortés of what is now Mexico City. That city was the Aztec Byzantium. Everyone, including Cortés himself, considered it the most beautiful city in the world. Among its delights were aviaries of marvelous, multicolored birds. Nearly every home had its own aviary. Now Cortés was driven out when he first entered the city, so two years later, he returned with his army and destroyed the entire place—including all the aviaries. He wiped out even the birds!

I want to share with you Barry Lopez's thoughts in this context because I feel they speak to the issue of the land, of the wilderness, and of our attitudes toward it. Lopez tells us that when we lose even the birds, we face losing the purpose of our ideals, our sense of dignity and compassion—even our sense of what we call God. He believes that eight thousand years ago, in the Fertile Crescent, we set aside the Mother Goddess tradition, but we can locate it again and creatively refine it in North America. The same could be said of Australia.

For Barry Lopez, the new world is still resonant with mystery. I get goose bumps at the thought of the parts of

Australia I have seen, especially the central part. I feel the truth of Barry's words for Australia. He calls for an enlightened response toward cultures that differ from our own, and by culture he does not mean just the human. He is also talking about wolves, birds, invertebrates. Barry believes that we can find the sense of resolution we have been seeking for centuries by moving away from the traditional narrow view of the value of life and beginning to respect other paths to perfection.

I find this to be an incredible outlook, and I lay it before you. Eight thousand years ago, when patriarchy began to overtake earth-based religions, our species took a turn away from nature and from God in nature. Now the reality is that you Australians are being invited—through the mystery still in your land, the spirits still on your land, and the Australian Aboriginal peoples not only outside you but in you, along with your Celtic ancestors—to take another look and recover even the meaning of God.

Let me turn now to the very rich topic of the Dreamtime. When new thoughts are first encountered, they are not always grasped immediately. So it was for me regarding the Dreamtime. I first read about it a few years ago, but it is only now just beginning to seep into me. There is such wisdom in this whole Dreamtime concept.

Let me begin by pointing out the connections between our biblical heritage, mysticism, and the Dreamtime. Elizabeth Cain has called our attention to the fact that there is no word for time in the Australian Aboriginal language. Everything is always now. This is exactly how Meister Eckhart talks. "God," says he, "is always in the beginning, making things new!" And he adds, "If you can return to the beginning, you will always be new, always be young, always be in touch with God." This is why our Scriptures begin with "In the beginning . . . "—both Genesis and John's Gospel. And all four Gospels begin with the creation story, a cosmic creation story, as I have demonstrated in my book, *The Coming of the Cosmic Christ*. The Cosmic Christ is celebrated in the first chapters of each of the synoptic Gospels, just as he is in the first chapter of John's Gospel.

Another phrase Eckhart uses is "living in the eternal now." What we find in the Australian Aboriginal understanding of time is pure mystical consciousness. We white people will never get it until we sink into our own mystical experience. That explains the clash between white and indigenous cultures.

We have to listen with our hearts, not just our heads. As Eckhart says, "God is creating the entire universe, fully and totally, in this present *now*."

"This is the Dreamtime," Eddie Kneebone says, "*now*." Eddie would undoubtedly feel that Meister Eckhart is an Australian Aborigine too!

All the stories of original creation are Dreamtime. It is all *now*. This view is, of course, scientifically correct. All nineteen billion years of history are behind us. They don't exist anymore. The original fireball is gone. The supernova explosion that gave birth to the elements of our body is gone. But it is present in today's sunshine, in today's photosynthesis, in our bodies and minds.

Every time an idea "goes off" in our brains, we make a connection. A light wave goes off, a photon; that light wave is a piece of the sun, and the sun is a piece of a supernova explosion that in turn was a piece of the original fireball. *The fireball is going off in your brain now*, because nothing that happened up to now exists anymore. There is no yesterday. It's like a wave coming up in the ocean: it brings everything with it.

What Eckhart is saying is verifiable by today's physics, *which is mystical*, and it's verifiable by the Australian Aboriginal tradition, *which is mystical*. (It is not, however, very verifiable in most church rituals or church thinking as yet. But you and I are going to make that happen—in politics and education too.)

There is definitely much in common between Eckhart's spirituality and that of the Australian Aborigine. The reason, I believe, is that Eckhart lived with the Celtic spirit in the Rhineland. Indeed, I would say that we have an Eckhart only because the Celts settled in the Rhineland. That settlement is behind what is called the Rhineland mystic movement. This fact also explains the emergence of a Hildegard of Bingen. Hildegard attended a Celtic monastery that was, by way of interest, a monastery for both sexes. Unlike the Jansenist Irish, the Celts were not all hung up on sex, and they had men and women residing in monasteries together, thus benefiting from their combined energy.

Again, another interesting fact here is that Hildegard had to break away because the men became very jealous of the great fame she achieved as a result of the books she wrote. Many women wanted to study with Hildegard in the monastery, but the men would not make room for them, even though they could easily have done so.

"Enough of this injustice!" cried Hildegard, and she left, taking with her not only her own dowry but also those of all the other women! For years the abbot wrote her poison-pen letters demanding that she come back—and be sure to bring the dowries back with her. Hildegard never returned. Instead, she started three women's monasteries. When she did reply to the abbot, her letter was all about injustice. That was the incomparable Hildegard.

So in the Celtic Rhineland mystical tradition, Meister Eckhart could write, "God is creating the entire universe, fully and totally in this present *now*. Everything that God created six thousand years ago (according to the science of his day) and even previous to that . . . God creates now *all at*

once." He goes on to collapse future and past into now:
"Everything of the past and everything of the present and
everything of the future God is creating in the innermost
realms of the soul." This is good Australian Aboriginal
thinking. And it is good physics too, because it is true.

What we give birth to is the future. If we continue destroying the wilderness, destroying our habitat, then the
future will be one of destruction. But if something in our
hearts and souls now creates instead of destroys, then the
future will be one of creativity and promise.

What emphasis all this puts on creativity, on the
choices we make with our divine powers of imagination! I
cannot listen to Australian Aborigines speaking for very long
without hearing the echo from their heart about the fact that
everything is happening *now*.

Dreamtime itself is right here now. When as a Christian
theologian, I hear the word *Dreamtime*, I hear Jesus talking
about the kingdom of God. "The kingdom and queendom
of God, the reign of God, is among you." (Luke 17:21) We
are in it.

In his explanation of Dreamtime, Eddie Kneebone makes
it clear that all living things are part of it, including the souls
and spirits of the ancestors that are in the trees, in the animals. Is not this the Christian doctrine of the communion of
the saints? This communion of saints is *here, now*. Hildegard is
sitting on your shoulder, urging you to be as stubborn as
she was in her time, and as creative. Eckhart too and all the
saints are here.

During my Vatican-imposed sabbatical, I did a vision
quest, which is a Native American ritual. You go into the
woods for twenty-four hours, fasting beforehand, and you
pray. It was a very powerful experience for me. One thing I
learned from it is that the Native American people believe
God does not make evil spirits; we humans do, and our
human institutions do. Moreover, the only avenue by which

an evil spirit can enter the human heart is through *fear*. That is their belief. Fear is the doorway through which evil spirits of others or of institutions enter our hearts. And prayer is geared to making ourselves strong enough to resist fear, or to enter into it without succumbing to it.

What amazing wisdom is embodied in this belief! Evil spirits come from humans, from institutions, and fear is the avenue of entrance.

Fundamentalism, which is spreading through all religions—Islam, Judaism, Buddhism, and certainly Christianity—is all about fear. Courage is at the heart of fighting the fear.

Another thing I learned on the vision quest was about the spirits of the place. All the leaves came alive during that twenty-four hours with images and animals. The whole forest was illuminated for twenty-four hours. There was even a Madonna up in the tree. When my director for the quest, Buck Ghosthorse, processed it with me afterward, he said, "You know, these spirits are the spirits of all the animals who have lived in this land." We're talking here about dinosaurs, crocodiles, polar bears. But the point he was making was that the spirits are present, and they are supportive. They want to see Creation Spirituality happen and expand with the human species, because it is to their advantage.

The communion of saints is on our side, but it does not involve just the two-legged ones. Thomas Merton—who has half a claim on being from Down Under, since his father was a New Zealander—says that every non-two-legged creature is a saint! (Something to remember when we're about to swat a mosquito! During the vision quest we were forbidden to kill any mosquitoes. At the time, I had thirty on me, and that proved interesting.)

The communion of saints, thus, takes in all creatures, and they all have soul. Our ancestors believed that. Only in the eighteenth century, with the Enlightenment and

Descartes, came the idea that humans alone have souls. Descartes held that if a dog were cut and it squealed, this would be a mechanical response only. That was the beginning of behaviorism—and of our Western medicine too. But Aquinas in the Middle Ages taught that animals and plants have souls.

I'd go even further. I think rocks and mountains have their own sense of soul—they just act a little slower. Today's physics tells us that every rock is a cyclone of activity. The atoms in the rock are jumping around. Indeed, everything is moving in the universe, everything is dancing the cosmic dance . . . except a few white Christians . . . in high places. . . .

I am connecting the tradition of the kingdom of God to the Dreamtime and the tradition of the communion of saints to the Dreamtime. Here is material for Australian theologians to work on. Eddie Kneebone declared that what the Dreamtime gives people is a powerful identity, a sense of their importance, a belief that they are valuable for what they are.

Another aspect of the Dreamtime is *cosmology*. It is a realization that we have a place in the universe. *Our lives are not trivial!* The young need to hear this. The Australian Aboriginal young people feel so dispossessed precisely because that message has been ripped away. Yet it was part of the original blessing, part of the cosmic gift.

At this point, I'd like to mention something Eddie Kneebone alluded to: the Australian Aboriginal feeling about the views of anthropologists. I resonate to this because the native people in America have the same feeling toward anthropologists. They're being told something similar to what Eddie spoke of: that their ancestors originally came from Europe, walked over the Bering Strait and settled in North America. About ten years ago, anthropologists were saying that Native Americans may have been in North America only

about six to eight thousand years. Later they said that the figure could be twelve thousand. But two years ago, in Florida,
they found a sweat lodge, upside down, and they carbon-
dated it back forty-two thousand years!

Buck Ghosthorse, the Lakota Native American whom I
mentioned earlier, comments, "Oh, we've no problem with
the theory that these folks came over the Bering Strait. The
point is that when they arrived, we shook their hands and
welcomed them!" Buck also used to quote his grandfather as
saying, "Don't worry about these white people. They're just
passing through!"

Another American Indian has remarked, "Sometimes I
just sit myself down next to a freeway and I watch all these
white people going places all the time, just going and
going—they're never there!" Yet part of the kingdom of God
motif of the Dreamtime is that we *are* there! That is what
Jesus is trying to tell us: the kingdom is already here, it is
among us! In the Western theological tradition, this is called
"realized eschatology."

We put so much energy into getting away from wherever we are, instead of putting the same energy into prepar-
ing our hearts to see the wonder that is already here with us,
where we are. Doing the latter is what is meant by simplify-
ing our lifestyle.

If the Australian Aborigines could be happy for thousands of years in the desert, with none of the so-called com-
forts of life, they must have something going for them. And
that something is a whole sense of *being there*.

THESE, THEN, ARE some reflections I wanted to offer in the
light of our own Western tradition. Perhaps this is the time
for us who are ex-Europeans to start cleaning up the mess
left by Western spirituality, in the name of empire, around
the world. We may need to do some meditating on how best
to do that and how to ritualize it. What has to be realized is

that we have inherited a dysfunctional spirituality from the recent centuries of Christianity.

The deeper roots of our Catholic tradition, however, tell a different story. Let us recall that it was the Irish, the Celts of the twelfth century, who re-Christianized Europe, brought it to life, made it creation-centered, and gave us our wonderful mystical traditions, from Francis of Assisi to Hildegard of Bingen.

In northern Italy alone there are over two hundred churches dedicated to Francis. The Celts were responsible for that! Francis is deeply Celtic in his spirituality. But we need to rescue Francis from being sentimentalized. (In the States, popular custom places him in backyard birdbaths!)

Sentimentality is not spirituality. It is spirituality's number one enemy. Carl Jung makes the point that sentimentalism and violence always go together: scratch a sentimentalist and you find violence. The issues related to violence, such as racism and injustice, are never dealt with in the sentimental context. Justice is not a category of sentimentalism. Syrupy emotion has nothing to do with a real passion for justice.

Thus we can affirm that the healthy intellectual history of Europe was led by the Celts. It was they who first translated the Eastern theologians for the Latin West. In fact, with regard to Thomas Aquinas, there is an interesting and not well known fact that bears this out. When Thomas was about seventeen, a student at the University of Naples, his main teacher was a Celt, an Irishman, and this man was teaching Aristotle to him—a very radical thing to do in those days! For Aristotle was a pagan scientist, and the Augustinian theologians who were the fundamentalists and sentimentalists of the thirteenth century—the people representing the establishment, the "empire" that Augustine had set up in the fourth century—these men were horrified at the thought of bringing in a cosmology from a pagan scientist like Aristotle. Moreover, the pope had actually forbidden

Christians to read Aristotle—and Naples is not very far from Rome!

Notwithstanding all this, Aquinas's Irish scholar was teaching him Aristotle, and Aquinas was to spend his whole life bringing Aristotle—the best scientist they could find in the thirteenth century—into the heart of Christianity. And with him, cosmology.

I am presently doing work on Aquinas's mysticism. We were always told that he was a rationalist, but he was not. His best mystical works have hardly ever been translated into English: his biblical commentaries and his commentary on Denys the Areopagite. All the Thomists through the centuries have come and gone, without bothering to translate the commentaries. Yet these commentaries are the least scholastic and the most cosmological. I have found some really wonderful things in these books!

Coming back to the Dreamtime, I want to repeat that I find it immensely rich. It is all about the ongoing creation story. And it's about mysticism, the eternal now, to which Jesus called us: the awareness of the kingdom and queendom of God being here. From this consciousness comes compassion. People realize that where there is unnecessary suffering, where there is injustice, there can be no kingdom and queendom of God. The Dreamtime is about opening our hearts to the joy of the present moment—that is, to realized eschatology.

In conclusion, I am convinced that here in Australia you are living a unique theological moment. This is the time to delve into the deep meaning of the Dreamtime. The only way to do it is through your own mystical tradition, which needs to be plumbed. It cannot be understood any other way.

III

CONTEMPORARY CULTURE

AND THE PRAXIS OF

CREATION SPIRITUALITY

CHAPTER 8

Howard Thurman:
A Creation-Centered Mystic from
the African-American Tradition

☾

The African-American spiritual tradition is rooted both in the cosmological religion of mother Africa and in the liberation tradition of Exodus and the Jewish people. In Howard Thurman, America can boast a spiritual genius and an authentic mystic in his own right who brought together some of the richest strands of African wisdom and American praxis. His Quaker mentor, Rufus Jones, who taught him the spiritualities of Meister Eckhart and Francis of Assisi, would be proud of his accomplishments in deep ecumenism. Thurman's powerful influence on Dr. Martin Luther King Jr. is a story that has yet to be told.

Experiencing Howard Thurman is for me like coming home. His life and his understanding of the spiritual journey profoundly attest to the Four Paths of Creation Spirituality. His passion for deep ecumenism, for justice, for a cosmic mysticism, all ring familiar bells when I read him. Of course, one reason for this is that as a young man he studied the mysticism of Meister Eckhart with the Quaker Rufus Jones. In addition, as a university student Thurman wrote a major study on Francis of Assisi, and he loved Henry Adams's *Mont Saint Michel and Chartres,* a classic work on the cosmological mysticism of the Middle Ages. In other words, Thurman found much nourishment in the mystical tradition of the medieval period, the West's last attempt at living a Creation and cosmic Spirituality.

Thurman, however, like every authentic mystic and unlike mere commentators on others' mystical experience, is deeply original. He does not come to Eckhart from a theory about mysticism; he comes to Eckhart from his own experience of the divine. Thurman is a mystic and a theologian in his own right.

Nevertheless, to demonstrate how much a part of the living creation, mystical tradition he is and to assist in the vast process of giving some organization to Thurman's voluminous writings, I would like here to lay out his teachings on spirituality using the Four Paths of Creation Spirituality as a structural starting point.

Regarding the Via Positiva, there is every evidence that Thurman was very much a nature mystic from his childhood days, growing up close to the land and sea in Florida. Consider this testimony from his autobiography: "As a child, the boundaries of my life spilled over into the mystery of the ocean and the wonder of the dark nights and the wooing of the wind until the breath of Nature and my own breath seemed to be one—it was resonant to the tonality of God. This was a part of my cosmic religious experience as I grew up."[1] His own experience as a wonder-filled child, as well as his peoples' experience from an African earth-based reverence for the cosmos, permeates this self-disclosure. Again, he draws on both sources of experience when he writes, "There is magic all around us—in the rocks, the trees, and the minds of men . . . and he who strikes the rock aright may find them where he will. . . . There can be no thing that does not have within it the signature of God, the Creator of life, the living substance out of which all particular manifestations arise." This is Cosmic Christ theology.

Thurman wrestled continuously with images of God, with how we can best name our mystical experience. One conclusion he reached strikes me as particularly powerful because I used the same terminology in my book, On Becoming a Musical, Mystical Bear, where I defined prayer as "a radical response to life." Thurman writes, "God is not merely the Creator of creatures, of all objects animate and inanimate; but also, and more importantly, . . . God is the creator of life itself. Existence is the creation of God; life is the creation of God." I hear echoes of Eckhart teaching "isness is God." Thurman calls us from the personal to the cosmic when he declares, "We are so overwhelmed by the personal but vast impact of the particularity of living objects that we are scarcely aware of a much more profound fact in our midst, and that is that life itself is alive." He insists that our "encounter with God . . . must be with One who is seen as holding within his context all that there is, including existence itself." This is panentheism.

Thurman was totally committed to the truth that all persons are mystics who can be broken through at any time by an encounter with the divine. And this experience forms the basis of life change and life decisions. "The incidents of a

man's [sic] life may, without a moment's notice, catapult
him into the midst of the experience which is completely ir-
radiated with the presence of God. In any wilderness the un-
suspecting traveler may come upon the burning bush, and
discover that the ground upon which he stands is holy
ground. Wherever such occurs, we may be sure that even
though the context itself may be casual or even random, the
experience itself is not." Thurman continuously returns to
this experience, the basis of all mysticism, as the center of
one's religious consciousness and work in the world.

THE VIA NEGATIVA is also richly developed in Thurman's
work. He wrestles with the question of asceticism and con-
cludes that "the religion of the inner life at its best is life affirming rather than life denying." But what about the need
to detach ourselves from those life forces that are fragment-
ing, divisive, and overly attaching? What about self-denial as
a means to the inner life? Silence is the answer, Thurman
teaches, "becoming still within." There "the individual becomes conscious of what is there all the time. 'Be still and
know that I am God' is the way the Psalmist puts it." When
one can learn to be still, "a strange thing happens. It is very
difficult to put into words. The initiative slips out of one's
hands and into the hands of God, the other Principal in the
religious experience. The self moves toward God. Such
movement seems to have the quality of innate and fundamental stirring." This is why Thurman can say that "religious experience in its profoundest dimension is the finding
of man [sic] by God and the finding of God by man [sic]."
And this is why the letting-go processes of our lives are in
the last analysis positive, not negative. "The mystical experience is only in a limited way life denying. It becomes in its
most profound sense life affirming."

Suffering is another dimension to the Via Negativa, and
Thurman feels that one's response to it is to admit its hold

on us and to take it directly to God. Our "acute hostility cannot be resolved or drained off until the individual faces God
with this fact." If we refuse to take our anger to God, "we
repress our true feelings about the evil with which we wrestle, and meanwhile our God becomes a sleeping ghost
among the stark hills of our own barren wasteland." What
happens when we take our pain and hostility to God? "A
kind of ultimate suction takes place which empties us completely." Emptying becomes a new source of energy, a new
encounter with the divine. It "has the possibility of 'ready-
ing' the spirit for religious experience."

THURMAN TALKS ABOUT the "inwardness of religion" and
the "outwardness of religion." I understand the former to be
Paths One and Two, the Via Positiva and the Via Negativa;
and the latter to be Paths Three and Four, the Via Creativa
and the Via Transformativa. The Via Creativa is celebrated in
many guises by Thurman, who approvingly cites a thinker
who said that imagination in humans is in fact the image of
God in us, "and those unto whom it is given shall see God."
To follow our religious imagination is to "operate from a
new center," one that is derived from our experience of the
divine. Thurman is talking about art as meditation and how
"when a man [sic] surrenders and has now a new center
which takes the form of a central demand, then his powers
are pooled, are focused, and may be directed to achieve impossible ends." With this surrender one "loses his life and
finds it." The self is not lost in this process; rather there occurs "an irradiation of the self that makes it alive with 'Godness' and in various ways. There is awakened the desire to be
Godlike. This is no vague pious wish, no moist-eyed sentimentality, but rather a robust affirmation of the whole spirit
of the man." Thurman calls what happens an "integration"
or "creative synthesis." One thing that happens is a loss of
the fear of death: "Death no longer appears as the great fear

or specter. The power of death over the individual life is broken." When we truly resurrect and lose our fear of death, we
enter into commitment. "There is no more searching question than this: under what circumstances would you yield
your life with enthusiasm?"

"That to which man is committed must be of such importance and of such supreme worth to him that in ex-
change for this sharing of his life, his physical existence is of
no consequence. A deeper and more integrated action results
from this surrender to the creative God. "The surrender of
the self at its center gives to the life a new basis for action. It
provides an integrated basis for action. Here at last man has
a core of purpose for his life and for his living." Here one
finds a "robust vitality that quickens the roots of personality,
creating an unfolding of the self that redefines, reshapes, and
makes all things new. . . . The individual knows that what is
happening to him can outlast all things without itself being
dissipated or lost."

The surrender carries us beyond our personal agendas to
being prophets (Thurman uses the word *martyr*) on behalf of
social transformation. Thus the Via Creativa leads to the Via
Transformativa for Thurman. He puts this explicitly when he
says that "the place where the imagination shows its greatest
powers as the *angelos*, the messenger, of God is in the miracle
which it creates when one man, standing in his place, is
able, while remaining there, to put himself in another man's
place. To send his imagination forth to establish a beachhead
in another man's spirit, and from that vantage point so to
blend with the other's landscape that what he sees and feels
is authentic—this is the great adventure in human relations."
Here Thurman is defining beautifully the truth of compassion. And in it lies salvation, for "to be to another human
being what is needed at the time that the need is most urgent and most acutely felt, this is to participate in the precise
act of redemption."

Thurman speaks of a "soul-shaking conflict of loyalty" that faces a person of compassion vis-à-vis his or her relationship to a group. The person of conscience often has to break with groups that once sustained him or her but have "become the custodian of conscience." The individual often sees deeper than the group into the suffering of others, into the "ethical mode of compassion."

Thurman, like Eckhart before him, is not hesitant to talk about our divinity, as when he says we "grow and unfold until goodness becomes 'Godness.' " The life and teachings of Jesus assist us in such a time of crisis because Jesus was "the for instance of the mind of God, . . . the mind that was in him becomes more and more clearly to me to be the mind that is God."

No matter how profound the personal experience of God, the biggest truth for Thurman is community: "The profoundest disclosure in the religious experience is the awareness that man is not alone. . . . What is disclosed in his religious experience he must define in community. That which God shareth with him, he must inspire his fellows to seek for themselves. He is dedicated, therefore, to the removing of all barriers which block or frustrate this possibility in the world." I can't help but feel that Thurman is revealing his own prophetic calling in this passage. He was truly a "mystic in action"—that is, a prophet. He translated mystical experience into social healing, which begins with social criticism. He himself criticized deeply the racist, classist, and sectarian character of Christianity as he experienced it, so cut up into denominational boundaries. Under these circumstances, church itself becomes a shameful "instrument of violence to the religious experience." He asked Gandhi what the greatest obstacle was to Christianity in India and reports his reply: "Christianity as it is practiced, as it has been identified with Western culture, with Western civilization and colonialism." Ultimately, for Thurman, deep ecumenism is the only future of religion. "It is my belief that in the presence of God there is neither male nor female, white nor black, Gentile nor Jew, Protestant nor Catholic, Hindu, Buddhist, nor Moslem, but a human spirit stripped to the literal substance of itself before God. Wherever man has this sense of the Eternal in his spirit, he hunts for it in his home, in his work, among his friends, in his pleasures, and in all the levels of his function. It is my simple faith that this is the kind of universe that sustains that kind of adventure, and what we see dimly now in the churning confusion and chaos of our tempestuous times will someday be the common experience of all the children of men everywhere."

Thurman wisely recognized that a strong Via Positiva— with its teaching, for example, that all of us are royal persons and sons and daughters of God—has vast implications in the struggle for justice. Speaking of sitting at the feet of his grandmother, an ex-slave, he tells us how "everything in me quivered with the pulsing tremor of raw energy when, in her recital, she would say, quoting a black preacher speaking to slaves: 'You—you are not niggers. You—you are not slaves. You are God's children.' This established for them the ground of personal dignity, so that a profound sense of personal worth could absorb the fear reaction. This alone is not enough, but without it, nothing else is of value." The Via Creativa also assists justice making because when one can "appraise his own intrinsic powers, gifts, talents, and abilities," he no longer sees the world or himself "through the darkened lenses of those who are largely responsible for his social predicament. He can think of himself with some measure of detachment from the shackles of his immediate world. Nothing can destroy the faith in life that follows from believing one is truly a child of the God of life." Thurman called for the individual to take his or her newly found center of creative power to his or her work worlds so that "wherever such a man is at work, wherever such a man is at play, there the rule of God is at hand."

I have touched on only some of Thurman's wisdom in light of the Four Paths of Creation Spirituality. His work, life, and teachings carry on the deep mystical-prophetic tradition of the West embellished richly with the uniqueness of his spirit and that of his people. He put candidly what most occupied his efforts in spirituality when he said, "All my life I have been seeking to validate, beyond all ambivalences and frustrations, the integrity of the inner life. I have sensed the urgency to find a way to act and react responsibly out of my own center. I have sought a way of life that could come under the influence of, and be informed by, the fruits of the inner life." And again, "I am concerned about the removing of the last barriers between the outer and the inner aspects of religious experience." The "inner" and the "outer" life—the mystical and the creative prophetic—this is the effort of all those committed to living out the Four Paths of Creation Spirituality.

NOTE

1. Citations are from Howard Thurman, *Mysticism and the Experience of Love* (Wallingford, Pa.: Pendle Hill Pamphlet 115, 1961); *The Creative Encounter* (Richmond, Ind.: Friends United Press, 1954); *Jesus and the Disinherited* (Richmond, Ind.: Friends United Press, 1981; first published 1949 by Abingdon Press); and *With Head and Heart: The Autobiography of Howard Thurman* (New York: Harcourt Brace Jovanovich, 1979).

CHAPTER 9

Liberation Theology
and Creation Spirituality

☾

Many people ask about the relationship between Liberation
Theology and Creation Spirituality. While I treat the subject
at far greater length in my book Creation Spirituality:
Liberating Gifts for the Peoples of the Earth, which
I wrote on my return from Latin America during my year of
silencing by the Vatican, this essay treats this important topic
quite succinctly.

For some time now I have been asked to contrast that movement of Christianity we know as Liberation Theology and that known as Creation-Centered Spirituality.

Liberation Theology and Creation-Centered Spirituality share much in common. Both movements seek to understand Christian love within the Jewish, biblical context of justice—there can be no love without justice. Or as Meister Eckhart puts it, "love will never be anywhere except where equality and unity are. There can be no love where people do not find equality or are not busy making equality." The goal of the entire spiritual effort in Creation-Centered Spirituality is compassion, and "compassion means justice" (Eckhart) and celebration. Both Liberation Theology and Creation-Centered Spirituality consider that a consciousness of faith needs to include a social, political, economic awareness that is critical and that offers workable and creative alternatives.

Both Liberation Theology and Creation-Centered Spirituality celebrate orthopraxis—the question of *how* we live our lives as an essential test of what we *say* we believe in. Belief is not a weapon for covering up truth or pain or injustice but is the opposite: our way of living out truth, justice, and compassion (the effort to relieve pain) in our work, our citizenship, and our lifestyles. Both Liberation Theology and Creation-Centered Spirituality insist on a working dialectic and mutuality between theory and practice. Ideas are too valuable to remain in the head alone, and experience is too basic to be relegated to being a shadow of ideas. Rather, the richest ideas come from practice, and practice in turn needs to critique ideas. There is no room for anti-intellectualism and the fear of ideas in authentic living and practice, on the one hand, and there is no room for idle spinning of ideas that are not grounded in practice and experience, on the other.

In addition, both Liberation Theology and Creation-Centered Spirituality emerge from the experience and wisdom of the *anawim*—the "forgotten ones." Liberation Theology has been born of centuries of colonialism and exploitation of the peoples of Latin America by the dominant powers of Europe and North American governments and giant corporations in alliance with military forces from without and within the countries at hand. Creation-Centered Spirituality comes to Christianity from the tens of thousands of years of experience of *anawim* peoples—namely women, native peoples, peasants, artists, and people of color.

No naming of differences will ever be complete because Liberation Theology continues to evolve, more and more in the direction of spirituality; Creation-Centered Spirituality is in its infancy in its self-awareness among Christians and in its practice as well as theory. Indeed, both movements appear to be converging, rather than diverging. Nevertheless, it will be useful, especially in this time of interchange, to outline some contrasts between Liberation Theology and Creation-Centered Spirituality.

1 First is the fact that Liberation Theology owes more to the German Enlightenment than does Creation-Centered Spirituality. Karl Marx, a genius and prophet born of the Enlightenment, offered much that is still useful today in terms of critique of social injustice and class struggle in particular, but the patriarchal Enlightenment leaves much out—for example, artists, workers who are not industrial workers, non-two-legged ones, the cosmos and creation, music, celebration, childlikeness, art, women. Creation-Centered Spirituality is far more ancient than Liberation Theology and owes more to native peoples of the Americas and Africa and Asia than it does to the European Enlightenment. While it absorbs Marx's passion and genius at social analysis and social criticism, it puts it into a larger, more cosmic setting than most liberation theologians do.

2 Liberation Theology tends to be patriarchal. Creation-Centered Spirituality is explicitly feminist, which means that it not only names the oppression of women in a patriarchal society but of men as well. Feminist values of making connections, of overcoming dualisms, of celebrating birthing, of cosmic rituals and recycling events need to play an ever larger role in community awakening. Wisdom is needed, not just knowledge.

3 Creation-Centered Spirituality insists on psychic justice as well as structural justice. The structural justice of the human psyche must itself be critiqued and transformed. What does this mean? It means that mysticism—what philosopher Joseph Pieper defines as "affirmation of the Whole" and what Rabbi Heschel defines as "radical amazement"—must be included as part of any valid social change. For society will not change radically by guns and by wars and by social class struggle—though the latter may be temporarily necessary. Rather, each person must undergo deep transformation at a psychic level. Creation-Centered Spirituality names this as a mystical awakening, an awakening of "right-brain" powers and creative powers. Injustice exists in the psyche itself when only one brain—the dominant left brain of analysis and techne—is allowed free reign or reward.

How can there be social justice without psychic justice as well? That is a question Creation-Centered Spirituality asks and answers. The answer to awakening right-brain activity is art as meditation. Art as meditation becomes an essential part of the orthopraxis of Creation-Centered Spirituality. Art awakens individuals to their empowerment and their responsibility for self-liberation. Art is the missing link between spirituality and social justice as it is between

cosmology and psyche (macrocosm/microcosm). Native
and peasant people know this truth. Liberation Theology, it
seems to me, underplays the need for a more maternal,
more mystical redevelopment of the human as essential for
justice happening and sustaining itself in a creative society.

4 Liberation Theology tends to be anthropocentric. There is
much in Liberation Theology that smacks of Newton's old
paradigm—for example, competition as an inevitable law of
nature; structure as more important than process; parts as
more important than the whole (there is no whole without
a mystical consciousness). In contrast, Creation-Centered
Spirituality listens carefully to what the new paradigms coming from post-Einsteinian science teach us.

Creation-Centered Spirituality is explicitly cosmic—
what physicists and biochemists teach us of the macro
universe and the micro universe is part of the global consciousness of our time. Ecology is intrinsic to Creation-
Centered Spirituality because all beings contain the divine
radiance (Hildegard) and the divine Christ (Paul). Energy,
healing, justice, and forgiveness are part of the wisdom that
the cosmos teaches us. Even though the majority of the in-
justices committed against earth and forests and soil and air
and water in the world today have been committed by "First
World" countries toward "Third World" ones, it is disap-
pointing how slow Liberation Theology has been to speak
out about this nonanthropocentric injustice. This injustice
will, even without human bombs, destroy the human
species and others along with it. The *anawim* of our world are
not just the two-legged poor but the rain forests and soil, the
whales and the trees, the birds and animals being wiped out
by human injustice and lacking a voice in an anthropocentric social system. Hebrew Scriptures and creation mystics
like Hildegard and Eckhart understand injustice as a rupture
in the cosmos itself. Justice is not human invention—it is

built into the universe itself. Humans are called to join creation.

5 Creation-Centered Spirituality speaks of "erotic justice," meaning that a patriarchal mode of abstract justice is not what will effect change in persons or society. An erotic justice is a deeply personalized justice, a response to the divine in every creature, the Cosmic Christ in every being. Gandhi said, "The individual is the one supreme consideration." Creation-Centered Spirituality celebrates and invites people to create celebrations of the original blessing, the royal personhood, the divine dignity of every individual. Embracing that dignity and creating a culture where it can be nourished and released is what guarantees a society of justice and peace, of creativity and compassion. Audre Lorde teaches that "eros cannot be felt secondhand." There is a need to defend the personalized right to eros and to justice and thus to resist the patriarchal definitions of justice as an abstraction.

6 Because Liberation Theology has emerged from Latin America (via Europe, of course), where there are a minimum of infrastructures within society—state, church, and military being the principal ones—it has tended in its thinking to big solutions. Thus, to combat big state you need big socialism or big church. Creation-Centered Spirituality would recognize E. F. Schumacher's option for decentralization, for smaller groups doing personalized politics and business as the answer to both unemployment and economic injustice.

Decentralization and small technology and small businesses that produce needed goods are key to the hopes Creation-Centered Spirituality holds for the renewal of work and society. To restore art as work (Nicaragua is doing this among the peasants in particular) is to heal much that is alienating in industrial work. Government too must become more and more localized and decentralized. And where it needs to be centralized, it should be centralized around nature's bioregions and not around anthropocentric and artificial boundaries.

The personal and the creative can rarely be unleashed in big systems. (Liberation Theology realizes this regarding church life in its birthing of base communities.) If Creation-Centered Spirituality is to renew the structures of First World societies, it must do so fully aware of the complex infrastructures of these societies. Thus, it finds fertile ground in practically all professions and institutions—wherever there are people willing to wake up, come alive, and let go. Dualistic rhetoric would be self-defeating in most of these instances. As Eckhart says, "a person works in a stable; he has a breakthrough. What does he do? He returns to the stable." Infiltration can go much further than confrontation, and small farming will do more for the lost soil and lost jobs at good work than will mass industrializing of agriculture by state monopolies replacing corporate ones. There is already much more power shared in the complex infrastructure of First World countries. It is necessary to turn and recycle that power for compassion.

7 Celebration is half of compassion for Creation-Centered Spirituality. The present time must contain seeds and intimations of the justice, peace, and rest that are to come. People are more awakened by pleasure than by duty, by joy than by guilt, by mutuality ritualized than by confrontation. Awe is the starting point—and with it wonder—of Creation-Centered Spirituality: the awe of our being part of this amazing universe. This awe deserves to be played out and ritualized, when ritual truly means festive folk-making once again. The awe is not that of a pseudomysticism of state or party but of our shared existence in the cosmos itself. Liberation Theology tends to lack this Via Positiva as a starting point for its theory and practice. Being an Enlightenment child, it tends to begin with the problem—always the human problem—of existence. Descartes's beginning philosophy with doubt is the equivalent of Augustine's beginning theology with original sin. Such beginnings do not lead to new creations or to awakening creative power in people and their societies. Celebration does.

8 Because Creation-Centered Spirituality is so ancient, it has lived through diverse economic systems. It is precapitalistic, as all mysticism is. Thus, it zeroes in less on class warfare than on healing in the broader context. It insists that there exist powers of healing in the human body and psyche and in the cosmic body that need to be tapped into if nonwar is to prevail over competition and dualistic struggles. There is more power in the human psyche than anthropocentric patriarchy ever dreamed. Gandhi and Martin Luther King Jr. demonstrated this by the success of their nonviolent protest movements. So too has Corazon Aquino. If war is to be rendered obsolete, then the human heart must be expanded. The practice of meditation, especially art as meditation, assists this expansion of the psyche and the consequent expulsion of war from the psyche and eventually from the cosmic psyche. "Imagination denied, war governed the nations," observes William Blake.

I do not see any of these contrasts between Liberation Theology and Creation-Centered Spirituality as rigid, but as signs of how each movement can be deepened and criticized in positive ways. Creation-Centered Spirituality seems very appropriate for First World cultures because there is an immense spiritual deprivation among the people. When this spiritual poverty is released, much energy will be unleashed.

The Third World's deprivation seems to be more in terms of material goods, for there people are still closer to the wisdom of the earth. But this wisdom is draining away very rapidly as Western consumerism and Western unemployment begin to taint the souls of these nations too. Thus, Creation-Centered Spirituality is important there as well so that in undergoing so-called technological development, these peoples do not surrender their souls to the vast spiritual desert that has followed the "development" of industrialized societies.

Hildegard says that being human consists of two things: justice and celebration. Where justice and celebration are happening, there Creation-Centered Spirituality is happening. And there liberation continues, as does creation itself.

CHAPTER 10

Meister Eckhart and Karl Marx: The Mystic as Political Theologian

(

Having studied with several Christian Marxists under Johannes Metz at the University of Munster in the late sixties, I was deeply curious about the roots of Marx's own political and prophetic thought and about whether there was any connection between him and the Creation Spirituality tradition. In Meister Eckhart, one finds such a connection—though Eckhart, like feminists in our time, is more inclusive in his critique of culture and religion: he critiques psyche and symbolism as well as political structures, although Marx's analysis of these structures is, of course, more thorough than Eckhart's.

I T IS A SHOCK to spiritualists who imagine that spirituality is
a term restricted to the "inner life" to learn that the last talk
the late Thomas Merton ever gave was entitled "Marxism
and Monastic Perspectives." In this talk, delivered two hours
before his death, Merton called the Marxist Herbert Marcuse
"a kind of monastic thinker" and declared that "the whole
New Testament is, in fact—and can be read by a Marxist-
oriented mind as—a protest against religious alienation."[1]
What the many proponents of spiritualist and sentimental
spirituality fail to comprehend is the inherent politics in all
mysticism. For all energy is interconnected, whether it be
energy of politics or of the flight from politics.[2]

Equally baffling to devotees of spiritualism will be the
title of this essay and the suggestion that spirituality and politics might go hand in hand. They do, of course. On the one
hand, spirituality is often used as a weapon (and a powerful
one it is) to repress political consciousness and assertiveness,
as the following observation of the historian Christopher
Hill makes clear, describing the role of the preacher in late
medieval society:

> The common people were permanently discontented, held
> down only by the preaching of the clergy and the swords
> of the nobility. If clergy or nobility lost positive enthusiasm
> for government policy a popular revolt might break out,
> like that of the Spanish comuneros in 1520 or of the Norfolk
> peasantry in 1549. But normally, as in these cases, once the
> point had been made and the government had learned its
> lesson, the commons would be bloodily repressed and
> preached against.[3]

On the other hand, spirituality has supported prophetic
movements, as is clearly the case with Meister Eckhart
(1260–1327), the German Dominican mystic and spiritual
theologian. No less a disciple of Marxism than Ernst Bloch
interpreted Eckhart's historical contribution to socialism in

the following manner: "In Eckhart the heretical, antiecclesi-astical lay movement of the late Middle Ages became articulate in German, which is a decisive factor in any socialist evaluation." Eckhart, in the name of mysticism, demystified the economic and political facts of life for the "common people" whom he inspired

> in the revolutions of the next two centuries, along with its predecessor, the mysticism of Joachim of Floris, Abbot of Calabrese—among the Hussites, and with Thomas Munzer in the German Peasant War; events, indeed, not notable ideologically for the rule of clarity, but ones in which the mystic fog was at least not of service to the ruling class.[4]

"To a healthy number of Marxists," writes Eckhartian scholar Reiner Schurmann, "Meister Eckhart appears as the theoretician of the class struggle in the Middle Ages." His is a "mysticism of the left" that "would designate the appropriation by man [sic] of his authentic good when he is alienated by the dogma of an inaccessible heaven."[5]

In this essay I want to concentrate on three areas of political consciousness in the life and preaching of Eckhart: (1) the merchant mentality, (2) how everyone is an aristocrat, and (3) his political condemnation. Before we examine these three areas, however, we need to deal briefly with certain general presuppositions in Eckhart's preaching.

GENERAL POLITICAL-MYSTICAL PRINCIPLES IN ECKHART

To do justice to all of Eckhart's mystical-political consciousness would be impossible in a single essay. The following themes of Eckhart are important for grasping the groundwork of his spirituality, and what is significant for this present study, they carry within themselves powerful

and profound insights as to the interrelatedness of spirituality and political consciousness. Since I have dealt with
them in greater length in another place,[6] I will only list
them here.

1 Because he has a theology of realized eschatology, heaven
is not projected onto another time or place for Eckhart but
has already begun within individuals. Bloch comments,
"This first insight into man's alienation of himself, namely,
that human treasures have been bartered for the illusion of
heaven, did not come about without some contribution
from mysticism."[7]

2 The spiritual journey culminates in a return to the world,
not in a flight from it. The return to creation means loving
one's neighbor. As Eckhart puts it:

> In contemplation you serve only yourself, in good works
> you serve many people. If a person were in such a raptur-
> ous state as Saint Paul once entered, and he knew of a sick
> man who wanted a cup of soup, it would be far better to
> withdraw from the rapture for love's sake and serve him
> who is in need.[8]

In his "Commentary on the Our Father," Eckhart explains
the expression *our daily bread*:

> Bread is given to us not that we eat it alone but that others
> who are indigent might be participants. . . . He who does
> not give to another what belongs to another does not eat
> his own bread, but another's at the same time with his
> own. Thus, when we eat bread acquired justly, we eat our
> bread; but when bread is acquired by evil means and with
> sin, we are not eating our own but another's. For nothing
> that we have unjustly is ours.[9]

3 Salvation is a We (not an I) salvation for Eckhart. He says,
"God has been the common Savior of the entire world, and
for this I am indebted to him with much more thanks than
if he had saved only me."[10]

4 Eckhart is a champion of the Via Negativa as an approach to God. He calls God the "non-God" and the "unnamable." This rejection of the language that culture or religion takes for granted for "their God" should be recognized for what it is with Eckhart: a political as well as a theological starting point. For to wipe one's mind clean of an inherited language is to wipe one's mind clean of an entire culture with its social and symbolic structures. The Via Negativa has profound political implications. It is a rejection of everything in order to start anew.

5 The kingdom of God theme, like that of realized eschatology, is personalized by Eckhart. In him there is no trace of ecclesiastical triumphalism, no confusion of church with the kingdom of God.

6 Eckhart dismisses dualistic relationships of God and people in favor of dialectical ones. All deep living is dialectical for him. He rejects subject-object relations with God that support most theisms in favor of a deeply shared panentheism. The panentheism is a political panentheism.

7 Marx objected to philosophers of contemplation who only wanted to gaze at the world as at an object. His philosophy, he insisted, would change the world. Eckhart too resists contemplation as a passive gazing at. Knowing for Eckhart is a "participation in being" and not a "gazing at" being.[11] He is a spiritual theologian and preacher, which is to say he seeks not "a theoretical dogma of what man is, but . . . a practical guide to what he must become." His is an effort to get persons to give birth, to become, to beget, to create—to change and to be changed. Our identity with God is operative and verb-oriented, not ontological or substantial.[12] Eckhart, like Marx, is action-oriented. His spirituality "is not oriented towards contemplation. It produces a new birth: the birth of the Son."[13] It is oriented, then, toward creativity and giving birth.

Having considered this brief outline of themes in Eckhart's spirituality, we can now turn to the three issues on which I want to concentrate in this essay.

THE MERCHANT MENTALITY

In his sermon based on Jesus' ejecting moneylenders from the temple,[14] Eckhart presents his case against what he calls the "merchant mentality"—a way of thinking and acting that infiltrates the deepest levels of a person, the space where God dwells or wants to dwell within us.

> This temple, in which God wants to rule in power according to His will, is the soul of man, which He formed and created just like Himself. . . . He made the soul of man so like Himself that in heaven or on earth, among all the glorious creatures that God so beautifully created, there is none which is so like Him as the human soul.[15]

Notice in this passage how Eckhart declares God's presence not to be in institutions, however magnificent or religious, but in people. People are the New Temple for Eckhart. It is because the merchant mentality has the power to touch us at our depths that it is so insidious and demonic. It can displace God from ourselves. "That is why God wants to have this temple empty, so that He alone may dwell in it. Hence this temple pleases Him so much, because it is so like Him and He is so pleased to be in the temple if He alone dwells in it."[16] God's dwelling with persons depends on their chasing the attitudes of buying and selling from their inner selves—a task that is not easy, for a merchant mentality will poison even good people and certainly religion itself.

> Who were the people who bought and sold, and who are they now? Take careful note of my words. This time I will only preach of good people. . . . All those are merchants

who refrain from grave sins and would like to be good
people and to do their good works to the glory of God,
such as fasting, vigils, prayers, and so forth.[17]

Eckhart declares that what makes otherwise good people
into merchants is an attitude of doing even pious works in
order to get "something in return" from God. "All such persons are merchants" he declares elsewhere, who want to
"trade with our Lord."[18] It is the mentality of getting that is
so devastating. "As long as we perform our works for the
sake of salvation or of going to heaven, we are on the wrong
track."[19]

What is a mercenary? What is a serf? Anyone who lives
a life of means instead of ends. "Those who seek something
with their works are servants and hirelings, or those who
work for a Why or Wherefore."[20] In other words, the merchant mentality reduces all living and thinking to problem
solving. It robs us of mystery living or living "without a
why." It is for this reason too that living without a why lies
at the very heart of Eckhart's spirituality[21] and why he himself could declare that "he who understands my teaching
about justice and the just person understands everything I
say."[22] Eckhart's critique of the merchant mentality becomes
a criticism of religion when it is itself a quid pro quo or a
God-give-me mentality. Why is Eckhart so disturbed by such
merchant attitudes? Because they miss the "glad and gratuitous" giving of God. The merchant mentality emphasizes
work over grace. Above all, it signifies a lack of freedom to
experience life in terms other than buying and selling, giving and getting.

> Truth needs no huckstering. God does not seek His own
> ends; in all His works He is free and untrammeled, and
> performs them from pure love. So does the man who is
> united with God: he is free and untrammeled in all his ac-
> tions and performs them to the glory of God alone.[23]

Furthermore, a merchant mentality produces a dualistic consciousness of before and after and erases the potential for "the highest truth," which is found in unitive experiences. The subject-object relationships of dualism that the merchant mentality generates are a contradiction to the unitive experience between God and humans. Unity, not separation, is the law of life. This interplay between God and humans cannot happen without "the continuous abandonment of both human and divine *eigenschaft*, property."[24] Since the divine-human interplay is truly play, it is just as truly without dualism. Eckhart's goal, then, is that we be free from the merchant mentality to the very core of our being. When you are so free, you are in touch with the divine.

> If you would be entirely free from huckstering, so that God will leave you in this temple, you should do everything that is possible in all your actions purely in praise of God, and should be as free as you were when you did not exist. You should ask for nothing in return.[25]

With this freedom, one is open to receiving divine gifts "anew in this Now . . . and begetting them again without hindrance."[26] All things—God included—come to those who do not fall victim to the commercial or merchandising mentality. You cannot enjoy life if your attitude is commercial.

Another objection Eckhart harbors against the merchant mentality is that the goods we buy and sell are external goods. Concentration on the external as object quite literally kills the divine in us. "Whatever motivates us other than out of ourselves is thoroughly an act of mortal sin," he declares.[27] In another sermon he develops further the lethal (mortal) aspects of materialism and how it kills even God:

> There is also a Something by which the soul lives in God, but when the soul is intent on external things that Something dies, and therefore God dies, as far as the soul is con-

cerned. Of course, God himself does not die. He continues
very much alive to himself. . . .

   Some people want to see God with their eyes as they see
a cow and to love him as they love their cow—they love
their cow for the milk and cheese and profit it makes them.
This is how it is with people who love God for the sake of
outward wealth or inward comfort. . . . Indeed, I tell you
the truth, any object you have on your mind, however
good, will be a barrier between you and the inmost
truth.[28]

   Still another objection to the merchant mentality is that
it creates a false sense of ownership. We own nothing, Eckhart insists. We are wayfarers who have been lent many gifts,
all of which are to be returned to the Creator. "We should
have all things as if they were lent to us, without any ownership, whether they are body and soul, sense, strength, external goods or honors, friends, relations, house, hall,
everything in fact."[29] Once again Eckhart is getting at our
relationships as being the fundament of spiritual liveliness.
But economics can poison our relationships, and we need to
resist what merchant attitudes can do to us. God is not a
giver of personal property or a canonizer of ownership. "As
personal property He never gave anything either to His
Mother or to any man, or to any creature in any way."[30] Instead of ownership of things, possession of God.

> Never has anything so fully owned by anyone as God will
> be mine with all that He can do and is. This ownership we
> should earn by being here without self-seeking and with-
> out everything that is not God.[31]

   Eckhart praises an attitude of reverence to life that is
built around this consciousness of living on time that is borrowed and gifts that are borrowed from the Creator. We have
been lent life from God—there lies the key to peaceful and
gentle living. He has a radical sense of how being and all the
gifts of living are ours *on loan* (*ze borge*).

Everything that is good and goodness itself was lent to him by God and not given. . . . He gives no good to the creature, but bestows it on him as a loan. The sun gives the air heat, but lends light to it; and therefore, as soon as the sun sets, the air loses the light, but the heat remains, because this is given to the air as its own."[32]

It follows that we are to be as lighthearted and as nongrabbing as the air is to the light that passes through it. Eckhart is deeply disturbed by a possessive instead of a "loan" mentality. In fact, he denounces *eigenschaft*—selfhood, attachment, property—"as nothingness because it darkens peregrine joy by making being into that particular being, man into that individual, and God into that divine person."[33] "Nothingness" is here used by Eckhart as a synonym for sin. We see then that the "merchant mentality" is an ultimate affront or sin to Eckhart's mystical view of living gracefully and with awareness of our receptivity.

Like his Dominican brother Aquinas who wrote that "there can be no joy in living without joy in work," Eckhart turns his attention to the important issue of finding joy in work. We do not work merely for pay but for ecstasy. He explores how "all man's suffering, all his works, all his life become happy and joyful."[34] Work is to be an end in itself and not just a means toward an end. For this is the way God, who "is still continually creating" the world, works.

Whoever is born of God . . . does all his work for the sake of working. God is never weary of loving and working. . . . He loves for the sake of love, works for the sake of work, and therefore God loves and works uninterruptedly. God's work is His nature, His being, His life, His happiness.[35]

Our work is to be patterned after God's work. For a wise person, "to work for God's sake is his being, his life, his work, his happiness." Authentic human work comes from within a person and not from outside. "If a man's work is to live, it must come from the depths of him—not from alien sources outside himself—but from within."[36] We are to love ourselves as well as God in our work.[37] To love self is to love God and to please God.

Eckhart's vision of spirituality does not repress or ignore injustice and human suffering but in fact demands awareness of it. Yet this sensitivity and awareness is only possible where the merchant mentality is lacking.

> What do poor people do who endure the same or more severe illness and suffering, and have no one even to give them water? They must seek their very bread in rain, cold, and snow from house to house. Therefore, if you would be comforted, forget those who are better placed and remember only those who are less fortunate.[38]

Love of neighbor is not based on society's definition of wealth but on the richness of our love of God. "The man who has Christ can give to all men of his riches and in abundance. We are to show by our good conduct that we are rich in Christ through his indwelling spirit."[39]

Eckhart does not hesitate to criticize the comfortable and the powerful:

> Some say: "Lord, I can indeed come in honor and wealth and comfort." Truly, if the Lamb had lived thus and had thus walked before us, I should rejoice to see you following Him in the same manner. But the virgin strides after the Lamb over rough and smooth ways, and wherever He steps.[40]

His argument against comfortable piety and spirituality is a Gospel one—namely that Jesus did not live and grow that way. Nor is philanthropy, even religious philanthropy, a substitute for love of neighbor.

> If a man were to give a thousand marks in gold, so that churches and monasteries could be built with it, that would be a great thing. Yet anyone would have given much

more if he knew how to esteem a thousand marks as nothing. He would have done far more than the other.[41]

Even dogs, he points out, know that love is more important than authority, and thus they are wise enough to put affection for their master ahead of that for king or emperor.[42] Is wisdom to be found where there is wealth, influence, and the comfort of the powerful? Hardly. "Now a master says that there is no man who is so foolish as not to desire wisdom. . . . If I am a rich man, that does not make me wise. But if I am transformed and conformed to the essence and nature of wisdom and become wisdom itself, then I am a wise man."[43] It is the power of transformation and conformation, of death and rebirth that are the ingredients of authentic wisdom and not the power of having power.

Still another criticism of the merchant mentality is that it destroys our capacity to receive. "The very best and highest things are really and in the best sense free gifts," Eckhart insists.[44] And these come from within us and cannot be measured by externals. In a real sense, our receiving is more important than our giving.

> I much prefer a person who can love God enough to take a handout of bread, to a person who can give a hundred dollars for God's sake. How do I explain that? . . . When the poor man extends his hand to beg the bread, he trades his honor in exchange. The giver buys the honor the receiver sells.[45]

Receiving, and our capacity to become bigger for the sake of greater receptivity, divine receptivity, are more important than giving. The problem with an activist merchant mentality is that it shrinks us up. It reduces the soul to the size of objects instead of expanding it to Godlike dimensions. "The soul is like that: the more it wants the more it is given; the more it receives the more it grows."[46]

In considering Eckhart's criticisms of the merchant mentality, criticisms that correspond to those of a Marxist like Erich Fromm at his best, we see that Eckhart is not moralizing about materialism. He is not treating the merchant mentality as an ethical problem. Rather, he sees materialism as a poisonous consciousness, a stumbling block to spiritual awareness—an *alienation*, to use his word. Nowhere does Eckhart complain that things are evil or immoral. Nor does he romanticize poverty (in fact, he criticizes conditions of poverty for how they degrade humanity). He directs his considerable energies instead to the heart of the demonic dimensions of materialism—that is, to its thing consciousness. Thing consciousness is a dualistic, subject-object way of thinking and acting that destroys our greatness and our oneness with self, others, nature, and God. Thus, for Eckhart it is our attitude toward things—an attitude most often taught by a merchant-mentality economic system—that makes us materialistic and, as he says, God slayers in the process.

In Eckhart's opinion, our drying up and becoming as puny as the objects we worship is not a moral fault but a spiritual catastrophe. For it means that God, who has chosen humankind in a special way to do big things within and among, is stymied. God cannot move, operate, or dance in a person who is as puny as a thing or in a society that worships thing-puniness. And God does want to dance for joy, Eckhart insists. "With each deed, however trifling, done out of virtue and justice, and resulting in justice, God is made glad—glad through and through—so that there is nothing in the core of the Godhead that does not dance for joy."[47] Thus the merchant mentality stymies not only human history but divine history as well; the continual unfolding of creation that God desires to do in a constant process of birthing is stymied. "Just as little as I can do anything without Him, He cannot really accomplish anything apart from me."[48] Eckhart's final word then against the merchant and materialistic mentality is not a fire-and-brimstone moral reprimand but an awesome, even divine, sadness. For he senses with a piercing sensitivity God's frustration that the divine work of continual loving and creating, a work that God "savors" and finds immense pleasure in, is being interfered with. It is as if God has no place to show divine love if men and women become obstacles along the way. God accomplishes through us or not at all. Eckhart's vision is staggering. No humanist ever imagined a more awesome view of the importance of human history than this.

But Eckhart does not stop with criticism of the merchant mentality. He offers an alternative way of living and of seeing, of interrelating whether by way of politics, economics, or religious practice. It is the way of *Abegescheidenheit*, a term he himself coined, and *Gelazenheit*. These terms have been variously translated as detachment, disinterest, solitude, releasement, letting go, letting be. Whatever are their most acceptable translations for our culture (and I prefer "letting go" for the former and "letting be" for the latter), we know what their opposites are. Their opposites are grabbing, hoarding, possessing, clinging. In other words, the way of *Abegescheidenheit* and *Gelazenheit* is meant to be an alternative to the way of rapacious, merchantlike having and thinking and acting. This way is a way of letting go of things—even our images of things and even our images of God—in order to experience experience once again. It is a way of letting things be as well so that when we experience, we truly experience what is there. This path or way of letting go and letting be is not a passive, quietistic sleep; it is an active, supremely awake and aware attitude toward all of life.

The path of letting go and letting be cuts to the quick of the merchant mentality. It is radically antimaterialistic, and Eckhart insists on applying it to all forms of materialism, in-

cluding religious ones. It means letting go of religious forms
of materialism that appear so often under the guise of pietis-
tic exercises, clericalism, caste privileges, spiritualism, or ecclesial triumphalism. Religious no less than profane power
trips are to be let go of.

HOW EVERYONE IS AN ARISTOCRAT

Having considered Eckhart's economic consciousness, we are
now prepared to examine his political consciousness. The
two are intimately related, for there was in Eckhart's time
and place a "merchant aristocracy."[49] Eckhart devoted an entire talk to the subject of "The Aristocrat."[50] The talk is an
exegesis of the scriptural passage from Luke (19:12): "A
certain nobleman went into a far country to receive for himself a kingdom, and to return." Eckhart begins his talk insisting that everyone is a nobleman or aristocrat.

> How nobly man is constituted by nature, and how divine
> is the state to which he can come by grace. . . . A large part
> of Holy Scripture is affected by these words. . . . In us is
> the inward man, whom the Scriptures call the new man,
> the heavenly man, the young man, the friend, and the
> noble man.[51]

Eckhart does not hide the biblical basis for his disturbing
thesis, and when he claims that "within us is the aristocrat"
he adds, "And this is what our Lord means when he says, 'A
nobleman went out into a far country and received for himself a kingdom and returned.' " In a society that was as aware
of privilege as was Eckhart's, the thesis that all are aristocrats
is a far from subtle rebuke of the caste system then prevailing.
But it is more than a rebuke—it is an imaginative alternative
that Eckhart is suggesting. According to historian Jacques
Heers, what characterized the popular uprisings of Eckhart's

period and place was that even when the "people" overthrew one aristocracy, another immediately took its place.[52] We see then how truly radical and imaginative was Eckhart's alternative: not to confront aristocracy but to recreate it entirely by baptizing all into it. Eckhart does not put down nobles and aristocrats, and he refuses to substitute a new dualism of the lowly over the privileged. Instead, with a dialectical imagination that only a mystic could muster, he makes the peasants into nobles. Instead, therefore, of putting down anyone, he elevates all. The practical fallout from such a democratic vision would, no doubt, express itself more stridently.

He elaborates on what the consequences are if all persons are indeed aristocrats (though one suspects that detailed elaboration was hardly necessary to the populace, just as, were a preacher to suggest today that "everyone is president of General Motors," the consequences would hardly demand involved elaboration). It means, says Eckhart, that "no one is nobler than you"—that there are no ladders that we need to climb or no chiefs on ladder tops that we need to please. It means we are equal, not ranked.

> What our Lord calls a nobleman the prophet calls a great eagle. Who then is nobler than he who is born, on one hand of the highest and the best that the creature has, and on the other hand from the inmost ground of the Divine nature and of His desert?[53]

Thus Eckhart reiterates his marvelous admiration for the nobility of the human person. Eckhart does not stop short of claiming that human beings give a home to the divine within them. For in us "God has sowed His image and His likeness, and . . . He sows the good seed, the root of all wisdom, all knowledge, all virtue, and all goodness, the seed of Divine nature. The seed of Divine nature is the Son of God, the Word of God."[54] Eckhart's theology of personhood does not concentrate on sin and redemption but on divinization.

In this regard he drinks fully of Eastern Christian spiritual theologies.

> The seed of God is in us. If it was cultivated by a good, wise and industrious laborer, it would thrive all the more and would grow up to God, whose seed it is, and the fruit would be like the Divine nature. The seed of a pear tree grows into a pear tree, a hazel seed into a hazel tree, a seed of God into God.[55]

We come in touch with our own divinity when we experience ego loss and ecstasy, provided we let ourselves go to these experiences of fullness. For the ego suspension that ecstasy is about is at the same time our God experience. One might say that full joy is our experience of God. Thomas Aquinas, Eckhart's brother Dominican and predecessor in the chair of theology for foreigners at the University of Paris, was also roundly criticized for considering ecstasy to be a result of love and not merely "supernatural" loves.[56] "How should man know that he knows God, if he does not know himself? For certainly this man does not know himself or other things in the least, but God alone, when he becomes blessed and is blessed in the root and the ground of blessedness."[57] But getting in touch with our divine origins has profound political implications, as Bloch recognized:

> One thing is certain: Eckhart's sermon does not intend to snuff man out for the sake of an Otherworld beyond him: . . . The revolutionary Anabaptists, those disciples of Eckhart and Tauler, showed afterwards in practice exactly how highly and how uncomfortably for every tyrant. A subject who thought himself to be in personal union with the Lord of Lords provided, when things got serious, a very poor example indeed of serfhood.[58]

How regular is this God experience for Eckhart? When does it happen? Is it only for heaven? By no means. For Eckhart, steeped in a consciousness of realized eschatology, heaven begins here on earth. The future is now. God is now. We know God (and not just *about* God) now. And here. Eckhart says: "Our Lord tells us very aptly what eternal life is: to know God as the only true God. . . ."[59] Notice the use of the present tense in his phrase "eternal life is to know God." The present-day experience of God is repeated by Eckhart. "He who follows and lives according to the spirit and according to its counsel belongs to eternal life. It is the inward man . . . that . . . always brings forth good fruit and never evil."[60] Again, eternal life has already begun for Eckhart.

The essence of the fullness of divine joy that Eckhart senses in the present life is one of cutting through the dualisms of subject-object. He insists on our cutting through the dualism implicit in our knowing *about* God, a dualism between knower and known, subject and object. "The nobleman receives and derives all his being, life and happiness solely and only from God, by God, and in God, and not from knowing, contemplating, or loving God, or anything of the kind."[61] Eckhart is not being anti-intellectual, for he never is; but he is, one might say, being antiacademic in the sense that he rejects the notion that knowledge *of* and the social advantages that accrue to the educated ever take precedence over knowledge *with*. He takes up the subject of the limits of knowledge that is knowledge *of* on another occasion. "One person who has mastered life is better than a thousand persons who have mastered only the contents of books."[62] The joy and beauty that we experience change us so that God "shines forth and sparkles" from us when we become the aristocrat we are born to be.

Eckhart recognizes two kinds of knowledge. One is characterized by "clearly distinguished ideas" (derived from Descartes's definition of truth as "clear and distinct ideas"), which might be called "evening knowledge." Another sees creatures not as separate entities that make for clear distinctions but as *interrelated*—that is, in their relationship to God in whom they live and move and have their being. This panentheistic manner of seeing reality is called "morning knowledge" and happens "when one knows the creatures in God . . . and in this way one sees the creatures without any differentiation and stripped of all images and deprived of all similarity in the One, who is God Himself."[63] Since interrelatedness, seeing the oneness of all things and their interconnections, is the essence of compassion,[64] we can call this dimension of aristocracy a compassionate consciousness. Indeed, compassion becomes the very definition of an aristocrat for Eckhart. "This is also the nobleman of whom our Lord said, 'A nobleman went out.' He is noble because he is one, and because he knows God and creatures in the One."[65] To know God and creatures as they are one is to know that God suffers when creatures suffer. Such knowledge is the beginning of compassion, which is an active effort to relieve creaturely and divine suffering. To know that God *and* the universe *and* people suffer together is to know how thoroughly political and nonprivatized some mysticism can be. "Indeed *anima mea anima nostra* has seldom or never been so highly thought of" as in Meister Eckhart's mysticism.[66] The redemption of one is the redemption of all.

Eckhart does not sentimentalize compassion; compassion for him is an awareness of our ontological togetherness, of the kinship of all creation and all being. "All creatures are interdependent," he declares, and it is for this reason that we serve one another.[67] Compassion for him means justice,[68] and it is the best of the names we can assign to God. "Wisdom and justice are the same in God."[69] "Since God is justice, you must embrace justice as it is in itself, as it is in God. Consequently, where justice is at work, you are at work, because you could not but do the works of justice. Yes, even if hell would interfere with the course of justice, you would still do the works of justice, and hell itself would not constitute any pain; hell would be joy."[70]

In this exegesis of Eckhart's profoundly political talk on "The Aristocrat" we have seen how a politically conscious spirituality demands the following characteristics: a redefinition of aristocrat; a belief in the nobility and basic equality of every person regardless of class or caste distinctions of any kind; ecstasy as an experience for all; realized eschatology as a taste of the end time already begun; eschatology as personal not institutional; interrelatedness as a way of knowing and living; and therefore compassion as the basis of human consciousness and activity—that is, as the definition of the human person at its best (as aristocrat). We have considered in this essay Eckhart's position on capitalism (merchant mentalities kill God in us, and they kill the joy of work and life), on class (there is none: we are all nobles), on democracy (all people give birth to God), on realized eschatology (heaven is now and is not to be projected into another life), on self-criticism as criticism of one's own institutions including religious ones; on human history as divine history. It does not take a great deal of imagination to suspect that not all of these ingredients to Eckhart's preaching would have sat well with each and every member of his society. Especially is this true when one considers that Eckhart in his day was "the most popular preacher in Germany"[71] and that his renown as a theologian lent fuel and status to his preaching. Since his was not a spirituality that sentimentalized the sins of society or church or their captains, it was bound to be observed closely in high places. Since his spirituality does not encourage ordinary persons to be masochistic and to be content to derive fulfillment in this life from waiting subserviently for a heaven after death, he was a marked man. His democratic suggestion that all are nobles, not only those born into power by blood or fortune or both, is hardly a lesson to go unnoticed by the aristocratic classes. His suggestion that the merchant mentality slays God and us must have disturbed many an influential seller, since Cologne in Eckhart's period was a European trade center par excellence. Not only did the German emperor Henry VII convoke an international gathering of the Lombard money-lenders in Cologne in 1309, which was attended by representatives of over seventy-seven European towns and cities, but Cologne also held the key to Germany's trade with England. "Its merchants forwarded English cloth by way of the Rhine valley toward the fairs in Frankfurt, in the cities of southern Germany, in the counties on the Danube, and even to the grand fairs of eastern Europe at Lvov and Krakow."[72]

What characterized the social problems of Eckhart's day? There was a population explosion that was especially manifest in the Rhineland area where Eckhart did the bulk of his preaching and counseling.[73] From the year 1303 until the eighteenth century, a "Little Ice Age" blanketed Europe with the consequence that the growing season was shortened and food was made scarce. After torrential rains in 1315, crops failed all over Europe, and famine became a reality for many. The expanding economies that characterized the twelfth and thirteenth centuries gave rise to the contracting economies of the fourteenth century, thus widening the division between the rich and poor. "Division of rich and poor became increasingly sharp. With control of the raw materials and tools of production the owners were able to reduce wages in classic exploitation. The poor . . . felt a sense of injustice that, finding no remedy, grew into a spirit of revolt."[74] The rural poor were the first to revolt when in 1320 the Pastoureaux (the shepherds' movement) broke out in the wake of famine. They were excommunicated by Pope John XXII and were eventually suppressed. It is worth noting that this pope, who is the same one who will play such a large role in

Eckhart's future, managed to spend 7,500 florins a year on his retinue's clothing, owned an ermine-trimmed pillow, and bought as a gift for himself forty pieces of gold cloth from Damascus at the cost of 1,276 gold florins.[75]

ECKHART'S POLITICAL CONDEMNATION

Meister Eckhart was subjected to an Inquisition first in Cologne and then, since that brought no substantial fruits, in Avignon where certain of his statements (or statements reportedly of his) were condemned in a bull issued by John XXII and dated March 27, 1329. He was already dead by this time, however, and had defended himself stoutly at his trial. This is not the place to enter into a theological debate on the fine points of Eckhart's thought since, in fact, more and more scholars agree that Eckhart was not heretical and that the Inquisition would have learned this had they bothered to study his whole works, including his Latin ones. Instead of delving into theological niceties, I wish to explore what might have been some other more political and economic motives behind Eckhart's trial and condemnation. It is not enough, for example, to demonstrate as scholars can now do how the Inquisition actually misquoted Eckhart in at least one crucial juncture and in doing so made him sound heretical, when actually his very words had been employed by a church council centuries before.[76] We are asking a more basic question: why the trial? Why this energy brought together against this preacher? Why the lies and distortions in the trial? Whence such violence?

Heresy and heretical trials are invariably bound up with more than a quest for intellectual purity. As Georg Strecher has put it, the words *heresy* and *orthodoxy* are terms usually applied to "designate movements in history." The terms are "theologically loaded slogans" since traditional orthodoxy

often "wields political as well as social and theological
weapons."[77] What is more to the point is to put the question, What did heresy mean in Eckhart's time and place? We
find a most revealing answer from A. Borst: "Heresy is most
often identified with the aspirations of the popular
classes."[78] And from Jacques Heers: "All the movement of
countryside revolts, religious and political heresies so fre-
quent and violent in middle Germany, Thuringia, and especially the Rhineland, were aimed not only at the Church and
its lords but also at the bourgeois."[79] The rising prices that
affected all of Europe in the High Middle Ages left the nobility "extremely weak" with its "economic foundation under-
mined." The nobility was going through a crisis of identity
and survival that included selling much of their land (often
to bourgeois) and marrying many bourgeois. "A strict definition of what constituted nobility" was now lacking, since
"the nobility in general was becoming much poorer."[80] The
bourgeoisie meanwhile continued to recognize the social su-
periority of noble birth. It was into this milieu of town-and-
merchant bourgeois power versus noble power that Meister
Eckhart imprudently thrust his message: "Damn the merchants and everyone a nobleman." If he had done this only
to academic audiences and in the clerical Latin tongue, that
would have been one thing; but to preach this message in
the vernacular of the peasant people was much too provoca-
tive. A heretic is often the theologian on the losing side, and
in his case Eckhart was hardly on the side of the powers that
were.

The least that can be said about the heresy trial of Eckhart is that the climate was hardly ripe for an objective consideration of his spiritual theology. Eckhart did not choose
to teach his spirituality in a vacuum of comfort and invul-
nerability. He was not ensconced in an ivory tower, either of
academic or ecclesial protectionism. He was a preacher who
preached. What were these times and what was the spirit of

the times into which Eckhart threw himself in order to recreate them?

It was a period of great conflict in society and church between ensconced and privileged institutions and movements of reform or renewal. There was a heated anticlericalism buttressed by an antimerchant and antimoney rhetoric that was directed against the comfortable clergy as well as certain temporal powers. The more vital of the proponents for greater justice for the poor were the Beghards and Beguines, who were very active in the Cologne area where Eckhart preached and taught. Indeed, so active were they that the archbishop of Cologne, Heinrich von Virneberg, put many of them to death by burning and drowning.[81] Eckhart himself preached in the vernacular, taking the revolutionary language of the Beghards and adapting it[82] in order to reach the lower classes with the kind of messages we have considered in this essay—namely, how every person is an aristocrat and how all baptized believers are "other Christs." His use of the vernacular in preference to Latin was itself a political choice on his part. No greater proof of this is required than the prominent role this played at his trial, where he was accused of corrupting the ignorant—namely, the lower classes. Twice in the papal bull condemning Eckhart mention is made of his "preaching persistently to simple persons." Eckhart had already received this criticism of his ministry and replied to it in the following manner:

> People will also say that such doctrine should not be spoken or written for the unlearned. To this I reply: if one is not to teach the unlearned then no one will ever be learned and no one will be able to teach or to write. For one teaches the unlearned to the end that from unlearned persons they may become learned ones. . . . "They who are whole," said our Lord, "have no need of medicine." The physician exists for the purpose of making the sick healthy.[83]

We have here a classic confrontation of those who want
to control by leaving the ignorant ignorant, and one who
wants to set free by educating the ignorant. One does not
trust the peasants; the other does. Eckhart practiced the
democracy he preached.

But Eckhart, poet and artist that he was, did more than
just speak to the peasants in their own tongue. Practicing his
theme of birthing, he actually created "a new vocabulary of
mysticism." The German language of the time "consisted of
a mass of dialects spoken by people who were for the most
part illiterate serfs."[84] Eckhart begot new words and language to correspond to the deep experience he felt was
available to all. Like Saint Francis before him, the language
Eckhart chose belonged to the people he chose to reach—
the disenfranchised. His choice of language reveals his eccle-
siology—one that is primarily of "the people of God," not
the hierarchies of Christendom.[85]

There was an institutionalized elitism in the intellectual
circles of Scholastic theology that Eckhart, like Luther who
was to follow him, also attacked. "Meister Eckhart turns
against Scholasticism. His preaching is seditious: it rises up
against the project of a culture which reduces the Indetermi-
nate to the disposition of man [sic], which makes it service-
able to spiritual comfort, collective security, academic
erudition, and institutions."[86] This was part of Eckhart's
message in his insistence on an anti-theism by way of a panentheism. To the extent that theologians only reinforced
the theisms and subject-object relationships of God and people and of people (the haves) and people (the have-nots)—
to this extent the anti-theism in his panentheistic God talk
was a distinct spiritual and political threat.[87] The people no
doubt understood very well Eckhart's telling remark, "I pray
God to rid me of God,"[88] for they too sensed that any God
that supported the oppressive situation in which they were

living was hardly worthy of being called God. Eckhart goes beyond God to the Godhead, which is to go beyond the immediately inherited God.

Eckhart, of course, was not alone in his efforts to renew church and society. Indeed, that was part of his problem. In the conflict that raged between German emperor and pope, the Dominicans supported the pope and the Franciscans supported the emperor. The archbishop of Cologne was a Franciscan and an "active partisan of the imperial cause" against the papal one.[89] This would not endear him to the Dominican Eckhart, who favored the pope. As we saw in his reference to dogs, Eckhart was not innocent of what has been called "indiscreet references" to the emperor-papal struggles in his sermons. Indeed, complaints were raised at the General Chapter of the Dominican order that was held in Venice in 1325 against unnamed German friars who were leading the simpleminded into error. The Dominican order would itself go through the throes of corruption and reform that characterized church and society at large. Eckhart and his disciple Suso have been described as the "promoters in the German provinces"[90] of the reform movement in their century, as the ill-fated Savonarola was to be the center of this movement from San Marco in Florence in the next. In this regard, it is significant that from its inception a century earlier the Dominican order had considered its vow of poverty not so much an ascetic practice as a political one. That is to say, the vow was a socioeconomic-political one of refusing to be part of the decadent feudal economy of the time, on the one hand, or the rising and equally nefarious capitalism, on the other.[91] Any Dominican involved in renewal of his own order would necessarily be facing the issues of capitalism head on. The sociologist R. H. Tawney saw this clearly when he declared that "the true descendant of the doctrines of Aquinas is the labor theory of value. The last of the schoolmen was Karl Marx."[92]

There were no small numbers of peasant people who believed the world—or at least the world they knew—was coming to an end. Plagues, famines, comets, depletion of male population from ill-fated crusades, papal-imperial battles were all seen as omens of the (or at least an) end time. "All spirituals from Suso to Catherine of Siena agree: the clergy are corrupt. What was new . . . was the spirit of revolt which fermented in the popular masses on the terrain of doctrine."[93]

Such was the cultural-religious setting for the trial of Meister Eckhart—a trial instigated by none other than the Franciscan archbishop of Cologne, whom we have seen in action three times previously. It should be remembered that the Franciscans, favoring the German emperor, were immensely hostile to the Dominicans (and vice versa) at this time. Indeed, so deep was their split that more than one scholar feels that the real reason for the condemnation of Eckhart was that it was a Franciscan "revenge" against the recent canonization of the Dominican Thomas Aquinas.[94] Nor should this be discounted lightly since Aquinas had been under a very heavy cloud indeed since his Parisian (1277) and two Oxford (1284, 1286) condemnations. So heavy was this cloud in Germany that Dominicans there reverted to a more Platonic and Augustinian spirituality in order not to be tainted with the suspect matter-oriented spirituality of Aquinas. Eckhart himself, however, tried to marry Augustine and Aquinas, and it is clear from this essay alone that he certainly did not repress Aquinas's creation spirituality. Indeed, at his defense, Eckhart compared his situation of being under suspicion to that of his recently canonized brother, Thomas Aquinas. To the Dominican order's everlasting credit, that order never abandoned Eckhart's defense as long as he was alive.

With the condemnation, much of Eckhart's holistic spirituality went underground to feed the imaginations of movements like Friends of God and the Beghards and Beguines.

Some of it surfaced in his follower John Tauler in particular, who in turn had a direct influence on Martin Luther. And not least among subsequent disciples, as we suggested at the beginning of this essay, was Karl Marx.

Ernst Bloch traces the Eckhartian influence on Marx in the following manner: from the revolutionary thinkers behind the Peasant Wars, such as Thomas Munzer and Huss, to the revolutionary Anabaptists, to the mystic poet Angelus Silesius, to the young Hegel, to the atheist Feuerbach, to Karl Marx. He sees in particular a great likeness between Angelus Silesius (who has been described as a "seventeenth-century . . . Eckhart"[95]) and Ludwig Feuerbach, whose position on religion Karl Marx borrowed almost in its entirety. James Clark, who is very cautious in this regard, concedes that it is "very plausible" that "some of the Beghards charged with heresy at Cologne" had quoted Eckhart in their own defense and that this "would explain Heinrich von Firneburg's (the archbishop's) attitudes toward Eckhart."[96] Thomas Merton has written his opinion of Eckhart's trial:

> He was a great man who was pulled down by a lot of little men who thought they could destroy him: who thought they could drag him to Avignon and have him utterly discredited. And indeed he was ruined, after his death in twenty-eight propositions which might doubtless be found somewhere in him, but which had none of his joy, his energy, his freedom. . . . Eckhart did not have the kind of mind that wasted time being cautious about every comma: he trusted men to recognize that what he saw was worth seeing because it brought obvious fruits of life and joy. For him, that was what mattered.[97]

It may well be that the greatest victim of his condemnation was not Eckhart but the mainstream of Christian spirituality. I do wonder whether Eckhart's condemnation did not make Luther's institutional rebellion inevitable. And what is more evident, the spiritualities that were to follow Eckhart, in particular the *devotio moderna*, Imitation of Christ, and flagellants, would be notable mostly for their sentimentalism, which includes anti-intellectualism, masochism, lack of political-social consciousness, and withdrawal from the vocation to change the world. "An entire work of interiorization is pursued at the end of the Middle Ages. The pilgrimage replaces the crusade, and the stations of the cross will soon replace the pilgrimage."[98] Henceforth *privatization* and *spirituality* would, with few exceptions, become almost synonymous terms in the West. Is Eckhart a "mystic of the left"? According to William Eckhardt in his study on compassion, left-wing freedom as distinct from right-wing freedom means freedom for the many instead of freedom for the few.[99] Given this criterion, Eckhart is clearly a "mystic of the left."

Like his sister, Joan of Arc, Eckhart paid a prophetic price for his trust in his own experience. His mysticism became prophecy for others and a cross for him. Joan of Arc spent five hundred years in the ecclesial darkness until she emerged as a canonized saint only in our century. I hardly think that Eckhart wants or needs such honors. After six centuries of being under a shadow, however, it might now be time to open our eyes to listen to the Gospel that this man who paid the price of a prophet was preaching. Ironically, Marx may assist believers to open their eyes, as Eckhart assisted Marx to open his. Spiritual-political theology akin to Meister Eckhart's is still claiming its victims in our own time. But at least they receive the support of those who went before. As Theodor Adorno has put it, "all those outside the sphere of management are pathfinders, trailblazers, and—above all—tragic figures."[100]

NOTES

1. Thomas Merton, "Marxism and Monastic Perspectives," in *A New Charter for Monasticism*, ed. John Moffit (Notre Dame, Ind.: Notre Dame University Press, 1970), 69, 76.

2. No one has demonstrated this more convincingly than Anne Douglas in her brilliant study on sentimentalism, *The Feminization of American Culture* (New York: Knopf, 1977). For spirituality and sentimentalism, see the conclusion of this book, "On Desentimentalizing Spirituality."

3. Christopher Hill, "Top People," *New York Review of Books*, 8 December 1977, 42.

4. Ernst Bloch, *Atheism in Christianity* (New York: Herder & Herder, 1972), 63ff. See also Alois M. Haas, "Maître Eckhart dans le miroir de l'idéologie marxiste," *La Vie spirituelle* (January 1971): 62–79; H. Ley, *Studie zur Geschichte des Materialismus im Mittelalter* (Berlin: Editions Planète, 1957).

5. Reiner Schurmann, *Maître Eckhart ou La Joie errante* (Paris: 1972), 11. Hereafter I will use the English translation of this excellent study on Eckhart, *Meister Eckhart: Mystic and Philosopher* (Bloomington, Ind.: Indiana University Press, 1978).

6. Matthew Fox, "Meister Eckhart on the Fourfold Journey in Creation Spirituality," in Fox, ed., *Western Spirituality: Historical Roots, Ecumenical Routes* (Notre Dame, Ind.: Fides/Claretian, 1979).

7. Bloch, *Atheism*, 65.

8. Raymond·Blakney, *Meister Eckhart: A Modern Translation* (New York: Harper & Row, 1941), 244, 14. Subsequent references to this translation will be abbreviated "Blakney" in these notes. Other translations employed in this article include James M. Clark, *Meister Eckhart* (New York: Thomas Nelson and Sons, 1957), abbreviated "Clark" in subsequent notes, and James M. Clark and John V. Skinner, *Meister Eckhart* (London: Faber and Faber, 1953), abbreviated "Clark and Skinner." In this particular instance as in endnote 10 below, Blakney's translation is more accurate than Clark's.

9. Meister Eckhart, *Die Lateinischen Werke*, eds. J. Koch et al., vol. 5 (Stuttgart: Kohlhammer, 1938ff), 11. Subsequent references are abbreviated *LW.*

10. Josef Quint, *Meister Eckhart: Deutsche Predigten und Traktate* (Munich: Carl Hanser, 1977), 77. Subsequent references are abbreviated "Quint."

11. C. F. Kelly, *Meister Eckhart on Divine Knowledge* (New Haven, Conn.: Yale University Press, 1977), 58.

12. Schurmann, *Mystic*, 13, 23, 28, 30, 47, 92, 233.

13. Ibid., 38.

14. "Intravit Jesus in Templum Dei et Ejiciebat Omnes," in Quint, 153–58, and in Clark, 127–32.

15. Clark, 127.

16. Ibid., 127.

17. Ibid., 127–28.

18. Blakney, Modern Translation, 240, 245.

19. Clark, 80.

20. Clark and Skinner, 53.

21. See Schurmann, Mystic, 113. The "without why" attitude lies at the center of Eckhart's spiritual theology—it is a mystery instead of a problem-solving attitude. It follows then that an antimerchant mentality also lies at the core of Eckhart's spirituality.

22. Meister Eckhart, Die Deutschenwerke, ed. Josef Quint, vol. 1 (Stuttgart: Kohlhammer, 1958), 105. The five volumes of this work were published from 1958 to 1976. Subsequent references are abbreviated DW.

23. Clark, 128.

24. Schurmann, Mystic, 110.

25. Clark, 128–29.

26. Ibid., 129.

27. Eckhart's "Defense." Cited in Schurmann, Mystic, 245.

28. Blakney, Modern Translation, 133, 241.

29. Clark and Skinner, 103.

30. Ibid., 103.

31. Ibid., 104.

32. Ibid., 128.

33. Schurmann, Mystic, 201–2.

34. Clark and Skinner, 135–36.

35. Ibid., 134.

36. Eckhart, DW, vol. 2, 708.

37. How close this theory of pride and work as an end in itself comes to the Buddhist philosophy of work may be seen in E. F. Schumacher, Small Is Beautiful (New York: Harper & Row, 1973), 53–63.

38. Clark and Skinner, 115.

39. Eckhart, LW, vol. 4, 195.

40. Clark, 221.

41. Ibid., 173.

42. Ibid., 147.

43. Ibid., 200.

44. Ibid., 171.

45. Blakney, Modern Translation, 235.

46. Ibid., 233.

47. Ibid., 246.

48. Clark, 249.

49. Jacques Heers, L'Occident aux XIVe et XVe siècles: Aspects économiques et sociaux (Paris: Presses Universitaires de France, 1970), 237.

50. Quint, 140–50; Clark and Skinner, 149–59.

51. Clark and Skinner, 149.

52. Heers, L'Occident, 235.

53. Clark and Skinner, 159. Eckhart does a play on the German words *Adler* (eagle) and *edler* (more noble).

54. Ibid., 150.

55. Ibid., 151.

56. For Aquinas's concept of ecstasy, see especially *De divinis nominibus*, c. 4, nn. 427–39; *Summa theologica*, I-II, q. 175, a. 2 ad 1. I have developed this creation-centered and typically Dominican, ecstasy-oriented spirituality in my book. *Whee! We, Wee All the Way Home: A Guide to a Sensual, Prophetic Spirituality* (Santa Fe, N.M.: Bear and Co., 1976). Eckhart notes that "this birth does not take place once a year or once in a month or once a day but all the time" (*DW*, vol. 2, 677).

57. Clark and Skinner, 157.

58. Bloch, *Atheism*, 65.

59. Clark and Skinner, 157.

60. Ibid., 151.

61. Ibid., 157.

62. Blakney, *Modern Translation*, 236.

63. Clark, 156.

64. See Merton, "Marxism," 80: "The whole idea of compassion . . . is based on a keen awareness of the interdependence of all these living beings."

65. Clark and Skinner, 156.

66. Bloch, *Atheism*, 64.

67. Eckhart, *DW*, vol. 2, 746. Eckhart is one of the few Christian spiritual writers to develop a true spirituality of compassion. See Matthew Fox, *A Spirituality Named Compassion* (San Francisco: HarperSanFrancisco, 1990 ed.).

68. Eckhart, *LW*, vol. 4, 126.

69. Eckhart, *DW*, vol. 2, 601.

70. Ibid., 708.

71. Clark, *The Great German Mystics* (New York: Russell and Russell, 1949), 9.

72. B. Kuske, *Quellen zur Geschichte*. Cited in Heers, *L'Occident*, 199.

73. Philippe Dolinger, "Strasbourg et Colmar Foyers de la mystique Rhé-nane," in *La Mystique Rhénane: Colloque de Strasbourg* (Paris: Presses Univer-sitaires de France, 1963), 4.

74. Barbara W. Tuchman, *A Distant Mirror: The Calamitous Fourteenth Century* (New York: Knopf, 1978), 24, 38.

75. Iris Origo, *The Merchant of Prato, 1335–1410* (New York: 1957), 8; see Tuchman, *Mirror*, 28.

76. I am referring, of course, to the critical question of Eckhart's being a pantheist. The sentence condemned is "Everything that is is God"— but Eckhart did not say that. He said, "Everything that is in God is God." This proposition was used as a solemn declaration by the Synod of Rheims in 1148 and is also found in Alan of Insulis, *Regulae Theologicae IX*, in Patrologia latina, ed. J. Migne, CCX 628. Thomas Aquinas, canonized three years before Eckhart's trial, also said, "That which is in God is God" (*Compendium theologiae*, 37, 41).

77. Cited in Walter Bauer, *Orthodoxy and Heresy in Earliest Christianity* (Philadelphia: Fortress, 1971), 313, 314, 312.

78. A. Borst, *Die Katherer* (Stuttgart: 1953). Cited approvingly in Heers, *L'Occident*, 348.

79. Heers, *L'Occident*, 360.

80. David M. Nicholas, "Town and Countryside: Social and Economic Tensions in Fourteenth-Century Flanders," *Comparative Studies in Society and History* (1968), 458f, 471f.

81. M. de Gandillac, *Maître Eckhart* (Paris: Aubier, 1942), 10ff.

82. Ibid., 23ff. Most of the Beguines were unmarried women asserting their rights in a society that did not want them. See Norman Cohn, *The Pursuit of the Millennium* (New York: Oxford University Press, 1970), 148–62. Dollinger establishes that Eckhart preached in their homes and corresponded with them ("Strasbourg et Colmar Foyers," 8).

83. Clark, *Meister Eckhart*, 14.8.

84. Clark, *German Mystics*, 22f.

85. See André Vauchez, "La spiritualité populaire au Moyen Age d'après l'oeuvre d'E. Delaruelle," *Revue d'histoire et de la spiritualité* 51 (1975): 285.

86. Schurmann, *Mystic*, 209; see also J. A. Bizet, *Mystiques Allemands du XIVe siècle* (Paris: 1957), 14.

87. John D. Caputo says that "Eckhart proposes a kind of mystical athe-ism" ("Fundamental Themes in Eckhart's Mysticism," *The Thomist* [April 1978]: 211) vol. 42, no. 2. For more on the relationship of atheism to politics, see Manuel-Reyes Matte, "Atheism as a Political Problem," *Listening* (spring–autumn 1970): 97–110. Vol. 5, no. 2.

88. Quint, 308.

89. Clark, Meister Eckhart, 21.

90. Bizet, Mystiques Allemands, 12ff.

91. See M. D. Chenu, Nature, Man, and Society in the Twelfth Century (Chicago: University of Chicago Press, 1968): "Poverty . . . represented both a rejection of the avarice and vanity of the new world and a liberation from the temporal security of the old regime. . . . It involved more than moral purification. . . . [It involved] rejecting out of hand an entire economic system" (235, 256).

92. R. H. Tawney, Religion and the Rise of Capitalism (Middlesex, England: Harcourt Brace & Co., 1969), 48.

93. Bizet, Mystiques Allemands, 12–13.

94. Cited by Gandillac, Maître Eckhart, 19. Clark characterizes the Franciscan-Dominican relationship at this time as one of "unconcealed hostility" (Meister Eckhart, 15).

95. O. Karrer, Meister Eckhart (Munich: Muller, 1926), 55. Cited in Thomas F. O'Meara, "Meister Eckhart's Destiny," Spirituality Today (December 1978): 349.

96. Cited by Gandillac, Maître Eckhart, 17. He also points out that as provincial minister of Saxony in Bohemia, Eckhart was much immersed in the milieu of the Brethren of the Free Spirit who were so dominant a force in Bohemia at that time.

97. Thomas Merton, Conjectures of a Guilty Bystander (Garden City, N.Y.: Doubleday, 1968), 53–54.

98. E. Delaruelle, cited in Vauchez, "Spiritualité populaire," 287. So thoroughly has the dualism of politics and spirituality taken over that even today commentators on Eckhart miss his political-economic consciousness. C. F. Kelly is an example. Kelly, a former monk, apparently wants to make Eckhart into a monk, while in fact he was a very active and politically embroiled Dominican friar.

99. William Eckhardt, Compassion: Toward a Science of Value (Oakville, Ontario: CPRI Press, 1972), 66–67, 257–258.

100. Theodor W. Adorno, Philosophy of Modern Music (New York: Seabury Press, 1973), 30.

CHAPTER 11

Otto Rank on the Artistic Journey as a Spiritual Journey, the Spiritual Journey as an Artistic Journey

☽

I consider Otto Rank to be one of the great spiritual giants of the twentieth century, a genius as a psychologist and a saint as a human being. Though vilified by his original community of Freudians, he never became bitter. He died a feminist and deeply committed to social justice in 1939. His work, more than any other psychologist's, provides the appropriate psychological basis for Creation Spirituality. This brief essay recounts just some of his deep contributions to increasing our spiritual awareness. In his last book, Beyond Psychology, he warns that we must move beyond psychology and look for cosmology and mysticism,

social justice and feminist wisdom if we are to survive as a
species. Rank sees his work as parallel to Einstein's. His deep
understanding of creativity makes him a mentor for all of us
living in a postmodern world.

IT IS NO SMALL thing to proclaim, as Christians and Jews do, that human beings are made in the "image and likeness of God." What does this *imago Dei* tradition mean? Does it mean that every human being is an artist and that in this discovery of one's vocation to create is found the Creator of all? Is the journey of discovering how one is an artist synonymous with the journey of discovering God?

These are a few questions that arise as a result of our pausing over the awesome belief that humans are the "image and likeness" of the Creator. Where might we turn to explore these issues more deeply? In this essay I would like to turn to Otto Rank and to share with the reader some of the implications for spiritual journeying that are contained in his extraordinary book, *Art and Artist*. Shortly before his death, the late Ernest Becker, Pulitzer-Prize-winning philosopher and author of *Denial of Death*, commented that Rank's *Art and Artist* was the most important book he had read in his entire lifetime.[1] I believe that Rank has left us a rich gift indeed and that *Art and Artist*, especially chapters 12 to 14, may well emerge as the most valuable psychoanalysis of the spiritual life in our time.

Rank was a disciple of Freud and a part of his inner circle in Vienna for over twenty years. In 1926 he broke with Freud, principally over the issue of Freud's treatment of the artist. Rank felt that Freud was a reductionist about artists, reducing all creative impulses and production to Oedipus complexes and the like. Rank's stand itself has tremendous implications for spiritual seekers, because theologians too have often been critical of Freud's reductionist surgery on all religious believers—as if because *some* believers look for a substitute father in God, *all* believers do. Or as if because religion can be and very often is an illusion, faith necessarily is; or as if because myth and illusion are important elements of spiritual journeying, spiritual journeying is necessarily a hoax all the time and everywhere.

RANK ON CREATIVITY

Rank went to live in Paris where he took up residence in the artists' *quartier* and devoted much of the rest of his life to counseling artists. An artist himself, he wrote novels, plays, and poetry as well as psychological studies, and counted among his circle of friends both Henry Miller and Anaïs Nin—in fact, he had a long relationship with the latter, and she writes the foreword to the current edition of *Art and Artist*.[2] She calls Rank a "rebel" for daring to stray from the orthodoxy of the great father figure, Sigmund Freud, and she points out how Rank is only coming into his own today because the disciples of Freud pursued a "relentless excommunication" of Rank that isolated him from the history of psychoanalysis. Rank was, Nin asserts, "a literary man" who was "preoccupied with social problems." His influence was great on the Philadelphia School of Social Work, and his analysis of what he calls the "genesis of creativity"—an exploration that is the goal of *Art and Artist*—does not lack a social dimension by any means. His psychoanalysis of the artist and, I would assert, of spirituality is a profoundly sociopsychological analysis. Among Rank's other books are his *Psychology and the Soul; Modern Education: A Critique of Its Fundamental Ideas;* and *Beyond Psychology*.

Rank makes several observations about creativity in modern culture that are so deep and ring so true that no contemporary spirituality can afford to ignore them. I shall discuss a few here.

Individualistic Ideology Rank complains that an ideology of the individual, fostered by a psychology that ignores art and society, is actually destroying art and spirituality and is responsible for the present impasse in spiritual consciousness. "For unless it has some collective or social basis—for instance, in religion, or, later, the 'genius-religion'—artistic creation is impossible" (*Art and Artist*, 389). It is a collective consciousness and not rugged individualism that gives birth to creativity, he is declaring. "Education or art can no more be supported on psychological ideologies than religion can be replaced by psychology. For psychology is the individual ideology *par excellence* and cannot become collective, even if it is generally accepted or recognized" (389). These comments, written in 1932, are prophetic indeed, for they warn of the idolatry of psychology and the reduction of spirituality to psychologism that is so prevalent in our own day, when psychological overkill has infiltrated many spirituality programs. There are actually programs in this country, for example, that demand CPE (clinical pastoral education) for a degree in spirituality, while ignoring cosmology and social justice; others that require spiritual direction understood as the poor person's psychotherapy. Theologian Krister Stendahl warns that it is the overpsychologizing of the Gospel that Dietrich Bonhoeffer has correctly called "cheap grace." Psychologism transforms "practically all of the immense and ferocious drama of history that we read about in the Bible into the kind of pastoral counseling and consolation in which God's mercy overcomes the fear of judgment."[3]

Today there also exists the dismal situation of persons who trumpet their commitment to "peace and justice" but totally ignore and even treat violently musicians and other namers of the collective unconscious or soul of persons.

"Peace and justice" promoters who ignore or attack artistic consciousness are in fact part of the problem, not the solution to global transformation, for they are born, as Rank teaches, of the ideology of individualism even when they protest otherwise. Peace-and-justice persons as well as psychologists and formation directors in religious orders would do well to listen to the sobering reflections of Arturo Paoli about the importance of the artist: "Beauty is the purpose of history; peace, harmony, unity, music are different words that express the same reality. To be religious is to give your life so that the world may be more beautiful, more just, more at peace; it is to prevent egotistical and self-serving ends from disrupting this harmony of the whole."[4]

Elitism as the Death of Art Rank criticizes the very pedestal that art has been consigned to in a culture that has, for all practical purposes, sold its soul to an ideology of the individual. He suggests that art has been prostituted by a consumer and materialistic society that wants to enshrine the artist much as superficial believers want to elevate the saints or their religious heroes. "The art-manias of modern society, with their overvaluing of the artist, indicate a decline of real artistic vigour, which is only speciously covered over by the last flicker of a snobbish enthusiasm" (427). Spiritual wayfarers might take to heart Rank's criticism and apply it to many areas of their own lives. For example, as regards art and the power of creativity, to what extent do our spiritualities succumb to "snobbish enthusiasms" and consign the name *artist* only to someone outside oneself or one's own circle? To what extent do we fail to nourish and nurture the artist within ourselves and among ourselves and fail to see how creativity is the very image and likeness of God coming to fruition?

To what extent do spiritually minded persons or spiritual systems fall into pedestal pieties as regards hagiogra-

phies and the writing of our saints' lives? If we are looking
for the perfect hero and saint to lead us from our slavery,
whether that hero be pictured as Dorothy Day or the latest
pope or someone else, and in the process we surrender our
unique and necessary vocation to be our own kind of saint,
we have missed the whole meaning of holiness. This same
flight from our responsibility for holiness and wholeness is
often projected onto institutions and institutional saviors by
religious persons on the American scene, where institutions
play so dominant a role in encouraging fads or what Rank
would call "spirituality-manias." The fads of art, religion,
and psychology are all criticized by Rank, who dares persons
to throw away art, religion, spirituality, or psychology as a
crutch and to start living them as integrated parts of one's
lifestyle, work, and personality. His challenge is overpower-
ingly biblical in its demands. He calls for sacrifice in the
form of surrender. "We are at one of those crises in human
history," he dares to say, "in which once again we must sacrifice one thing if we want the full enjoyment of another. . . .
There seems to be a spiritual law whereby nothing can be
wholly won or enjoyed without something being given up
or sacrificed for it" (428–29).

How are we to sacrifice and surrender? We need to do it
by our freely chosen decision, for "surrender means not an
imposed necessity, but a freely chosen decision." What do
we surrender? Traditional forms, says Rank. "The surrender
of traditional forms no longer means a loss to us, but a liberation of creative force from the chains of old ideologies"
(429). The salvation of the individual, for Rank, is the liberation of the individual's creative potential. The true art, for
Rank, is the development of one's full person. In the past we
all too often surrendered the body in our search for our soul
or fullest energies; we are now invited to participate in a
new creation, a new humanity. "The new type of humanity
will only become possible when we have passed beyond this
psychotherapeutic transitional stage, and must grow out of

those artists themselves who have achieved a renunciant attitude towards artistic production." As spiritual people and as
artistic people (they are one and the same for believers in
humanity's *imago Dei* theme), we need to let go of (one is
reminded of Meister Eckhart's way of *Abegescheidenheit* and
Gelazenheit) and let be what one cherishes the most: for the
artist, art; for the spiritual person, spirituality; for the psychologist, psychology. Only this letting go, this seed dying,
will produce fruit and fruition. "The creative type who can
renounce this protection by art and can devote his whole
creative force to life and the formation of life will be the
first representative of the new human type" (431).

GOD—THE ONE TO
WHOM WE GIVE THE GIFT

For Rank, an artist is one who wants to leave behind a gift.
But "the artist's gift is always to creation itself, to the ultimate meaning in life, to God."[5] God then is the ultimate gift
receiver for the artist, and this is why all other protections
from art must be let go of. The work we do in art must itself
be renounced in the long run, since "it cannot give salvation."[6] If God is the one to whom we give the gift, then
there is an inherent Eucharist or thank-you based on experience and memory of that experience that is deep within all
our efforts to create. The gift of creativity contains within itself a need for a eucharistic thank-you offering for the gift
and gifts of living. God is "The One We Thank: The Receiver
of the Gift" of our work and creativity.

Fear—The Biggest Obstacle to Spirituality Rank devotes
considerable time and attention to the major obstacle that
our outer structures (culture) and our inner structures (psychology) erect to prevent spirituality and creativity from
happening. In one word, that obstacle is fear—the fear of

surrender, of suffering, of exploring, of fear itself, and above all of death and of life. The fear of life "has led to the substitution of artistic production for life, and to the eternalization of the all-too-mortal ego in a work of art. For the artistic individual has lived in art-creation instead of actual life, letting his work live or die on its own account, and has never wholly surrendered himself to life" (430). If one substitutes for the term *artistic person* the expression *religious person*, one begins to see the depths of Rank's insight vis-à-vis spirituality. How often—in parishes or novitiates, in religious houses or in ecclesial bureaucracies, in liturgies or in the ministry we are involved in—we have substituted religious productions for life. How often well-intentioned spiritual persons have failed to surrender wholly to life and have lived their religious creation instead of actual life. What Rank is speaking of, mystics have also spoken of in the past: that compulsion and overattachment are most insidious, indeed most demonic, when they consist of attachment to "good works," whether of liturgy, prayer, ministerial duties, or the like. Rank is counseling what all solid mystics have counseled: a letting go.

For Rank, the history of human art is the history of the human soul or, more accurately, of the effort at creating soul by humans. The single biggest obstacle to soul making for Rank (not to discount the obstacles created by individual ideologies and elitism) is the inability to live a dialectical life, one that accepts both a collective and an individual life, a socially involved and a solitary life. The dialectic between enjoying life and working at creating life forms a veritable crucifixion for the spiritual person, with the nail of creativity driven through one hand and the nail of the need to live fully driven through the other. "The basic conflict of the creative personality is that between his desire to live a natural life in an ordinary sense and the need to produce ideologically—which corresponds socially to that between individuality and collectivity" (416). The holy or whole person, whom Rank calls the productive type, will find a "middle way" or a dialectic to accommodate both tensions in his or her life. "Whereas the average man [sic] largely subordinates himself, both socially and biologically, to the collective, and the neurotic shuts himself deliberately off from both, the productive type finds a middle way, which is expressed in ideological experience and personal creativity" (416). But the dialectic that represents the balance in the spiritual person's life "is difficult, impermanent, and in all circumstances painful," warns Rank (415). It is this fear of suffering what all birthers must suffer that accounts for so little creativity or so little of what Creation Spirituality would call the *imago Dei* in human history.[7]

Prophecy, Success, and the Need for Solitude There can be no in-depth or spiritual living without solitude. Rank understood this, and in his characteristically insightful way, he offers reasons why this is the case. The spiritual person—in Rank's terms, the creative person—struggles "against the community of living men and against posterity" (406). The prophetic struggle of the spiritual person is one of trying to escape "collectivizing influences by deliberate new creations" (406). This struggle of the artist against community is often misunderstood by persons within the community, who respond with envy and jealousy at the power and beauty that is often born of such struggle. For certain individuals, steeped in a mere individualistic ideology, imagine that the spiritual person is struggling against them personally. Nothing could be further from the truth. The spiritual person's struggle is a struggle against social ideologies and especially any which postpone life and living. More often than not it is a struggle against oneself insofar as the "self" or ego has incorporated such ideologies. When persons in a group overreact to the spiritual person's struggle, it invariably takes the form of envy and jealousy, a collective condemnation of the creative person's success. "The assumption that the artist seeks only success and fame originates with the unproductive type, who may not only be eager for it himself, but also be actuated by the belief that the artist wants to become famous, whereas really he himself wants to make him famous so as to participate in his immortality" (407). Thus the notion that spiritual greatness seeks fame and success is itself a projection by the unproductive, or what Rank calls the neurotic, individual who has surrendered his or her vocation to greatness. This surrender of bigness corresponds with a flight from life and therefore with an exaggerated need for immortality or bigness after life. Thus the spiritual person enters as hero or savior or saint to play the role of immortalizer for those too afraid to live bigly.

Rank insists that, in fact, every true creative person knows that success is the enemy of holiness. "Success is therefore a stimulus to creativity only so long as it is not attained," he warns (408). Thus, the need for solitude—to get away from any fame or success that comes with being true to the *imago Dei* in one. The real reason for spiritual productivity, according to Rank, is not fame or immortality but rather it is "a means to achieve actual life, since it helps to overcome fear." One might, if a theologian, substitute *eternal life* for *actual life* in the sense of eternal life already begun, of realized eschatology, of the kingdom and queendom of God already begun.

In this regard it is noteworthy that Jesus, who was himself so creative both in his message and in his style of choosing the message in his parables (Rank calls all style ideology), was so intent on preaching the coming of the divine reign *now*. "Thy kingdom come on earth as it is in

heaven," he teaches people to pray. Look, too, at the amount
of preaching that Jesus devoted to the overcoming of fear.
Faith is said to drive out fear, and so does love. And the
Father-Creator of all watches over even the sparrow falling
from the nest, so there is no need to fear. Rather, there is a
time, a new messianic time, in which to create. New light is
shed on the crucifixion insofar as there is Gospel evidence
that it was Jesus' success, his large crowds and his being listened to, that aroused religious leaders against him. "He
tried to make himself a king," they complained, thus fulfilling one of Rank's observations. Since "a community is always hungry for material for its own eternalization, . . .
outstanding individuals . . . then become the pioneers and
victims of this collective immortality, whether they will it or
not. . . . Fame might then be taken as an expression of regret
on the part of the community which has annexed this man
and his work as its own" (411).

Thus there is still another need for solitude on the part
of a creative person (Jesus' being driven out to the desert so
often), and that is to escape the collective-immortality impulses of a community—impulses that may be expressed
positively or negatively.

There are powerful and long-lasting lessons here for
those who live "in community"—that they not define community too narrowly and materialistically, as physical near-
ness and togetherness, for example. For to do this would be
to reduce "community living" to nonliving or what is in
fact a flight from life and from spiritual depth and greatness.
In such "community" there would be no saints whatsoever.
True spiritual living includes the dialectic of solitude and social interaction that Jesus or any spiritual person lives.

Creating Solitude is not a one-way goal for the spiritual
person, however. It is only half of a dialectic; the other half

is giving birth. And this, for Rank (as for Meister Eckhart),
is, when all is said and done, the better half. "The highest
type of artist [read: spiritual person] is he who can use the
typical conflict of humanity within himself to produce collective values which though akin to the traditional in form
and content—because in principle they spring from the
same conflict—are yet individual, and new creations of
these collective values, in that they present the personal
ideology of the artist who is the representative of his age"
(361–62). In other words, the ultimate vocation is to serve
others by responding creatively to the needs of one's times.
Such birthing demands sacrifice on the giver's part that is
often unnamable and unknown. In other words, the creative person takes upon himself or herself the sins (that is,
dualisms) of his or her generation and times and tries to
recreate from them.

The artist experiences a deep sense of vocation or calling. For such a person his or her "calling is not a means of
livelihood, but life itself. . . . The artist does not practice his
calling but is it. . . . The artist needs his calling for his spiritual existence" (371). Thus, entering into creativity reveals a
profound meaning of vocation: one becomes one's work,
and work intersects with one's deepest conflicts and sufferings. One's work "reveals his struggles in love and life,
which in the productive type spring from the impulse to
create, and not vice versa. This conflict arises from an inten-
sification in him of the general human dualism" (371). The
artist thus becomes his or her calling with all the pain that
implies. Prophetic work is born through this very conflict,
for it is "only through his inner conflict that the artist gains
the courage, the vigor, and the foresight to grasp the im-
pending change of attitude before others do so, to feel it
more intensely, and to shape it formally." The more committed to one's vocation one becomes, "the less capable the col-

lective ideologies are of carrying it (especially in the case of religion), the more internal the struggle of the cultures becomes, and the great artist finally has to carry it personally, in artistic development and in human suffering" (369). The "carrying it" here might well refer to the cross that Jesus and many prophets before and after him have borne figuratively or literally. The conflict between outward and inward freedom is "one of the essential dynamisms of all artistic creation" (366), and the rooted person who is creative learns this lesson of dialectical living early.

Play Rank believes that the play impulse is the soundest starting point for understanding the psychology of the creative (or what we are calling the holy or spiritual) person. There is, Rank declares, a profound "purposelessness" in all true art (103)—much, I would suggest, as all adult prayer is basically useless. It is our wasting time, letting time and ego go, that constitutes our adult prayer. The neurotic, who for Rank is the *artiste manqué*, the frustrated artist who cannot create because fear dominates, needs above all else to learn humor and play from the creative person. The saint manqué must learn the same from true contemplatives, who are always humorous people. "The neurotic must first learn to live playfully, illusorily, unreally, on some plane of illusion—first of all on the inner emotional plane. This is a gift which the artist, as an allied type, seems to possess from the outset" (109).

I do not know any dimension to contemporary spirituality that concerns me more, nor do I know any more fundamental test of authentic mysticism or prophecy than that of humor and play. The prophet or social-justice type who lacks a sense of humor is dangerous to be around, for there is a hint in that lacuna of a dualistic rather than a dialectical individual. The mystic who cannot laugh is a bogus mystic intent on using mysticism as a contemplative crutch, just as

the prophet who cannot laugh is a bogus prophet using
"peace and justice" as a new moralism and orthodoxy test.
Time and time again I have met graduates of spirituality programs around our country who could not laugh! I feel pity
for them and fear for their spirituality programs. These
overly somber types—or what Rank would call ideologues
of spirituality—remind me of Jesus' complaint with the
people of his time: "We pipe to you and you do not dance;
we sing dirges, and you do not mourn." God save us from
the neurotics who preach a spirituality sans humor and play-
fulness. The neurotics who cannot take play into their spirituality ought to take Rank's advice and learn from more
spiritual people how to laugh again.

SUMMARY

This has been a brief introduction to Otto Rank's exploration
of psyche, society, and spirit. "There is," as Ernest Becker
maintains, "no substitute for reading Rank" and, of all his
works, "*Art and Artist* is the most secure monument to his genius."[8] I hope the reader has learned enough of the depth of
Rank's analysis to pursue his or her own reading of Otto
Rank. I believe that *Art and Artist* is not only the most solid
psychoanalysis of the spiritual life that I know of but also
that its conclusions open up whole new avenues for Chris-
tology and understanding the person and the history of
Jesus (who was, after all, not a king but an artist). We also
have in this book one of the authentic mystical documents
of the twentieth century. It is a creation-centered mysticism,
however, and thus people or spiritualities who do not recognize extrovert meditation as meditation might pass it by.[9]
That would be a great loss, for as Evelyn Underhill testifies,
"the artist is no more and no less than a contemplative who
has learned to express himself, and who tells his love in

color, speech, or sound. The mystic, upon one side of his nature, is an artist of a special and exalted kind, who tries to express something of the revelation he has received, mediates Reality and race. . . . [Artists] participate in the Heaven of Reality."[10]

NOTES

1. See Ernest Becker's treatment of Rank in *The Denial of Death* (New York: Free Press, 1973). A classic biography of Rank is Jessie Taft, *Otto Rank* (New York: Julian Press, 1958). Ira Progoff acknowledges Rank's contributions to spirituality in *The Death and Rebirth of Psychology* (New York: Delta Books, 1964).

2. Otto Rank, *Art and Artist* (New York: Agathon Press, 1975). The book was written in 1932. Subsequent references (page numbers only) to this work will be in parentheses in the text.

3. Krister Stendahl, *Paul among Jews and Gentiles* (Philadelphia: Fortress Press, 1978), 98.

4. Arturo Pasli, *Meditations on Saint Luke* (Maryknoll, N.Y.: Orbis, 1977), 6.

5. Cited in Becker, *Denial of Death*, 173.

6. Ibid.

7. I have explored Rank's analysis of the fear of creativity in much greater detail in "Creativity and Compassion," chap. 4 in *A Spirituality Named Compassion and the Healing of the Global Village, Humpty Dumpty, and Us* (San Francisco: HarperSanFrancisco, 1990 ed.).

8. Becker, *Denial of Death*, xii, 171.

9. See Matthew Fox, "The Case for Extrovert Meditation," *Spirituality Today* 30 (1978): 164–77.

10. Evelyn Underhill, *Practical Mysticism* (New York: Dutton, 1915), 27.

CHAPTER 12

Deep Ecumenism,
Ecojustice, and Art as Meditation

☾

Art as meditation is the primary prayer form in the Creation
Spiritual tradition. Here I interact with the great "bible" of art
as meditation, M. C. Richards's book, Centering in Pottery,
Poetry, and the Person. I discovered her book after I had
launched the Institute in Culture and Creation Spirituality at
Mundelein College in Chicago in 1976, and I found that her
work assuaged my doubts and loneliness in attempting a curricu-
lum in which art played the major role. (The first person I hired
when I started the institute was a dancer, Tria Thompson.) Was
I crazy? M. C. Richards assured me that if I was, I was in good
company.

I N MY BOOK *The Coming of the Cosmic Christ,* I define deep ecumenism as "the movement that will unleash the wisdom of
all world religions—Hinduism and Buddhism, Islam and
Judaism, Taoism and Shintoism, Christianity in all its forms,
and native religions and Goddess religions throughout the
world." I also comment on the practical implications of this
awakening to the mystical or wisdom dimension of our spiritual heritage: "This unleashing of wisdom holds the last
hope for the survival of the planet we call home. For there is
no such thing as a Lutheran sun and a Taoist moon, a Jewish
ocean and a Roman Catholic forest. When humanity learns
this we will have learned a way out of our anthropocentric
dilemma that is boring our young, killing our souls, trivial-
izing our worship, and exterminating the planet."[1]

Deep ecumenism is needed today to bring forth the wisdom of all the world religions for the critical issues that our
species faces at this apocalyptic moment in earth history: the
issues of ecological disaster, already being intimated where
the hole in the ozone layer is being felt, for example, and
where the warming of the earth is making the Sahara desert
expand even into southern Europe; issues of youth despair—a despair apparent not only in so-called Third World
countries but on the Native American reservations and in the
inner-city ghettoes in the United States as well as among
drug-addicted youth of the middle class throughout the
West; and issues of global peace and justice, such as the
pressing need to reinvent work so that all humans may have
good work.

The heart of the contribution that an awakened mysticism can make is a rediscovery of the sense of the sacred,
and with it the imagination and energy that a sense of the
sacred brings to the task of reinventing relationships of all
kinds—work (and its counterpart, unemployment), politics,
economics, religion. When persons encounter the sacred,

they are more ready to let go (this is something so-called First World people in particular must do in our time). Letting go is a valued part of the spiritual journey; it is part of the Via Negativa. When persons can let go, they are also more ready to interfere, which is how Rabbi Heschel defines the primary work of the prophet. Thus social transformation depends on our renewed capacity both to let go and to interfere. To do this constructively requires authentic creativity as well.

Deep ecumenism, then, is about something deeply practical—it is about shared praxis, the art of praying together. To pray together is a far deeper and more demanding way of interacting than merely reading theological position papers at each other. Deep ecumenism has to do with opening the heart up—which is, after all, what authentic prayer does. As Rainer Maria Rilke put it early in this century, "the work of the eyes is finished; go now and do heart work." Deep ecumenism is about shared heart work; it is the coming together of spiritual practitioners to do heart work together no matter what our particular religious backgrounds.

We have been engaged in this kind of praxis of deep ecumenism at the Institute in Culture and Creation Spirituality (ICCS) since its foundation sixteen years ago in Chicago and in a special way since our arrival in Oakland, California, eight years ago. At ICCS we study the Sophia or Wisdom tradition of our ancestors in a course on "Wisdom and Movement." How important it is that we not subject our most mystical and cosmological sacred texts to mere left-brain analysis and exegesis but that we pass the truth through our bodies. By doing so all new truths come home to us—and by "us" I don't mean just Westerners but everyone who has a body as well as a heart to pray with. (A well-kept secret in the West is that the heart is in the body. How then can we do heart work without the body?)

Another way we celebrate Sophia or Wisdom is by sharing in the new creation story from today's science. This rebirth of cosmology is a poignant contribution to deep ecumenism for several reasons: first, because these stories are being held as truthful around the world—in India and throughout Asia; in Africa, Europe, and the Americas. Just as all tribes of humans kept themselves together by their shared creation story in the past, so today our species is being gifted with a single creation story from science that can make us a tribe. This is no small thing, for without a common creation story we will never come to a common morality. It is when people share a common beginning that they can begin to agree on a common goal and on the moral path to that goal.

The new creation story is deeply mystical, for it is deeply awe inspiring, and awe is mysticism. It is a story of the unconditional love of the universe that has brought about our planet and our species and those other creatures with whom we share this planet. Therefore, the proper response to this story is through art, for the proper way to respond to mystical experience is always by way of silence (when we are struck with awe, we are struck with silence) and by art. The finest way to tell the story is through ritual, which is the most community-oriented of all arts. Any response other than art (for example, dogma) is too superficial to express our experiences of the Great Mystery, the ineffable. The new creation story affirms that our lives are bathed in the Great Mystery—every element of our bodies was birthed in a supernova explosion 5½ billion years ago; all the organs of our bodies have their 18-billion-year story to tell. The stars, the one trillion galaxies, the sun and the moon, the mountains and waters and forests and fish—all have their sacred and revelatory story to share. It is time to put these mysteries into ritual. It is ritual—not academia—

that will educate our species in its creation story. Words are not enough, for, as Rilke put it, "words are the last resort for expressing what happens deep within us."

Deep ecumenism is not only elicited from an encounter with the new creation story from science. It takes place when we gather to pray in sweat lodges or in other ancient prayer forms practiced by the native peoples of the world. At ICCS we do sweat lodges and Native American rituals of many kinds; we do wicca circle dances and spiral dances; we do Sufi dances and other Dances of Universal Peace; and we do African drumming and African dance and learn about that tradition's rites of passage. All this awakens in the soul an awareness of cosmic ritual and a remembrance of how we once had it in the West—certainly among our Celtic ancestors, for example, who also had sweat lodges, circle dances, the Green Man, the Goddess, and a living sense of the divine in all things (and therefore of the Cosmic Christ, who is the divine element, the divine "I am," in every creature). It is because of this cosmic sense that we are touched still by the wisdom of Hildegard of Bingen, Meister Eckhart, Francis of Assisi, Nicolas of Cusa, Thomas Aquinas, and Julian of Norwich—persons affected directly and indirectly by the sense of microcosm and macrocosm in the Celtic tradition. Our times are times for rediscovering and retelling the story of how nature is indeed a source of divine revelation. If we fail to do this—and the proper way to do the telling is through ritual—then we will continue our destruction of nature.[2]

At the Institute in Culture and Creation Spirituality, students and faculty are involved together in deep ecumenism as we gather around the fountains of wisdom emanating from our numerous and wonderful spiritual traditions. But special attenton is paid to the cosmological and Goddess and Green Man awakening of the twelfth and early thirteenth

centuries. For this renaissance comes closer than that of any
other time to paralleling the renaissance emerging in the
1990s. We also draw on the biblical mystical tradition, especially that of cosmic wisdom or the Cosmic Christ. Faculty
and students at ICCS are from Catholic, Protestant, Jewish,
Hindu, Muslim, African, Native American, and wicca backgrounds or are New Age persons and seekers who have not
been touched by religion or who have left it. We can all
learn together in such an ecumenical environment.

ART AS MEDITATION:
THE DOOR TO DEEP ECUMENISM
AND THE ACCESSING OF THE SPIRIT

How do we awaken persons to their capacity, however dor-
mant and underdeveloped, for ritual praxis and mystical expression of a deep and justice-oriented kind? What about
people who have been deeply wounded by fundamentalist
religion and are recovering Christians, for example?

Art as meditation is the primary form of prayer in the
creation-centered tradition, and to practice it and undergo it
opens the door to the praxis of deep ecumenism. After all,
ritual itself is a practice of art as meditation. At our institute
we invite many artists, who have themselves undergone a
paradigm shift vis-à-vis art (seeing it as spiritual practice
and not as product-oriented) to lead our students in art as
meditation. These art forms may include any of the following: painting, improvisation, arts as healing, clay, writing,
walking in nature, drumming, singing Hildegard of Bingen's
music, Eastern chants, massage, and so on. No matter which
of these practices a person chooses to take there is a common experience to them all. They are all experiences of
prayer, and no one way is "Roman Catholic" or "Protestant"

or "Buddhist." Art is deeply ecumenical—that is, universal.
No church can lay claim to owning art as process.

Art is not only the most appropriate expression for mystical experience; it can also be the process that elicits the experience of mysticism in the first place. When art is entered into as process and not as product, art becomes a "Way" (from Christ's words in John's Gospel: "I am the Way"), a path, and not—as the message we receive in a capitalist society tells us—as a product or goal.

One reason why art as meditation is so useful in our time is that it opens us to the Spirit. Where is the Spirit? Where is the Spirit that we need to encounter and that reaches out to touch us at this critical point in history? The Spirit is to be found primarily in the depths; it is in the "innermost part of our being," as Meister Eckhart put it. It is down more than up. Spirituality is about journeying down—down into the depths of self and society; down into the pain, darkness, emptiness, silence, guts, and lower chakras of our experience. Down to where the breath begins, in a deep place, at our diaphragms; down where compassion is felt—in the guts of our beings. This journey downward is ignored when theology and religion operate only with the left hemisphere of the brain, where words are operative and light reigns. God is the deep ground, as Eckhart puts it, and God is "a great underground river that no one can dam up and no one can stop." Deep ecumenism is about journeying into this underground river to drink of the wet waters of wisdom. Grief too is found in our depths, where there is rage and sorrow as well as silence and transcendence. After all, as Eckhart says, "God is at home; it is we who have gone out for a walk." Spiritual praxis is always in some way a journey home, a return to our depths where the "inner person" or the "true self" (Alice Miller) reigns as opposed to the "outer person" or superficial person or "false self." As

Eckhart puts it, the inner person is "the soil in which God has sown the divine likeness and image and in which God sows the good seed, the roots of all wisdom, all skills, all virtues, all goodness—the seed of the divine nature (2 Pet. 1:4). The seed of the divine nature is God's Son, the Word of God."[3]

The question that arises about the Spirit is not so much where is the Spirit—for the Spirit is everywhere. A more pressing question is how do we make an inner journey into the Spirit. How do we access the Spirit depth? I believe that the most accessible route to the Spirit, the least elitist and the most available route, the deepest and most authentic route, is that of art as meditation. Through art as meditation, we come in touch with our own experiences of depth—our experiences of joy and our experiences of suffering. But we do not stop there—rather, by accessing the depths of the experience we also access the means out of the depths of awe and grief into the light of day, namely creativity. By journeying into our experience by way of art as meditation we come in touch with our images once again and our power for imagery: this is empowering. It gives us our souls back, and our responsibility to express them. In the process, the Spirit returns—through our imaginations and through our hands, bodies, voices, songs, color, clay, words of poetic truth. As Eckhart puts it, "the truth does not come from outside in but from inside out and passes through an inner form."[4] We get in touch with the truth through art as meditation and we also get in touch with a form by which to express our truth.

The ecumenical aspect to all this is the discovery that all truth is one—that "my truth" is "our truth" at the level of spiritual experience. As the fifteenth-century Indian mystic Kabir put it, "now beyond caste or creed am I!"[5] No one owns such breakthroughs of Spirit; they are universal, for no one owns the Spirit and no religious tradition has a monopoly on it. Indeed, the Spirit far exceeds any one tradition, and that is why all practitioners need to have their hearts open for the Spirit to enter in and tell us truths—some of them new and some of them ancient—that we all need to hear today.

Introvert Meditation Contrasted to Art as Meditation

It is useful to examine in greater depth the role of art as meditation in our spiritualities, since this way constitutes the primary prayer form in the Creation Spiritual tradition. It is also important to point out how "new" this ancient form of prayer appears to be in light of the privatizing of spirituality that occurred during the Enlightenment period, due to rationalism, pietism, and the West's penchant for an introspective conscience. In a celebrated article, "The Apostle Paul and the Introspective Conscience of the West," Krister Stendahl, dean of Harvard Divinity School, demonstrates how profoundly introspective Western spirituality became under the exaggerated influence of Saint Augustine and how this introspection has distorted our reading of biblical spirituality.[6] One price the West has paid for too much introspection is the gradual privatizing of meditation, so that the word *meditation* very often means exclusively an inward journey into the self. The combination of this Augustinian introspective bias with such introverted meditation runs the risk of becoming spiritualism. Such intensive introspection is not biblical, for it fails the test of being Christian—namely, compassion understood as celebration and justice making.[7]

There is, of course, a role that introspective or concentrative meditation can play. It is mostly the role of enhancing self-awareness, which is no small matter in a society as superficial, materialistic, violent, and insecure as our own.

All meditation, whether ascetic or aesthetic, is about waking us up. It is about overcoming the an-aesthetic in our lives. It is about awakening us to the awesome, God-filled, and often demon-ridden reality of which we are so integrally a part. The Chilean psychologist Claudio Naranjo and the American psychologist Robert Ornstein, in their study *On the Psychology of Meditation*, contrast what they call introvert meditation with extrovert meditation. (Their "extrovert meditation" is what I call "art as meditation.") For the sake of brevity and visual as well as intellectual contrast, I will list how they contrast the two meditation forms here.

Introvert	**Extrovert**
just sitting	surrendering to experience
concentrating and repeating (e.g., chant, mantra)	letting go
interiorizing an externally given form	expressing an inner form to which one is attuned
turning off	opening up
Apollonian	Dionysian
inner directed	outer directed
imagery is given	imagery arises spontaneously
a way of detachment	a way of surrender

While both methods have as a common purpose openness to experience, art as meditation is said especially to instill an "attitude of reverence toward all of existence."[8] This bears a direct relationship to a creation-centered spirituality, which emphasizes the grace of beauty everywhere and the interrelatedness of all things. Thomas Merton's spiritual journey, which gradually employed more and more art as meditations, including photography, drawing, and writing, has been traced as a journey that "turned finally from mysticism of introspection . . . toward the mysticism of unifying and unitary vision."[9] No wonder his last talk was on Marx and monasticism, compassion and spirituality!

In considering this list of contrasts between introvert and extrovert or art as meditation, we should understand clearly that the former, not the latter, is outer directed or dependent on imagery given from the outside. Thus the word extrovert does not mean "for extroverts" or "outer directed." It means flowing from the deepest and most creative center to the full world all around us. There are important political consequences to this, as we shall consider.

Art as meditation concentrates on present experience. In this way too, it would seem attuned to communion with and sympathy for current suffering and current ills—one more evidence of its link to prophetic spirituality. Introvert meditation is more a replenishment of energy by "taking a vacation," as Ornstein puts it. In this respect, introvert meditation can actually assist extrovert meditation and, in an indirect way, sustain prophetic living and action. An example of art as meditation is given from the Tibetan tradition.

> The street cleaner has to take his task of sweeping as the starting point for meditation. So, likewise, must the potter take his task of producing clay utensils on his potter's wheel and the cobbler, his handicrafts. Here, again, therefore, it is evident that one may do what he will so long as he is clearly aware of what he is doing. Every activity is of equal value as a basic for dharama exercise.[10]

We learn that the key to art as meditation, then, is discipline and awareness.

Two Kinds of Art as Meditation

Meditation is by no means restricted to a journey inward; it can also be a journey outward either to behold the grace and beauty of God in all creatures or to create such beauty. Thus there are two kinds of art as meditation: that which experiences communion with divine appearances around us and that which seeks to create divine insights into truth, beauty, and unity or its social counterpart, compassion. The first kind I will call C or communion meditation. It concentrates on outside images not as objects but as experiences of communion. Consider a dog with a bone, a musician listening to music, a nature lover with leaves, a lover with the beloved, a scientist with a microscope. Thomas Merton testifies to the deep power of such meditation: "The mind that responds to the intellectual and spiritual values that lie hidden in a poem, a painting, or a piece of music discovers a spiritual vitality that lifts it above itself, takes it out of itself, and makes it present to itself on a level of being that it did not know it could ever achieve."[11] To be taken to a "level of being we did not know we could achieve" is to be taken to the sacred mountain top. Theophanies occur there. We all—and especially the young—deserve to be taken to such epiphanies.

The second kind of art as meditation, that of centering by way of making or doing, I will call M. This form of art as meditation may take the form of photography, which allows the viewer to see creation in a more disciplined and therefore more nearly complete way (Thomas Merton relied heavily on this method in his arsenal of spiritual disciplines), dance, filmmaking, ikebana (Japanese flower arranging), making pottery, gardening, lovemaking, tai chi, playing a musical instrument, composing poetry, studying (Thomas Aquinas was big on this), nursing, drawing, painting, sculpting, calligraphy, cooking, journal writing, running. The list could go on and on, for the issue in art as meditation is not what is being done or what is produced but the total presence, body and spirit, in the process of creating.

What both C and M kinds of meditation hold in common is that they are forms of concentration and centering by way of an aesthetic rather than an ascetic discipline. They do not call for withdrawing our senses from creation but for utilizing them in a transformative vision of creation. Eros is

a part of the process—indeed, eros undergoes its own discipline in the process of art as mediation. As such, these ways
of meditation are presumed in a creation-centered spirituality that, being profoundly panentheistic and therefore aware
of how all of creation is bathed in God's grace, seeks to
awaken us to that fact. Art as meditation does not seek so
much to "find God in the soul" as to find the soul and how
the soul—and all else—is in God. For the heart of panentheistic and creation-centered belief is that all is in God and
God is in all. The two kinds of art as meditation, C and M,
are integrally related, just as the person watching and enjoying the dance (C) is related to the dancer (who is very likely
meditating in form M).

Elements of Art as Meditation

The world-renowned potter, poet, and philosopher M. C.
Richards wrote a book in 1964 that can rightly be called the
bible of art as meditation. (A revised version appeared on
the twenty-fifth anniversary of the work in 1989.) Here I
wish to dialogue with that book, exploring more deeply the
elements of art as meditation. It appears that the following
energies are put in motion and harmony in such meditation
activity.

1 Bodiliness and Passion Art as meditation does not cut one off
from one's senses as introvert meditation does. Rather, it engages the senses in a total and disciplined effort, and from
this engagement an altered state of consciousness results. The
body is not forgotten but rather drawn into such meditation
experiences. As Mary Richards puts it, "it is in our bodies
that redemption takes place. It is the physicality of the crafts
that pleases me: I learn through my hands and my eyes and
my skin what I could never learn through my brain."[12]

Because art as meditation is about doing, it is about materials. Therefore it involves matter and the transformation of matter and the transformation of energy by way of matter. Therefore it is about struggle or, as the poet would put it, about fire.

> To live as artists in the moods and materials of life! . . . Not to sell ourselves short as less interesting, less beautiful and stirring and mysterious than the things we make—less visionary and hopeful and intact. And to realize that we do not win our depth and our inner form and our texture and our truth of being without the fire. Ordeal by fire. There is no substitute for transformation of the body. (Richards, 105)

On hearing about art as meditation, some persons respond that "the interest in arts is middle class." Our materialistic culture may have made art into one more commercialized object for the consuming classes, but in fact the making of beauty and the discovery of beauty in body and other materials and the awareness that body and matter as well as energy and matter are all parts of the cycle of energies in our world—these are not middle-class truths. They are classless truths. No class has a monopoly on the body. Indeed, it is body awareness that most often results in sensitivity to the body politic. Never were prophets out of touch with their own bodies.[13] What is middle class is our taking for granted, as Joseph Pieper has wisely observed and to take our bodies for granted is indeed bourgeois—and art as meditation can destroy this neurosis by waking us up finally to the truth of our body and the truths that our bodies can teach us.

Art as meditation, being bodily, cuts through the awesome and demonic dualism of body versus soul that so much ascetic spirituality of the past centuries of Christianity has taken for granted. But happily art as meditation does not

offer a mental or conceptual critique of body-soul di-
chotomies so much as an experiential one. In it one learns
that it is "impossible to distinguish between body and soul:
between the living being and the shape it takes" (Richards,
102). The form that one listens intently to, that one gives
birth to, is itself, in Richards's terms, a "bodying forth."

> Incarnation: bodying forth. Is this not our whole concern?
> The bodying forth of our sense of life? Is this not a sense
> fully as actual as our sense of touch, which quickens not
> only in our skin but in our hearts, when we say that we are
> "touched" by another's kindness? . . . That is what form is:
> the bodying forth. The bodying forth of the living vessel in
> the shapes of clay. (Richards, 38–39)

Richards's use of the term *incarnation* is deliberate. We
Christians of the West usually only mouth those words and
then return to the safety of our heads, whereas authentic
spirituality calls for a deep bodying forth, a genuine belief
expressed in action of the holiness of our own incarnation,
our bodily natures, and our connection with one another
and with all of creation by way of our shared bodiliness.

2 Prophecy Claudio Naranjo calls extrovert meditation the
"way of the prophets." Why does he call it that? I have already alluded to some reasons: because art as meditation
does not divorce sin from social sin. It develops bodily
awareness and with it awareness of the body politic. In addition, art as meditation is about doing. So is love and the
doing of justice. One does justice by undoing injustice, as
one does a pot or a poem or an act of love. By developing
awareness, all forms of meditation overcome what psychologist Ornstein calls "habituation," or our getting too used to
the way things are. Is this not the source of the prophets' insights—that they refuse to take injustice for granted as society and its institutions so easily do? Yet the dehabituation of

art as meditation differs from that of introvert meditation
because the former concentrates its energies on the world
outside oneself—not outside as in a subject-object relationship but as integrally a part of one's whole existence.

Of the biblical prophets whose lives we know something about, all were persons who practiced art as meditation. Hosea was both a farmer living on the land and very
likely a baker; Amos was a shepherd and dresser of sycamore
trees, thus a herdsman and a gardener.[14] Jesus was a carpenter and son of a carpenter. A poet whose spirit and eyes were
keenly aware of nature's lessons from the tiniest mustard
seed to sparrows that fall from nests to herdsmen separating
sheep from goats, Jesus wove these patterns into his poetry—that is, his parables.

Rabbi Heschel reveals a negative reason why art as meditation is the way of the prophet: because, as he says, the prophet speaks not from an inner peace and calmness (the
introvert way) but "charged with agitation, anguish, and a
spirit of nonacceptance" (Heschel, 6). It was his keen concentration on "how man behaves"—in other words, his art
as meditation—that made Jeremiah the prophet he was
(Heschel, 117). Heschel describes the prophetic person, not
in terms of inner peace, but in terms of action and doing.
The sympathy of the prophet is "the opposite of emotional
solitariness. . . . Not mere feeling, but action, will mitigate
the world's misery, society's injustice, or the people's alienation from God. . . . The prophets were not in the habit of
dwelling upon their private experiences" (Heschel, 309).
The prophets, we see, were not overly introspective, as so
much of the West has become.

We need to reflect on the political implications of an exclusively introvert meditation practice. Politically speaking,
the loss of art as meditation has not been a disadvantage for
fascist or imperialistic ambitions of nation or person in the

past few centuries. The reason for this is that introvert medi-
tators do not make good prophets—indeed, they hardly become prophets at all. They do make very ample passive
citizens, however, for they have withdrawn to another
world—one where peace, harmony, and unity exist oblivious of justice, injustice, or compassion. Introvert meditation
has been urged on millions of citizens in our century by the
likes of Franco, J. Edgar Hoover, and others. Introvert meditation, we recall, takes its images from others—more likely
than not from the very makers of the status quo. In such a
situation, spirituality becomes pacification rather than awakening and fits perfectly into the plans of those who feel
themselves born to control others.

The prophets, far from setting spirit off from body, were
in fact sensual, passionate persons. Theirs was not an ascetic
mortification of the senses. "Asceticism was not the ideal of
the biblical man. [sic] The source of evil is not in passion, in
the throbbing heart, but rather in hardness of heart, in cal-
lousness and insensitivity. . . . We are stirred by their passion
and enlivened imagination. . . . It is to the imagination and
the passions that the prophets speak, rather than aiming at
the cold approbation of the mind" (Heschel, 258). Niet-
zsche observed in the prophets—not unlike Richards's observation regarding the one who practices art as meditation—a "kind of consecration of passion."

The prophet, rather than turning inward for peace and
calm, turns outward for God—God who is both beautiful
and demanding of justice where it is lacking. This is ultimately why prophetic spirituality requires art as meditation.
"What the prophet faces is not his own faith. He faces God.
To sense the living God is to sense infinite goodness, infinite
wisdom, infinite beauty. Such a sensation is a sensation of
joy" (Heschel, 143). Thus we learn that the true prophet is
not at all oblivious to beauty or to joy and the ecstasies of

living but finds them more in creation and in creating than in inward journeying. Indeed, it is the intensity of this joy that drives the prophet on to see it shared with all and not hoarded immorally by an elite few. This vision fires the prophet. As a result the prophet's images "must not shine, they must burn." Prophetic words are "designed to shock rather than to edify" (Heschel, 7). Thus, the prophet's task, like meditation's task, is to wake people up—not to inner peace but to social injustice; not to perfect repose with the One but to relieving the burdens of others, so that oneness among people—that is, love and justice—might begin to happen.

Mary Richards testifies what the throwing of pots did for her social consciousness while observing racial prejudices on a beach in North Carolina.

> The irony blinded me like a too bright light, as I saw those palefaces trying to get black, and in their laws not letting that black face drink at their faucets. My entire feeling about the sun was affected. That's what I mean: you take it all in, the politics and the recreation and the social attitudes, the environment and spring. . . . How can we keep our recreation and our politics and our philosophy separate? How can we not see what our eyes behold? As our perceptions become more and more coordinated, we grow in justice. (Richards, 78)

Richards here underlines the often forgotten insight: to sensitize one's perceptions (which is what art as meditation does) is to sensitize one's capacities for learning where true suffering lies. By sensitizing perception we train for compassion and prophecy. Furthermore, Richards sees institutional sin as a projection of the lack of beauty, or the underdeveloped beauty, within all of us—the lack of centering, therefore. The implication is, of course, that were we to enter into centering and the making of beauty we would enter into a more humanized existence.

Humanity can kill itself without lifting a finger, without
even pressing a button. All it has to do is turn itself off.
And then get "kicks" by "turning on." The picture is
everywhere to be seen. Genocide. The bomb is only a detail. The big boom on the firecracker we've been fiddling
with for centuries. The mess in social justice, the mess in
medicine, the mess in agriculture, the mess in foods and
drugs, the mess in education are symptoms of the mess in
the human soul. Who do we think we are? . . . What is the
human? What is the human being's work, what is the
human's pleasure? (Richards, 114)

The issue of work that Richards raises is an immensely
important prophetic issue of our time. Not only because unemployment has become a raging mortal sin spawned in the
entire so-called free world of late capitalism, but also because so much of the work of the employed is demoralizing
for worker and others alike. Richards elaborates on how extrovert meditation can put wholeness back into our work
cycle.

The craftsman works from an immediate life sense. There
is little reason in our culture to make pottery or furniture
or fabric or jewelry by hand except out of an intuitive
sense of one's own being and the being of others, and a
love of the work. Surely there is no social or economic reason: no status, not much money, no security. . . . Material
prosperity and professional success, which are so much
touted, often fall short of satisfying the person as much as
he had been led to expect. (Richards, 109)

Art as meditation teaches the sacredness of work.

There have been so many compromises, so many moments
of falseness in the interests of expediency and the public
image, that by the time the body is well dressed and
housed and fed and delighted, the simple heart will have
gone out of it. Working in the crafts can help to make a
man bold in his honor, perhaps because he has very little
else to lose! (Richards, 109)

What Richards is hinting at is more than a change in our work world. She is hinting at a change in our economic presuppositions as well. From the wheel, she seems to be saying, will be born an economics that values the process and not just the product. But in truth, she tells us, the birth will be from persons committed to such a priority, though their energies and insights may come from the wheel.

Art as meditation is also about a new kind of power—not a repression of power and its delights, not a grabbing for a certain kind of grabbable power, but an entry into a new kind of power. It is a power that is act-oriented and process- or verb-oriented instead of object- or thing-oriented, the basis of a materialistic and violent cultural power. The word craft, Richards explains, "comes from the German word Kraft, meaning power or strength. . . . We can't fake craft. It lies in the act. The strains we have put in the clay break open in the fire. We do not have the craft, or craftsmanship, if we do not speak to the light that lives within the earthly materials; this means ALL earthly materials, including people themselves" (Richards, 12). It is as if José Argüelles is correct when he predicts that "when man [sic] is deprived of the power of expression, he will express himself in a drive of power."[15]

Still another dimension to prophetic art as meditation is its feminist energies. Only an all-male and aggressively patriarchal spirituality in flight from earth, sensuality, and mother would define meditation exclusively as psychic withdrawal from our senses and distrust creativity as a meditation form. Feminist author Adrienne Rich approves of the hypothesis of anthropologists that "the deeply reverenced art of pottery making was invented by women, was taboo to men, was regarded as a sacred process."

> The making of the pot is just as much a part of the creative activity of the Feminine as is the making of the child. . . .
> In pottery making the woman experiences . . . primordial

creative force. . . . The manufacture of pots, like most op-
erations in primitive society . . . partakes of a ritual or religious character. . . . The pot's identity with the Great
Mother is deeply rooted in ancient belief through the
greater part of the world.[16]

The birthing that is characteristic of extrovert meditation will be a threat to any culture or any individuals who
are not at home with the mothering or nurturing qualities
within themselves.

3 Imagination Theologian Gregory Baum in his important
study on theology and sociology makes a far-reaching observation when he comments that "while in classical Catholic
theology it was supposed that faith resides in the intelligence, it may be more realistic and ultimately more profound to say that faith resides in the imagination."[17] If faith
resides in the imagination, then education for faith means
training, exercising, nurturing the imagination. How is this
to be done? Art as meditation is one sound way, as Richards
testifies.

> I would place the development of imagination among the
> primary goals of education. Imagination is the ability to
> picture in the mind what is not present to the senses. . . .
> Imagination in the craftsman works in various ways. There
> is much to ponder on here. He does not always build to-
> ward a prior vision. Often images come in the process of
> working. The material, his hands—together they beget.
> (Richards, 14–15)

Richards links imagination with prophetic consciousness
and acting, when she talks of "Moral Imagination." "We are
not always able to feel the love we would like to feel. But we
may behave imaginatively: envisioning and eventually creating what is not yet present. This is what I call Moral Imagination" (Richards, 92). Imagination is the special gift of the
prophet. "From the child's ability to imagine grows as well

the adult's capacity for compassion: the ability to picture the sufferings of others, to identify. In one's citizenship, or the art of politics, it is part of one's skill to imagine other ways of living than one's own" (Richards, 115). But imagination presumes union with, not withdrawal from, matter and sensuality.

> It is the transformation, in their metaphysical vibrancy, and in the life they lead through the senses: the colors of dry and wet clay, the sensations of weight when it is solid and hollow, the long course of the fire, expectations fulfilled and the surprises, imagination already stirring toward the next form, the broken shards, the ground-up slabs. (Richards, 143).

One gets the impression from Richards that the potter (or any other artist as meditator we might think of) is driven by imagination, almost a victim, a prisoner, of his or her own imagination no less than a sailor is driven by the wind and a prisoner of it.

Art as meditation is not afraid of ideas or people with ideas. In fact, it seeks ideas out and gets high on them. Art as meditation is not anti-intellectual, as so much of our society and spiritualistic religions are. In it art becomes again what it truly is: a search for truth, an authentic way of living the intellectual life.

4 Dialectic Healing of Dualism In art as meditation is a healing of dualisms that our society takes for granted, such as inner and outer, male and female, body and spirit, parent and child, mother and father, work and play, work and art. The discovery of a holistic or dialectical consciousness is a finding by doing and by process, not by definition and conceptualization. Thus Richards comments, "Life is bipolar. Everything contains its opposite. . . . Because of the law of polarity, if we devote ourselves too exclusively to one pole, our world will tend to go flat. It is not a formula we are involved in, but a mystery" (Richards, 96, 116). The centering process is itself dialectical—that is, a process that unseparates what we have inherited as separate. The potter not only pushes the clay but is pushed by it; the writer not only writes his ideas but the ideas write and form and shape the writer. The same holds for lovers or for students (who are also teachers) and teachers (who are also students). From this dialectical process the birthing actually takes place—in us and in the cosmos.

The healing dimension to art as meditation, then, is less "taking a vacation" or getting away from it all than it is a reentry into the organism of existence, a reentry into polar activities, a becoming one with such activities and therefore becoming dialectical oneself. Richards testifies to this. Even in her writing, she says, she "pushes as far as I can push, to birth and death, life and death, getting them centered, unseparated. . . . Always I try to go toward, not formulation, but organism" (Richards, 5). Instead of being a problem, paradox is recognized as a law of the universe—a path we all need to take if we are to be at home here.

5 Disciplines Art as meditation teaches us the "discipline of freedom," according to Richards. Freedom is not the same as "anything goes" or libertinism or personal anarchy. It is "freedom with order," as Pablo Casals so fondly and fervently insisted. It is this discipline of freedom that art as meditation teaches. It is a freedom beyond words, a freedom to play and create and give birth. "Pottery has helped my poetry because I was less instructed in the handicraft and therefore less inhibited. I permitted myself a kind of freedom in the use of clay which I would not have known how to find in the verbal world." What is this brand of disciplined freedom that art as meditation can teach? It involves the freedom to play. But it is won of hard, sweaty, earthy, sensual work. It is the freedom to feel again. "We must be able to have fun, we must feel enjoyment, and sometimes long imprisonment has made us numb and sluggish. And then we find out that there are, paradoxically, disciplines which create in us capacities which allow us to seek our freedom. . . . We become brighter, more energy flows through us, our limbs rise, our spirit comes alive in our tissues" (Richards, 22).

A related discipline to that of freedom is that of responding and of yielding. We learn the difference between control and aggression on the one hand and response and assertiveness on the other. "We redeem [our energies] not by wrestling with them and managing them, for we have not the wisdom nor the strength to do that, but by letting the light to shine upon them" (Richards, 35). A letting be is learned in art as meditation—a letting be and therefore a letting go, a yielding. Since "responses are values" for Richards, our very capacity to learn response instead of superficial reply or control-oriented grabbing is itself a spiritual discipline that is learned. Discipline is itself hard work, sometimes unpleasant even when its goal is the beautiful. But this too is learned in art as meditation—to persevere with the difficulty no less than with the fun of discipline. "The discipline comes in when we have to pay attention to what we don't like, aren't interested in, don't understand, mistrust, . . . when we have to read the poetry of our enemies—within or without" (Richards, 64).

IT IS NOT only religion that has rendered the West overly introspective and introvert in its meditation forms. Society has contributed much by, for example, accepting Descartes's cerebral definition of truth as "clear and distinct ideas" and setting up entire educational systems under his tutelage, so to speak, wherein people actually begin to believe that they are because they think. The Industrial Revolution has rendered the machine more efficient than the imaginative hand. Capitalism, by idolizing efficiency before fun, has formed a very unholy alliance with industry, which has effectively driven the artisan and craftsman or craftswoman underground or simply financially "under" altogether. So much art as meditation could be taken for granted before the printing press, for example, or before textile factory works, or before plastic assembly lines, or before the rural flight to the cities (every family farmer is an artist who enters into rhythm with the soil and seasons). In short, cultural changes and upheavals have contributed substantially to the Western loss of meditation by centering and creating.

Art as meditation is deeply ecumenical because all peoples regardless of religious tradition share these elements of our existence in common: body; prophecy; imagination; dialectical consciousness; discipline. To explore them as we must in art as meditation is to take deep journeys together into the common underground rivers of wisdom. Art as meditation puts demands on body, imagination, and body politic that are visionary and therefore biblical demands. A prophetic action of faithful persons in our time and culture would be to return balance to the word *meditation* by recovering the spirit of creativity as a spiritual discipline. After all, our Scriptures announce that a new heaven and a new earth will be born. Perhaps the Potter of potters (Isa. 64:8) can give birth through us only if we have ourselves learned what giving birth is through the practice of art as meditation.

In the praxis of art as meditation there is another aspect that is radically ecumenical and it is this: the materials for this meditation are not controlled in any way by any religious denomination. Who ever heard, for example, of Anglican clay or Buddhist paint or Roman Catholic body or Hindu breath or Sufi words or Lakota stones? Thus the material or "stuff" of art as meditation is everyone's and no one's. It is an unconditional gift of the universe. When one prays in a sweat lodge with the Lakota people and water is poured on the hot rocks and steam emerges, that steam is the presence of the Spirit, but it is an ecumenical Spirit insofar as it is not "Lakota" steam—it is just steam. There is not a Christian Spirit or a Buddhist Spirit or a Lakota Spirit. There is only one Spirit. One is reminded of Thomas Aquinas's teaching that there is no such thing as "Christian grace" but just grace.

CONCLUSION

Part of a journey downward is the greening of our souls that takes place when the depths are stirred up and breath or Spirit is allowed to roam again, to "blow where it wills." After all, the green things of the earth all have roots—they derive their nourishment from the dark recesses of the deep, dark earth. Why would the greening of our souls operate any differently? Instead of the dry soul of what Hildegard of Bingen calls "carelessness" and indifference to injustice and moral outrage, the greening of our souls is about awakening both our passion for life and our outrage at that which abuses life. This is a natural spiritual journey—the journey from passion to compassion; from eros as love of life to eros as passion for justice (since injustice harms life). If God is "Life, per se Life," as Aquinas puts it, then to defend life is to defend God. But to defend life we must be living—we must be alive. Being alive is breathing and knowing that we are breathing; it is breathing and being grateful for our breathing (one who is not grateful is not yet alive, for gratitude is born of awe, wonder, and reverence). All spirituality is about becoming alive. Spirit means *ruah* or breath, after all, and to be unspiritual is to be at home with death, boredom, ennui, acedia, inertia, passivity. It is to lack the energy for doing good things, as Thomas Aquinas puts it. Spirituality as praxis then is about recovering the ways to become alive. In art as meditation lies an educational revolution.

In art as meditation people come alive again. They learn to feel, to listen to their own truth and their deep experience, but also to listen to the truth in others. Passion and compassion do come together in art as meditation. A time of a global renaissance requires a global spirituality. Nicolas of Cusa foresaw this five centuries ago:

> Humanity will find that it is not a diversity of creeds, but the very same creed which is everywhere proposed.[18]
>
> There cannot but be one wisdom. . . . Humans must therefore all agree that there is but one most simple wisdom whose power is infinite; and everyone, in explaining the intensity of this beauty, must discover that it is a supreme and terrible beauty. . . . Even though you are designated in terms of different religions, yet you presuppose in all this diversity one religion which you call wisdom.[19]

One is reminded of Hildegard of Bingen's observation that "wisdom resides in all creative works."[20] Little wonder that we must return to art as meditation if we are to recover the wisdom that is the core contribution of all the world religions and that our species requires so desperately today.

NOTES

1. Matthew Fox, *The Coming of the Cosmic Christ* (San Francisco: HarperSanFrancisco, 1988), 228.

2. Rainer Maria Rilke, *The Selected Poetry of Rainer Maria Rilke*, trans. and ed. Stephen Mitchell (New York: Vintage Books, 1984), 135.

3. Meister Eckhart, "Vom edlen menschen," in Josef Quint, *Meister Eckhart: Deutsche Predigten und Traktate* (Munich: Carl Hanser Verlag, 1977), 141.

4. Meister Eckhart, "Omne datum optimum et omne donum desursum est," in Quint, *Meister Eckhart*, 170.

5. Sehdev Kumar, *The Vision of Kabir* (Concord, Ontario, Canada: Alpha & Omega, 1984), 14.

6. See Krister Stendahl, *Paul among Jews and Gentiles* (Philadelphia: Fortress Press, 1976), 78–96.

7. See Matthew Fox, *A Spirituality Named Compassion* (San Francisco: Harper & Row, 1979).

8. Claudio Naranjo and Robert E. Ornstein, *On the Psychology of Meditation* (New York: Viking Press, 1972), 91.

9. Luke Flaherty, cited in Suzanne M. Schreiber, "Thomas Merton: Man of Contemplation and Creativity" (Chicago: Mundelein College, n.d.), 3. I am much indebted to this unpublished thesis.

10. Naranjo and Ornstein, *Psychology*, 199.

11. Thomas Merton, *No Man Is an Island* (New York: Harcourt, Brace, 1955), 34.

12. M. C. Richards, *Centering in Pottery, Poetry, and the Person* (Middletown, Conn.: Wesleyan University Press, 1964), 15. Subsequent references to this work will be cited by author and page number in the text. M. C. Richards joined the faculty of ICCS as artist in residence in 1992.

13. See Matthew Fox, *Whee! We, Wee All the Way Home: A Guide to a Sensual, Prophetic Spirituality* (Santa Fe, N.M.: Bear & Co., 1981), 139–58. The way of natural or creation ecstasies spoken of in that book (3–12, 81–88) is the way of art as meditation.

14. Abraham Heschel, *The Prophets* (New York: Harper & Row, 1962), 39, 28. Subsequent references to this book will be cited by author and page number in the text.

15. José Argüelles, *The Transformative Vision* (Berkeley: Shambhala, 1975), 218.

16. Adrienne Rich, *Of Woman Born* (New York: Norton, 1976), 96–97.

17. Gregory Baum, *Religion and Alienation* (New York: Paulist Press, 1976), 244.

18. Nicolas of Cusa, "De Pace Fidei," in *Opera Omnia*, ed. Felix Meiner (Leipzig: 1932), vol. 6, 17.

19. Ibid., vol. 4, 11.

20. Heinrich Schipperges, trans., *Hildegard von Bingen: Welt und Mensch* (Salzburg: Otto Müller, 1965), 107.

CHAPTER 13

The Spiritual Journey
of the Homosexual . . . and Just
About Everyone Else

☾

This essay was originally delivered as the keynote address at a
Dignity convention in Seattle, Washington, in 1983. (Dignity
is the Catholic association of gays and lesbians.) The conference
was hosted by Archbishop Raymond Hunthausen, who was later
disciplined by the Vatican for doing so. My troubles with the
Vatican began then too, when the extreme right-wing group of
Catholics in Seattle (known as CUFF, Catholics United for the
Faith) sent documents to the Vatican deploring my presence at
the conference. If I had it to do over, I would do it again.

THIS PAST SUMMER I had the privilege of teaching with Sister Jose Hobday, a Franciscan sister and a Native American. One day she took me aside with great seriousness and said she had a question she had to put to me as a representative of white society. "I cannot understand," she began, "the hang-up in white culture and church toward the homosexual. In our native traditions we don't even have a word for 'homosexual.' And it is well known among us that often the homosexual was the most spiritual member of a tribe, who played powerful roles as counselors to some of our most important chiefs." She went on to explain how in her ministry of retreat giving, the people she encountered who were "the most beautiful Christians of all" were very often homosexual men and women. This had been my experience as well.

Obviously, what Sister Jose was witnessing, as an outsider in the white person's world, was homophobia. If we lived in a society or a church that was not homophobic, we would need no essay on the topic I have chosen to write on. If our society and our churches accepted the homosexual for what he and she is, there would be no wagging of tongues and lifting of eyebrows about "Homosexuality and Spirituality." In itself the homosexual's spirituality is not different from anyone else's; however, here lies the rub. All spirituality is incarnational—that is, grounded in the locality of subcultures and culture. Sadly, churches can become too much like the world and can fall into sins like homophobia in bending over to imitate the world and its ways. For this reason the experience of the homosexual growing up in Western culture and most Christian denominations has indeed affected his or her spirituality or way of life. It has, for example, profoundly affected such a person's self-image. It has profoundly affected his or her relationships—how many homosexuals, for example, have either (1) felt the need to keep the "deep, dark secret" from their parents and siblings, thus

introducing a basic dishonesty into their family relationships, or (2) had to, by coming out, cut ties altogether
with parents or other family members, or (3) had to hide
their own sexual orientation even from themselves until
after marriage, thus hurting other innocent people? Self-
knowledge and self-discovery are the first steps along the
spiritual way, according to the teachings of the mystics, yet
self-discovery regarding one's sexuality has seldom been en-
dorsed in the churches.

This lack of self-esteem that the homosexual growing up
in a homophobic society or church suffers is of inestimable
significance for one's ongoing spiritual growth or lack
thereof. For without trust, which includes trust in oneself
and in one's body and in nature, there can be no full development of a psychological or spiritual kind. The pain and
suffering that a homosexual in a homophobic culture undergoes can be either redemptive or alienating. It redeems
when it leads to a sensitive vulnerability that allows the homosexual to identify with the sufferings of other oppressed
persons—Jews, the blacks, the Native Americans, women in
a patriarchal society, the *anawim* of any description. When the
homosexual can grow through her or his suffering, a great
spiritual richness is attained. Compassion is gained. When,
however, for any number of reasons a homosexual cannot
pass through the pain that homophobic cultures rain on him
or her, then a psychospiritual arrest can happen and the homosexual becomes a scapegoat, a self-fulfilling prophecy of
a homophobic society, a broken and essentially lonely person who, in his or her alienation, truly feels like an alien, a
stranger in a sick society. In the alien's effort to please that
society, he or she falls prey to its worst sins: power over,
power under, sadomasochism, consumerism, hatred of
body, inability to sustain relationships, adolescent arrest, and
egoistic quests for perfectionism and immortality. Like the

slave who has imbibed the ideology of his slave master, the homosexual then fulfills the prophecy of the heterosexual, plays out the worst stereotypes of the repressed homophobic conscience, and gives to the sexist homophobic society a weapon of great strength: "See," it will say, "I warned you about the homosexual."

SUPPOSITIONS REGARDING SPIRITUALITY AND THE HOMOSEXUAL

In this essay on spirituality and the homosexual I wish to make explicit three suppositions:

1 In using the term *homosexual*, I do not mean to negate the uniqueness, the decision making, the diversity of persons both women and men who are homosexual. Just as there is not one lifestyle of "a black" or "a woman," so too homosexuals come in great varieties of colors, vocations, lifestyles, talents, woundedness, journeys. Nevertheless, to be homosexual in a culture that is excessively conscious of sexuality in the first place and that is excessively heterosexual and therefore homophobic does create a common ground for speaking of that emergent movement of persons demanding their sexual liberation and who call themselves gay and lesbian. Carter Heyward, speaking of her experience of coming out, writes:

> I knew that coming out was, for me, not first a statement about who I sleep with but rather a statement about what I value in human and divine life: learning to stand on common ground; a process at once sexual, political, spiritual, economic; a relational journey both individual and collective.[1]

As stated earlier, I do not believe the homosexual has a spirituality distinct from that of a heterosexual, a bisexual, or anyone else. Yet because the cultural situation is so different for a homosexual, there is all urgency about his or her finding and living out a spirituality that often escapes the more comfortable lifestyle of the heterosexual. Because the homosexual has often encountered deep pain and personal anguish earlier in life than the heterosexual, it is very likely that the homosexual has fallen more deeply and sooner either into divine grace or into demoniclike compulsions. An example of the latter would be the high rate of alcoholism among homosexuals, especially among homosexual men.

2 In saying that the homosexual's spirituality does not differ significantly from the heterosexual's, I am not saying that differences in spirituality do not per se exist. But the most basic difference in spirituality is not that between homosexual and heterosexual, it is between fall-redemption spiritual theologies and creation-centered spiritualities. The fall-redemption tradition begins with the doctrine of original sin and sees all of salvation history through those glasses. Jesus, in this tradition, came primarily to wipe away original sin. This tradition, represented by Augustine in the West, is essentially dualistic and noncosmic—there is no Cosmic Christ in Augustine's spirituality. In this regard it is important to point out that the homosexual has been a special victim of the fall-redemption spiritual tradition. Indeed, all oppressed groups have been. For in this tradition an awesome silence prevails about prophecy, social justice, and human liberation. Essentially introspective,[2] this tradition begins its theology with sin and personal guilt. It has proven an invaluable tool for maintaining the status quo, especially as regards the human propensity in the West for equating guilt with sexuality. It should never be forgotten that Augustine, who named the term original sin by mistranslating Romans 5:12,[3] actually posited that original sin was passed on in the sexual act by the male's sperm. Christian theology ought to meditate long and hard on the subtle implications of this sexual/original sin philosophy for the homosexual, who in a real sense is taught very early in society and church that his or her sexual feelings and orientation are inherently sinful—that is, originally. Of all people, the homosexual must let go of the fall-redemption spiritual tradition and the sooner the better.

The homosexual will recognize in the creation-centered spiritual tradition the kind of liberation with discipline that he or she needs to live a spiritual life, one that culminates in transformation of self and society into compassionate human celebrators and justice makers. This tradition, which is the oldest spiritual tradition of the Bible, for the Yahwist author of the Hebrew Bible wrote in these terms, begins not with original sin but with original blessing.[4] Can you and I, can the homosexual and the heterosexual, believe that he or she is an original blessing? There is where authentic faith lies: in learning to trust the gift and beauty of one's own unique and original existence—an existence that is itself gratuitous and does not need justifications of a moral kind to earn a blessing. This tradition is a cosmic tradition and sees salvation history as integral to the history of the universe, of nature, of human history, of our bodies. The whole cosmic body and the body of Christ are in the process of healing, redeeming, forgiving, releasing. Trust is the basic psychology of this tradition and not guilt. Learning to trust the cosmos, oneself, God, and others while remaining vulnerable, childlike, mystical, and beauty-oriented—these are the steps on such a spiritual journey. Trust alone, psychologist William Eckhardt teaches, can lead to a way of life that is compassionate.[5] Lack of trust, his seven-year study on compassion demonstrates, cannot lead to compassion. Self-love leads to compassion, not self-hatred. "Have compassion toward yourself," says Meister Eckhart, the great spokesperson of the creation-centered spiritual tradition. For how will

Christians ever manage to fulfill Jesus' injunction to love others as we love ourselves if we have not learned to love ourselves?

3 Homosexuals, like heterosexuals, like all saints, sin too; but being homosexual is not one of these sins nor is it the "original sin." Homosexual sins are no different from any one else's sins, for the fact of being homosexual is not one of these sins. Otherwise the Creator, who as far as we now know has created approximately 10 percent of the human race homosexual, would be a sadistic and vicious God. And that, we know, cannot be the truth, since faith teaches us how delighted, how thrilled, how exuberant She was and is with creation and its ongoing blessings. And among those blessings human beings, whether heterosexual or homosexual, especially delight God. "God finds joy and rapture in us,"[6] says Meister Eckhart, writing out of a profound absorption with the Wisdom tradition of the Scriptures.

While the sins of homosexuals are in themselves no different from those of heterosexuals, bisexuals, and so on, nevertheless, because sinlike language and all else that is human and incarnational is to an extent culturally determined, the homosexual, by being driven into underground and marginal living situations, may find temptations to some sins more often than those in so-called straight society. For example, the sin of consumerism. There is a general dictum of economics that reads, The more you make, the more you spend. This "law" seems to hold rather valid among middle-class persons in a consumer society. To the extent that the homosexual finds himself or herself (1) in a middle-class situation and (2) in consumer society, a special access to the sin of consumerism exists. Why? Because many homosexuals are not parents and to that extent are spared the financial burdens, many of which are joys, that parents have in providing for their children's needs and upbringing. This kind of economic independence sets the middle-class gay person up as an easy target for advertisers, who are the missionaries of consumer religion in our time. The insatiable greed for the latest fashion and consumer product must be resisted by the homosexual of the middle class.

The sin of self-hatred is easier for a person to fall into if one has had to deny his or her sexual identity for years, even with those friends and relatives who are closest to one. The sin of self-hatred is easier to succumb to when bad theology teaches a person that in effect God loves you less because of your sexual identity or even that God loves you only on condition that your being does not lead to action—a horrible dualism that a true Scholastic could never countenance, since even that intellectual tradition instructs that *agere sequitur esse*, "we will act according to our being."

Another sin that the homosexual may be especially tempted by is the sin of ersatz immortalities. Because the homosexual qua homosexual has not parented children and because children for centuries have represented immortality in the West, the homosexual is thrown into a very profound and significant search for immortality, for a gift to leave behind, as Rank puts it.[7] Rank points out that in healthy persons this gift often takes the form of art and creativity. But in an unhealthy and materialistic society the first temptation is to look at material goods or their amassing as a sign of immortality. In this respect the sin of clinging, the fear of letting go, the sin of pyramid building, of excessive pursuit of material security, or of prolongation of the idol of youthfulness would seem to hit the homosexual subculture with particular vengeance and would need to be resisted strongly.

THE HOMOSEXUAL AS *ANAWIM*

Liberation Theologians have raised the consciousness of the people of God as to how the biblical God works through the lowly and the *anawim*—those without a voice. The Spirit of God works through these people; they assist in bringing about divine healing to a world battered by sinful humanity. Mary, the mother of Jesus, sings of this relationship in Luke's Gospel when she declares:

> He has scattered the proud in the imagination of their hearts,
> He has put down the mighty from their thrones,
> and exalted those of low degree;
> He has filled the hungry with good things,
> and the rich he has sent empty away. (Luke 1:51–53)

Gustavo Gutierrez, commenting on this passage, writes, "The future of history belongs to the poor and exploited. True liberation will be the work of the oppressed themselves; in them, the Lord saves history. The spirituality of liberation will have as its basis the spirituality of the *anawim*."[8] The early church was a scandal to the Jews, as was the fact that Jesus died on the cross a scandal to Greek and Jew alike. The cross and Easter assure that the oppressed would henceforth be in charge of their own lives. Mary represented such a scandal, since she called herself a "handmaid." Scriptural scholar Raymond Brown writes, "In the early dialogue between Christians and Jews, one of the objections against Christianity is that God would never have had His Messiah come into the world without fitting honor and glory born of a woman who admitted that she was no more than a handmaid, a female slave."[9]

I maintain that the homosexual is indeed a representative of the sexual *anawim*, of the dark or shadow side, the underside, the dispossessed side, the persecuted side of the

Western consciousness as regards sexuality. Culture knows very little about sexuality and even less about homosexuality and what causes it; after all, it was only in the last century that humanity learned that women contribute an ovum to the process of human fertilization and thus are not merely passive receptors of the male seed. But instead of maintaining a respectful silence about the mystery of homosexuality, society and very often religious believers too have felt themselves anointed to pontificate on the morality or immorality, the "naturalness" and "unnaturalness" of homosexual activity. This presumption on the part of a clear majority that it can judge the morality of a 10 percent minority constitutes a social scandal from a theological point of view. We know for certain that the God of the Bible, while we do not know Her reason for creating so varied a species as humankind, is biased in favor of the *anawim*.

The Good News that breaks through for the believer in the Gospel of Jesus is that, strange to tell, it is right here in the space of oppression where God is to be heard, that God is indeed among the poorest and the least in a special way and that it would behoove the majority to listen to the minority. Writes Latin American theologian Segundo Galilea, "The 'least' are not only individual persons in Latin America, but human groups, marginal subcultures, social classes, or sectors. There is in them a collective presence of Jesus, the experience of which constitutes a true contemplative act."[10] In other words, when Jesus announces in Matthew's Gospel that we are to relieve the suffering of the little ones, and in the process we will find God in and among the little ones, he is announcing Good News to the homosexual. And it's Good News for the heterosexual too when the dominant society is (or becomes) still and learns from the oppressed (and therefore learns wisdom and compassion) and lets go of the repression and object making of persons different from oneself. This Good News in turn brings the Good News of celebration, for when letting go occurs, celebration among all persons, homosexual and heterosexual, can happen once again; it also brings the Good News of justice making, for only when those in power let go of their claims to unjust social structures are the poor set free.

And it brings the Good News of creativity, for, as psychologist Otto Rank demonstrates,[11] creativity is only possible when diversity is allowed. When diversity of sexual orientation is admitted by the public as a whole, then authentic creativity can emerge from both heterosexual and homosexual worlds alike. A case in point is John Boswell's study, which demonstrates that the most fertile of all Christian periods in the West occurred during the hundred-year period from 1050 to 1150 when homosexuality was allowed its space and time and place in society and church alike.[12]

Tolerance becomes the key to creativity not because it is a pious virtue to practice but because its presence indicates a willingness by all citizens of society or church to let be. By letting homosexuals be homosexual, the heterosexual is freed from homophobia and can channel her or his energies into creativity, at the same time that the oppressed homosexual is freed to let himself or herself contribute what he or she can to culture's growth and development. Since grace builds on nature and since recent studies of homosexuality indicate that fully 10 percent of a culture is homosexual, then it is imperative that we let nature be nature and let homosexuals be homosexuals. When this is allowed to happen, grace may break through in many forms for all persons of culture and church. And homosexual and heterosexual alike will be able to bless and not curse one another. But for this to happen, it must be emphasized that a majority (90 percent) has no right to dictate the private morality of a 10 percent minority any more than a minority has a right to forgo all moral responsibility and interconnection with the majority. The Gospel that announces that the *anawim* bear special gifts to the people of God at large must be allowed to break through society's projections on gay and lesbian people in order to set all peoples and the Spirit itself free.

With this freedom goes increased responsibility. Ernest Becker warns that the opposite of guilt is not innocence but responsibility.[13] When the homosexual is freed to be himself or herself, what are some particular areas of responsibility that he or she is called to? One such area would be the liberation of other sexually oppressed peoples. It should be remembered, advertisers notwithstanding, that the majority of the human race does not find itself in a sexually fulfilling lifestyle. This is the case with prisoners and members of institutions such as mental hospitals; with handicapped, with widows, widowers, divorced, and sometimes other single persons. A good test of the homosexual's spiritual liberation, since it is "by their fruits that you will know them," will be that person's dedication to the liberation of other persons. This liberation and compassion may take the form of active organizing or of simply being with and offering affection, time, and presence to the lonely of society. If compassion is not the result of gay and lesbian liberation, then that liberation has not been at all radical, at all spiritual. It has been merely an ego or personal liberation and not a liberation of the Self, which is by nature bound to all selves, human and others, of our holy universe.

THE SPIRITUAL JOURNEY OF THE HOMOSEXUAL IN FOUR PATHS

The creation-centered spiritual journey rejects the threefold and all-too-familiar path of the Neoplatonic tradition, whose steps are named purgation, illumination, union. Instead, it offers a fourfold path, which is named in the following manner: (1) creation—the Via Positiva; (2) letting go and letting be—the Via Negativa; (3) birthing and creativity—the Via Creativa; (4) new creation—compassion and social justice—the Via Transformativa.[14] Since I have already stated that in my opinion the homosexual's journey and task are no different essentially from those of any other loved creature of God, I do not intend to demonstrate that the creation-centered spiritual journey is that of the homosexual or vice versa. What I would like to ask is this, however: given the unique cultural context and milieu in a homophobic culture for the homosexual, is it possible that, emerging from the depths of such a journey, the homosexual or sexual *anawim* is indeed graced with a special insight as to the stages of the creation-centered spiritual journey? Might indeed this insight be one way in which the grace of God is breaking through the *anawim*'s experience to enlighten the rest of society in our time? I shall answer this question by looking at the homosexual's experience of each of the four paths.

The Homosexual and the Via Positiva

Inherent in the Via Positiva is a theology of blessing, of experiencing the ecstasy and blessing that all life is. "Isness is God," said Meister Eckhart, and here lies the great miracle of existence. The goodness of creation, its essential trustworthiness and voluptuousness, is praised by the psalmist and other writers of the Wisdom tradition of Scripture. Ours is a world "thoroughly worthy of trust," writes Wisdom scholar Gerhard von Rad.[15] Beauty overwhelms us at every turn toward creation and nature—it is awesome, it is frightening, and since, as Simone Weil observed, beauty has everything to do with terror, Nature is beautiful and not merely pretty or nice. The ecstasies of creation—nature, friendship, art, poetry, dance, work that is noncompulsive, noncompetitive sport, sexuality[16]—all these are available to heterosexual and homosexual alike.

But a question arises: is it possible that the homosexual has experienced a unique challenge to his or her trust of nature and creation and this at a rather early and prelogical age, precisely when it came to his or her sexual orientation? All of a sudden, the gay or lesbian person must face the question of whether creation is "very good" (Gen. 1:31)— except for his or her creation. But one does not "choose" one's sexual preference. It is part of creation indeed, of nature. Homosexuality is unnatural, as the Greeks and Scholastics called it, only to the heterosexual. The homosexual undergoes a deep crisis regarding creation. This crisis may result in behavior that is immature and ego-oriented; or it may go the other route—it may begin the deepening and hallowing route that true spiritual depths are made of. It may result in greater, not lesser, trust of self, body, nature, cosmos, and God. If that be the case, and my pastoral experience has taught me it often has been, then the homosexual will bring a hard-won and deeper appreciation of beauty and gratitude to the banquet of life and will be able to pronounce from the depths the words of Meister Eckhart: if the only prayer you say in your whole life is "thank you," that will suffice.

The struggle for self-trust that the homosexual embarks on is a profound one, and it culminates in the recovery of a theological theme that brings Good News to all persons: that every child of God is a royal person—that is, a person endowed with divine dignity and with divine responsibility.[17] Until persons, whether heterosexual or homosexual is of no consequence here, come to grips with their royal personhood with all the beauty and responsibility that it contains, they will not work so that others who are different from them can also attain their dignity and nobility.[18]

The Homosexual and the Via Negativa

Like any member of an oppressed group, the homosexual will know a lot about darkness, loneliness, nothingness. And about letting go and letting be. The homosexual child must let go earlier than most children of the parental, social, or psychological role models that society gives one in the sexual sphere. Such a person will have to let go of the option of marriage as a lifestyle. The sacrament of "coming out" is a kind of letting go: a letting go of the images of personhood, sexuality, and selfhood that society has put on one in favor of trusting oneself enough to let oneself be oneself. Just as the slave had to empty himself or herself of the slave master's language and thinking and value system, so too the homosexual undergoes emptying, of a profound personal and social kind, of projects and projections that heterosexual society has insisted on. This emptying and letting go and letting be can lead either to a deeper and more vulnerable, more compassionate sense of belonging with others who suffer unjustly, or it can lead to a cynicism, a rage, a hoarding of consumer idols (including sexual consumerism) on the part of the homosexual. If it leads to the former, it is certainly a blessing in disguise, a school of wisdom learned by suffering, a theology of the apophatic God, the God of darkness, whom the straight world needs so desperately to hear more about.

Part of the profound letting-go process that all people must undergo in their spiritual growing is the letting go of pain, of enemies, of hurt, and of guilt. The choice to wallow in one's pain or in one's guilt is a deliberate choice, as can be the deeper option, which is to let go and move on. Of course, before one can let go of pain, one must first admit to it, stop denying it, and allow pain to be pain for a while. The homosexual who has allowed pain to be pain and then let go of it brings healing to others, for all persons suffer pain. Yet judging from our culture's constant flight from pain, straight society is not terribly adept at moving beyond it. Those who have undergone deep experiences of the Via Negativa, as many homosexuals have done, can bring prophetic insight about pain and letting go to the greater society.

The Homosexual and the Via Creativa

Creativity is always ex nihilo—that is, it is always from nothing and from our experiences of nothingness. It is out of the dark. The darkness of letting go and letting be is the precursor to the energy of birth and rebirth. People as astute as Otto Rank put the question, Why are so many homosexuals in the arts? I would reply that the first reason is that such a high percentage of homosexuals have undergone the Via Negativa, having to let go of parents and families and self-archetypes so early that they have been emptied and hollowed out for the great birthing that follows. Rank's own answer, that homosexuals by not having children search for other expressions of immortality and art is one of them, does not contradict my observation. For in fact the birthing of beauty and truth in all the ways that art can do so—dance, pottery, music, poetry, drama, to name a few—is in fact the birthing of alternative children. These are the gifts the creative person wishes to leave behind. Both heterosexual and homosexual persons are creative—all, after all, are made as images of God the Creator—but the homosexual is driven to birth continually by a powerful experience of the Via Negativa as well as the need to create a different lifestyle for himself or herself. Living marginal existences is conducive to creativity, while comfort seldom is. One is reminded of Eckhart's image, which he derives from the prophet Isaiah: from eternity God lies on a maternity bed giving birth. . . . What does God do all day long? God gives birth.[19]

The Homosexual and the Via Transformativa

Hopefully, the direction in which the homosexual takes his or her love of beauty and creation, wisdom from suffering, and creative possibilities is not just the direction of creating more trivia for a consumer-oriented society. Hopefully, this ever-deepening spiral of the spiritual journey will culminate and crescendo where Jesus told us it ought always to crescendo—in compassion. "Be you compassionate as your Creator in heaven is compassionate," said Jesus at the end of the Sermon on the Mount in Luke's Gospel (6:36). Compassion does not mean to feel sorry for people or to treat them as superior or inferior, as the English language has come to mean by the word. Compassion means justice, declares Meister Eckhart, and that is precisely the biblical tradition. But compassion also means celebration. Both justice and celebration rejuvenate society and transform it. Without celebration, justice workers become too serious, exhausted, and without a taste of the future. In short, in a capitalist and consumer society they become like capitalism itself: joyless and imageless. Without justice making, on the other hand, celebrators become bored at their own parties, incestuous, consumers. And celebration, instead of a return to the simple gifts of creation reexperienced with the art of savoring, becomes one more consumer item—boring, violent, expensive.

While heterosexuals as much as homosexuals are called to the justice making and the celebration that compassion is about, still it can be said that a movement of *anawim* who have themselves experienced the oppression of injustice boasts a unique capacity to understand the journey of other victims of injustice, whether of a racial, economic, or sexual kind. While all persons are called to recover the art of celebration, who can teach us more about celebration than those who have learned to celebrate in the midst of sadness and oppression? Who will know more about the value and the purposelessness of savoring pleasure than those who have . had to face the critical question of whether life is beautiful or not? Who will know more about the beauty of creation and new creation than those who have been told verbally and nonverbally by religion and society that the way they were created was a mistake, or was even sinful?

ADDITIONAL GIFTS
FROM THE HOMOSEXUAL

If it is true that the homosexual represents a certain form of the *anawim* and if it is true that the homosexual has often been involved in an ever-deepening journey along the creation-centered spiritual pathway, then it must follow that the Spirit of God wants to bestow gifts on the nonhomosexual people of God by way of the homosexual. The pity of dualism and sexism that keeps the homosexual underground is that the majority of God's people become deprived. And often de-praved. The slave master suffered as much from the system of slavery as did the slave but, alas, imagined he did not. At least the slave knew he was not free. How many homopho-bic persons and institutions know what they are missing by oppressing gay and lesbian persons? In addition to driving such persons to what is sometimes an exaggerated system of segregation and lifestyle, a homophobic culture banishes healthy role models for the one out of ten children who are homosexual.

In addition to gifts from the homosexual that have been alluded to in this essay, I would like to conclude with some others that deserve our attention and meditation. Jesus taught us to love our enemies. If, as Sister Jose Hobday has observed, white culture has made a special enemy of the homosexual, then it is time to start meditating on what kinds of graces and blessings might come our way if we were to embrace instead of condemn the sexual *anawim* in our midst.

1 *Sexual relativity.* I think that it is more than a coincidence that the gay and lesbian liberation movement is occurring in a time and culture that is passing from a scientific myth of Newtonian absoluteness to that of Einsteinian relativity. There is a relativity about sexuality that is not well served by those who, like Newton, feel they can know the unbending laws of nature. Plato said that homosexuality is unnatural because animals don't do it—the problem is that he did not know what animals do and do not do when it comes to sex. One prophetic gift from the homosexual will be to teach humility to those who, like Plato, presume to know exactly what is and is not natural. And what is natural varies with different groups. As Alfred North Whitehead, working out of an Einsteinian and not a Newtonian worldview, put it, the laws of nature develop together with the societies that constitute an epoch.[20] The Einsteinian epoch we are moving into will include an acceptance of the relativity of sexual lifestyles. And with this acceptance, we will become aware that the essence of sexuality is relationship and the quality of relationships—not absolutist laws and principles à la Newton. Eckhart taught that relation is the essence of a thing. This corresponds beautifully with Einstein's teaching on the theory of relativity.[21]

2 *A faith built more on relationship than on institution.* Because the homosexual has not been welcomed qua homosexual into ecclesiastical institutions, that gay or lesbian person who has remained active in any ecclesial community has had to look deeper than the institution itself for answers to the questions of faith: what matters? Does anything matter? There is a well of creativity to be tapped from persons who have learned to live marginally in institutions; they could be a powerful force in revitalizing those very institutions.

3 *A witness to the power of difference as a basis for creativity.* The homosexual stands as a witness to how people can indeed be different. Otto Rank criticizes the West, and America in particular, for equating equality with sameness, whereas in fact authentic equality consists in admitting one's difference and thereby allowing others their uniqueness and difference. And, Rank insists, creativity comes from differences and not from sameness. Minority groups, the *anawim*, are more creative because they have touched nothingness in their being emptied, but also because they have been made painfully aware of their being different. When a society can allow for difference, it will, as Boswell demonstrates the medieval church did, celebrate creative rejuvenation.

4 *Recovery of the body as spirit, of sensual spirituality, of nonreproductive love.* Behind the dualism of body versus soul or of spirit versus matter that has heinously infiltrated Christianity from Hellenism lies the dualism that spirit is about soul and not body. That is not the case in biblical teaching, where the word too often translated as soul, *nepesh*, indeed means all of the following: throat, neck, desire, life, person.[22] The homosexual, by not equating sexuality exclusively with procreation, as Augustine did, allows for the energies of Spirit to flow once again, to overcome dualism that neither Jesus nor the prophets ever imagined, to allow passion its proper place so that compassion might be born.[23] Furthermore, by removing sexual expression from a dominantly reproductive motif—as if sexual love needs to be justified by having babies—the homosexual, like the author of the Song of Songs, teaches society to pause long enough to savor life and its divine delights. In this way homosexual love is an affront to capitalism, which is per se production-oriented and has never developed an art of celebration.[24] Otto Rank believes that humanity is emerging from the sexual era when the quest for immortality or soul was expressed in an exaggeration of family or of its opposite, celibacy. In this era sexuality was in fact taken too seriously by all of us. As we emerge from the sexual era, we need those who can teach us the lighter, more playful, less serious, and less goal-oriented side to sexuality—the mystical side. Here, as Masters and Johnson have found, the homosexual offers a gift to the heterosexual community and society as a whole.

If it is true, as Gutierrez writes, that the spirituality of liberation will have as its basis the spirituality of the *anawim*, then the issue of First and Third World liberation, of feminist and male liberation, of North American as well as Latin American liberation, of white as well as black, brown, red liberation cannot be joined without the sexual *anawim* being listened to.

I wish to conclude this essay with portions of a letter that I received from a gay man who was part of a Dignity retreat I gave recently.

> It is only by finally coming to terms with being gay—and letting myself be gay—that I have begun to see the incredible pain and magnificent pleasure of being a living person. . . . That struggle—which I fought the whole time—is opening my life in a way I never thought possible. It has given me the chance to work at my whole life and to say I don't have to be like everyone else in the rest of my life's aspects either.
>
> Living as a gay man has let me feel love and passion and pain I didn't know I was capable of. But it all makes life an experience worth living.
>
> I wonder if I can now translate some of that into my work life. I'm struggling to put passion into what I do for a living. [In my work as a lawyer] I am outraged and feel great helplessness. [Other lawyers] don't understand human needs and don't seem to care.
>
> So I struggle with vocation—but thanks to being gay I can honestly say that I am becoming awake.

It is my experience that the broken world in which we live and which is so overtly heterosexual needs all the awakening that it can get. Perhaps it is not too late to begin to listen to the *anawim* in our midst.

NOTES

1. Carter Heyward, "In the Beginning Is the Relation: Toward a Christian Ethic of Sexuality," Integrity Forum (Lent 1981): 3.

2. See Krister Stendahl, "Paul and the Introspective Conscience of the West," in Paul among Jews and Gentiles (Philadelphia: Fortress Press, 1978), 78–96 for an important critique of how Augustine's introspective conscience has distorted Western theology's reading of the Bible.

3. Herbert Haag, Is Original Sin in Scripture? (New York: Sheed and Ward, 1969). His conclusion is no.

4. See Claus Westermann, Blessing in the Bible and the Life of the Church (Philadelphia: Fortress Press, 1978).

5. William Eckhardt, Compassion: Toward a Science of Value (Toronto: CPRI Press, 1973).

6. These and other sayings from Meister Eckhart can be found in the following books: Matthew Fox, Breakthrough: Meister Eckhart's Creation Spirituality in a New Translation (Garden City, N.Y.: Doubleday, 1980); and Matthew Fox, Meditations with Meister Eckhart (Santa Fe, N.M.: Bear & Co., 1982).

7. Otto Rank, Art and Artist (New York: Agathon Press, 1975).

8. Gustavo Gutierrez, A Theology of Liberation: History, Politics, and Salvation, trans. Sister Caridad Inda and John Eagleson (Maryknoll, N.Y.: Orbis Books, 1973), 207–8.

9. Raymond E. Brown, The Birth of the Messiah (Garden City, N.Y.: Doubleday, 1977), 364.

10. Segundo Galilea, "Liberation as an Encounter with Politics and Contemplation," in Richard Woods, ed., Understanding Mysticism (Garden City, N.Y.: Doubleday, 1980), 533.

11. Otto Rank, Beyond Psychology (New York: Dover, 1958), 54 ff.

12. John Boswell, Christianity, Social Tolerance, and Homosexuality (Chicago: University of Chicago Press, 1980).

13. Ernest Becker, *The Denial of Death* (New York: Free Press, 1973).

14. I have outlined these paths in the following works: "Meister Eckhart on the Fourfold Path in the Creation-Centered Spiritual Tradition," in Matthew Fox, ed., *Western Spirituality: Historical Roots, Ecumenical Routes* (Santa Fe, N.M.: Bear & Co., 1981), 215–48; and in *Breakthrough*, passim; and in the introduction to *Meditations*.

15. Gerhard von Rad, *Wisdom in Israel* (Nashville, Tenn.: Abingdon, 1978), 306.

16. I have dealt with these natural ecstasies as the basis of our mystical experience in *Whee! We, Wee All the Way Home* (Santa Fe, N.M.: Bear & Co., 1981), 45–54, passim.

17. See Helen Kenik, "Toward a Biblical Basis for Creation Theology," in Fox, *Western Spirituality*, 39–68.

18. The prophetic responsibility of royal personhood is laid out in Meister Eckhart's sermon, "Everyone an Aristocrat, Everyone a Royal Person" in Fox, *Breakthrough*, 510–30. Such themes of liberation had much to do with Eckhart's condemnation. See Matthew Fox, "Meister Eckhart and Karl Marx: The Mystic as Political Theologian," in this volume.

19. Fox, *Meditations with Meister Eckhart*, 88.

20. Cited in Donald W. Sherburne, *A Key to Whitehead's Process and Reality* (New York: Macmillan, 1966), 93.

21. Cf. Matthew Fox and Brian Swimme, *Manifesto for a Global Civilization* (Santa Fe, N.M.: Bear & Co., 1982).

22. Hans Walter Wolff, *Anthropology of the Old Testament* (Philadelphia: Fortress, 1981), 11–26.

23. See Fox, *Whee! We, Wee*, 1–28.

24. Norman O. Brown, *Life Against Death: The Psychoanalytical Meaning of History* (Middletown, Conn.: Wesleyan University Press, 1970), 234–322.

CHAPTER 14

AIDS and the Quest
for an Authentic Spirituality

☾

This was originally a talk sponsored by the AIDS Project network of the diocese of Oakland, California, in the spring of
1991. The event was a fund-raiser for the organization, which
has to raise all its own funds. The two persons whom I cite in
the talk, Michael and Matt, have since died of AIDS.

I WANT TO TALK about AIDS and our quest for authentic spirituality. I use the word quest deliberately in this title because it tells a true story. We're not there yet. We're not there as a people, we're not there as a church—that is, a believing people—we're not there as a species. We are only on the way. We are pilgrims on the way to an authentic spirituality, and the irony is that AIDS is helping us to make this journey to an authentic spirituality. I'll be citing several mystics, the great Meister Eckhart of the fourteenth century; Mechtild of Magdeburg, social activist, feminist Beguine of the thirteenth century; John of the Cross of the sixteenth century. And I'll also be citing some people with AIDS who are mystics of our time—because Creation Spirituality teaches that we are all mystics, we're just not all awake to it yet, and sometimes it takes AIDS or some other peril to wake us up to our deeper selves.

Matt Furlong is a man with AIDS. He published a wonderful interview in Creation Spirituality magazine several years ago about his experiences. One of the things Matt said in that interview was "AIDS is God's way of getting my attention. I guess pain was the only way God could get through to me. . . . As much as I wish I could have learned another way, I have to admit that AIDS has taught me some important lessons. I wouldn't trade AIDS with anything else I've experienced in life, for it has taught me what life is all about."

There was another man with AIDS named Mike who was a student in our program at the Institute in Culture and Creation Spirituality in Oakland, California. When I told him that I was writing about AIDS, he said, "Tell them that AIDS is a gift—it is a gift to society and a gift to the individual with it, because it will result in our being more honest about our sexuality, and it demands a critique of the oppression in our society and of how the oppressed have internalized that oppression with self-hatred, shame, and low

self-esteem." He pointed especially to the internalized oppression of gays and lesbian people, of women, and of
African-Americans. He himself is gay; he said, "I wonder if a
lot of gay men have AIDS because they choose unsafe sex as
a way of expressing their self-hatred." I asked why it is a gift
to the individual to have AIDS. He said, "Because the journey of AIDS is so deep, the journey one undertakes with
AIDS is so deep."

This is a spiritual journey for all of us, for we are all living with AIDS. It is a mystical and a prophetic journey.

What do I mean when I use the term *spirituality*? I mean
living life in depth, living out of our true self, the inner self,
what Saint Paul and Meister Eckhart call the inner self: the
Cosmic Christ, that unique image of God that each of us is
in our depth. Paul and Meister Eckhart make the distinction
between the inner person and the outer person. And Meister
Eckhart says the outward person is the old person, the
earthly person, the person of this world who grows old
from day to day. His or her end is death. But the inward person, on the other hand, is a new person, the heavenly person in whom God shines. God is shining inside every one of
us, inside every creature. Hildegard of Bingen in the twelfth
century said, "Every creature is a glittering, glistening mirror of God." But our species has to find that mirror.

We can cover up the inner person with the outer person.
And how does this happen, that the inner person gets overcome, or neglected, or covered up? Essentially, I think, it happens because of wounds and our vulnerability, especially as
children. We are such a vulnerable species. You know, a horse
gets born and two and a half years later it is ready to run and
win a million dollars for you. A human gets born and twenty-
four years later it drags itself home from college wanting a
free phone and a free bed. And all those twenty-four years we
are vulnerable. Because we are vulnerable, we have to start

paying attention to the wounded child inside us. In her book *Dream of the Gifted Child*, Alice Miller, who has worked for over twenty-six years with the addicted youth and the criminals of Germany, says, "It is the middle class especially who are busy denying they have a wounded child inside." And she comments on how we create a false self that overtakes our true self in order to please those very people who wound us. We live out our life at the level of the outer person or the false self. And this is why we have to pay attention to the wounds. In the wounds are the truth and the power.

It is my experience that a lot of people with AIDS have a lot of wounds in the stories of their lives. Drug addicts have a lot of wounds, homosexuals stereotyped in a homophobic culture like ours have a lot of wounds. The issue is one of authentic self-love versus self-hatred. Again, Matt Furlong in his interview speaks explicitly to this when he says, "I had no self-esteem. I was consciously suicidal at times. I come from a very troubled background. We grew up in a pretty sick situation, but because we had nothing to compare it to, we thought it was normal. My dad was an alcoholic and so are four of the five children in my family. My dad never tried to instill a sense of self-worth in us as kids. I understand now that my dad also suffered from a lack of self-esteem— he just passed it on to my generation. When I'm able to get some distance from it, I realize that he was wounded too. Sometimes our choices are pretty limited." There's great wisdom in that, and there's compassion and there's understanding that if a child grows up wounded and has not been able to take care of these wounds, that child will pass it on as an adult, and sometimes the wounded child will turn into a killer adult—if nothing else, a killer of oneself through self-hatred. And so the cycle continues.

This is why the advice of Jesus is so radical. We are to love others as we love ourselves. It is so simple and so deeply difficult, because a human cannot learn love without love.

It is here that the new cosmology is so helpful to a full spirituality in a time of AIDS for it is a story about unconditional love.

A couple of weeks ago I was on a panel in Boston dealing with spirituality and healing. Maya Angelou, the wonderful African-American poet, and Dr. Scott Peck, a psychiatrist, were on the panel. He made this point: "Unconditional love only lasts with a new baby until it can talk back." Initially, I thought this was kind of a pessimistic statement, and then I realized that if we look at the human condition only within an anthropocentric context (that is, only within the question of whether the baby is talking back to the parents or not), then indeed unconditional love is a rarity. But if we look at the whole story of our existence, of our entire home, we realize that our home is a trillion galaxies big and has a history of at least fifteen to seventeen billion years. When we hear the new creation story that we're being taught at this very time in history, it is a story, strangely enough, about unconditional love—the unconditional love of the universe that prepared for every one of us coming here.

Dr. Beverly Rubik, a biophysicist, says that about seventeen or eighteen billion years ago the universe began as a pinpoint of fire—in fact, it was smaller than a pinpoint— and it expanded. This fire expanded for 750,000 years, and in it was created carbon and hydrogen and oxygen and nitrogen and phosphate and sulfur—the beginnings of the atomic world. Each step along the line was critical, she points out; even after the fireball disappeared, decisions were made constantly that were critical if life was to emerge on this peculiar planet. And she's always using this new phrase, the *anthropic principle*, which means, in the lay person's language, the universe has been a setup for life from the first second of its existence. There has been a conspiracy in the universe from the first second of our existence that we would happen! She says this truth has scientists giving up

atheism because science cannot explain all the awesome hap-
penings on behalf of life in the past eighteen billion years.
She says divinity must be behind all of it, mind must be in
all of it, wisdom is in all of it. Our blood cells undulate like
drums, everything is in motion, atoms are dancing too. She
points out that Professor Paff, a German physicist, has
demonstrated that every atom contains light or photons. And
so we are biophoton emissions. Photons and light are emit-
ted by DNA. We are beacons broadcasting light to the ends
of the universe. "We are electromagnetic bioinformation
systems, coherent lightlike laser beams, we are biolasers. We
radiate, we are radiant beings."

These are the words of a scientist in our time, who of
course is also a mystic. When I hear this language—these
images of light, the photons in every atom—I get déjà vu
about our tradition in the West of the Cosmic Christ, of the
light that is in every being, the Christ who is light in every
being. And I think of Hildegard's words that every creature is
a radiant being.

And so at this very time when we wonder if there is unconditional love any place, we are learning in fact that we
were unconditionally loved as a species and as individuals
beginning eighteen billion years ago by the universe itself.

AIDS is about our immune deficiency, not only in our
species but as a planet. The whole planet today is undergoing a kind of immune deficiency syndrome. I see humans
with AIDS as something like the canaries that miners used to
send down into the mine shaft to see if the air was lethal or
not. AIDS is a testimonial to the fact that the earth system at
all levels is suffering from immune deficiency. The seals of
the North Sea that died by the hundreds a few summers ago,
the whales and dolphins often beaching themselves, the
trees, the grasses, and the forests—they're dying in our
midst, at the very moment when our species, with our na-

tion leading the way, is bent on external defense spending of unimaginable amounts. We are spending nearly three hundred billion dollars a year on weapons in our country alone, while in fact we are ignoring the intrinsic defense systems— the immune systems of our species and indeed of the earth itself.

Do you remember the time when we were able to eat food without vitamin supplements? When food itself contained healthy, nutritious strength within it? AIDS is about our entire relationship to creation. It is about how we have been taking healthy creation for granted, including the immune systems of our bodies and the immune systems of our planet, feeling that we have to play God to control outward defenses when in fact we should be struck by awe, by the interconnectivity and the inner strength of all earth systems, including the marvel called the human body.

Why is it persons with AIDS tell me they are gifted by it? I am reminded of Meister Eckhart, who said, "All things praise God, even suffering and evil can praise God and bless God." Again, turning to the interview with Matt Furlong, he says, "I'm angry at the justice that was not done toward me, . . . and that is not being done toward young people today. As paradoxical as it may sound, getting in touch with my anger has really been a source of healing for me. I am not in denial anymore." Mystics talk about the Via Negativa, about entering that place of darkness that includes anger, and facing it, not running from it. My student Michael told me about his "day of rage." All day long he felt nothing but rage, rage toward his condition, rage toward himself, toward his family, toward society. And he said he just stayed with the rage all day because that's what he had learned at ICCS: he had learned that this is what the mystic in us can do. He let the rage be rage. He didn't cover it up with morphine or anything else. And he said he felt a great purgation, a great cleansing the next day, a great awakening. Like Matt, he was not in denial anymore.

Anne Wilson Schaef, in talking about addiction and the addictive society, says that "denial is a major defense mechanism." Denial makes our society work, and acknowledging the denial is an essential part of healing our entire society so that we can see again, so that we can see the beauty of our existence once again. Meister Eckhart says, "God is the denial of denial." That means the moment we can deny denial, divinity erupts. Because divinity is always here. As Eckhart says, "God is at home; it's we who've gone out for a walk." But we're way out for a walk when we are in denial. And to get back home again is to deny the denial and thereby release the divine. The truth comes out in our true selves when that inner self, that mystic self that wants to play again in the universe, comes out—where it has always wanted to be.

Matt Furlong says, "At times with this disease I've had an incredible insight into the unity of all things—from the grains of sands to the clouds in the sky. In my journal I wrote thank you for my pain—without it I would never have met you—and thank you for my joy—without it I could not express you—you and I are one." That experience of the oneness of things, of our oneness with the grains of sand and with the stars and with history and with one another, and with the shared pain and the shared ecstasy of the world—this is a mystical experience. And as Matt points out, it is part of the AIDS journey, it is part of all human journeys that are taken at the level of death and not superficially. This phrase from Matt speaking to the creator, "you and I are one," is absolutely identical to Meister Eckhart's language in the fourteenth century when he speaks of "breakthrough." He says, "In breakthrough I discover that God and I are one." And so the breakthrough experience is part of the AIDS journey, and it is part of the human journey.

Eckhart says that there are two kinds of birth that a person undergoes. The first one is our birth into the world. He says, "When I was born, when I flowed out of the Creator, all creatures stood up and shouted, 'Behold, here is God'; they were correct." Now, this man had worked through his wounded child to be able to say something like that! There's a rabbi (and remember that Jesus was taught by rabbis, not by Christian theologians) who says that every time a human goes down the street, hosts of angels precede that individual shouting, "Make way, make way, make way for the image of God." That's what it's all about, that's how we were born. And as Paul says, "our life is growing brighter and brighter into an image of God." So life is not just about trying to keep clean that original image of God; it's about investing in it, having it grow brighter and brighter, a fuller and fuller Cosmic Christ.

Now the second birth that Eckhart wrote about he calls "breakthrough." He says this is a birth into God. What he means is that this is our waking up, it is our conversion, our *metanoia*, our change of heart, our seeing the world in a new way, seeing it through God's eyes—which are the eyes of our true self, of our inner child, of our mystic child. Eckhart says, "The eyes with which I see God are the same eyes with which God sees me." Breakthrough is about a new birth in us—a rebirth. And Eckhart says, "As often as this birth takes place the only begotten child of God is born there." And so this rebirth, this breakthrough can take place in us and through us many times every day. The way to breakthrough, however, is very often the Via Negativa, the way of darkness: the way of emptying, the way of letting go, the way of suffering and pain.

The mystics help us to name this deep journey, and I want to share a few images from that wonderful mystic, Mechtild of Magdeburg, a lay woman who was active in the thirteenth century working with the sick and the young people. She was hounded because she was not married and because she was not a nun in a convent; she was a Beguine inventing a different lifestyle for women who were serving others. They were hounded out of cities, they were accused of being prostitutes, and so forth. And so she faced a lot of political oppression in her lifetime. She kept a journal, and that is what I'm reading from. In the Via Negativa, she asks questions: "Do you wish to have love? If you wish to have love then you must leave love." This is the paradox that all mystics and all experience tell us about: if we must have love, we will have to leave love at times. She says, "There comes a time when both body and soul enter into such a vast darkness that one loses light and consciousness and knows nothing more of God's intimacy. At such a time when the light in the lantern burns out, not even the beauty of the lantern can any longer be seen." She is talking bout the dark night of the soul, about how dark things can get. Not only is the light out but even the form of the lantern is invisible in the intense darkness. With longing and distress she says, "We are reminded of our nothingness. At such a time I pray to God, 'Lord, this burden is too heavy for me,' and God replies, 'I will take this burden first, clasp it close to myself, and that way you may more easily bear it.' Still, I feel that I can bear no longer the wounds I have been given. My enemies surround me; how long must I remain here on earth in this mortal body as a target at which people throw stones and shoot and assail my honor with their evil cunning? God has wounded me close unto death. If God leaves me unanointed I could never recover. Lord, I will tear the heart of my soul in two and you must lay yourself in the wounds of my soul. I am ill and I long deeply for the drink which Jesus Christ himself drank. God replies, 'I was always to be your physician, bringing healing and ointment for all

your wounds.' From suffering I have learned this, that whoever is wounded by love will never be made whole unless
she embrace the very same love which wounded her." The
paradoxical wisdom of the mystics that we need at times is
to embrace the darkness, to befriend the pain.

What we are reminded of by AIDS is that the dark night
of the soul is real. It is an experience that every one of us has
many times, whether we do or don't have AIDS, and certainly at this time, when we're all living with AIDS. For all
pain is everybody's. All pain is connected, all experiences, all
things are interdependent in this universe.

I remember once when I took Michael from his hospital
room out to the park nearby. He hadn't been outdoors since
he entered the hospital three weeks before. And he saw every
flower; every single one he remarked about. We sat on a wall
and looked down, and he saw a man running. And he said,
"Wow, isn't that something to be able to run." He had entered the hospital with pneumonia; he was coughing and
could barely breathe. We take for granted the flowers, we take
for granted being able to breathe, we take for granted being
able to run. And that is our failure. This is why we need crisis
to teach us to see again. Molly Rosh is one of my favorite
people. She's a grandmother of nine who has done nonviolent protest against nuclear weapons, and the last time she
was in prison she tells a story of how they used to take the
inmates out for an hour in the prison yard and let them walk
around a tiny plot of mud. And the third week she noticed
how many species of wildflowers there were. And it was the
wildflowers that kept her alive in those months in prison.
When she was released, she was so alert to tiny wildflowers;
when she drives down the highway she sees them in the
cracks in the sidewalk. And the next time she's arrested it will
be for reckless driving because she's avoiding running over
these little friends who befriended her in prison.

To cease taking for granted is the first step toward being a mystic. The German philosopher Joseph Pieper says, "The definition of bourgeois culture is taking for granted." People with AIDS do not take for granted. None of us should.

Breakthrough happens by way of the Via Negativa, which is always a lesson in letting go. It is also a kind of resurrection experience. A couple of years ago, I was working on a book about Thomas Aquinas's mysticism. No one's ever taught me about his mysticism, and I figure since he was condemned three times before they canonized him, he must have had something interesting to say. And I've been finding it. Aquinas says, "Let us not put off rising until our death, let us do so now since Christ rose on the third day. . . . Let us again rise to a new and glorious life; a new life is a life of justice." He says, "The power of Christ's resurrection does not extend just to the resurrection of bodies but to that of our souls." A new creation is born because of resurrection, and so I think this theme is very powerful and very important—that we are called to a resurrection now, to an awakening, to breakthrough. And the resurrection of the body, which follows our experience of death, will take care of itself if we have learned to live fully in this lifetime. Again Matt Furlong says, "It's funny"—now, that's another way for the mystic to say it's paradoxical, be prepared—"It's funny, but the day that someone told me I was going to die was the day I realized that I was alive. I want to live until I die." Those are the words of a mystic, my friends, a mystic with AIDS in our time and in our city. If no one's ever told you this, I want to tell you now, people—we're all going to die. So let's live until we die. As Otto Rank says, "the artist is the one who wants to leave behind a gift"—to leave behind gifts, that is the evidence that we're living. Not that we're massing or hoarding things, property, money, or ego trips, but that we're giving away gifts, blessings, building community with one another—that is proof that we're alive, that we've undergone the first resurrection. That we've cut through the denial that addiction has put upon us. And Matt says, "I've learned that I make myself, I become myself through my choices; through all of this, I've come to know God." In our creativity we make ourselves, we birth the Christ who is that image of God in us, and that is the Via Creativa, the way of creativity that is part of the break-through.

So the issue for every one of us is not whether we will die—we're all going to die, our culture will die, even our species will very likely die someday. The issue is when we die, will we have done our work or not. Or as Jesus said on the cross when he died, "*Consummatum est,*" meaning "My work is finished." His work was done so he could die. What is our work, what is our destiny, our calling, our vocation? That is the question that a resurrected person thinks about. John of the Cross, a great mystic and poet, says, "My only work is love, love is my only work." I suspect that has something to do with all of our work and with all of our being here.

The mystic turns into a prophet—the prophet is the mystic in action. And as Heschel says, "the prophet inter-feres." In our culture, so overcome with addiction, to be a mystic is to be prophetic because it is to interfere with ad-diction—to say no, that we can live without addiction. This is how Anne Wilson Schaef defines the essence of addiction: she says, "An addiction keeps us unaware of what is going on inside of us. We do not have to deal with our anger, our pain, our depression, our confusion, or even our joy and our love because we do not feel them or we feel them only vaguely. If we do not choose to arrest the addiction we shall die." And not just as individuals will we die but as a species, and as a people and as a nation and as a church.

And so the mystic in us refuses to be out of touch with our experience of love and awe and wonder and delight and refuses to be out of touch with our experiences of darkness

and fear and anger. We enter into all that. AIDS then raises
questions about our defense spending in our addiction to
militarism. It raises questions about our dispirited civilization, our spiritual impoverishment, our fear of death, and
what goes with it: our fear of life. As Matt Furlong says, "I
have learned that humans are really afraid of life. We are
afraid to let go, we are afraid to lose control. I've accepted
the fact that I used to spend a lot of time running away from
myself and from God, from what life was really all about. I
have learned that all the distractions, all the destructive behavior I used to engage in was motivated by the fear of looking within. The fear of doing my homework." Our
homework is our heart work. As the poet Rilke says, "the
work of the eyes is finished; go now and do heart work."

AIDS is a time for heart work for everybody. Spirituality
is about heart work, and prayer is about strength, building
up the heart so it's strong, so that the door of fear does not
let the evil spirits in.

This is so important because our culture today and our
species are being overrun by fear. Fundamentalism in all of
its forms is about fear. Thomas Aquinas says, "Those who
are in great fear are so intent on their own passion that they
pay no attention to the suffering of others." I've noticed this
about all fundamentalists—injustice and justice are not in
their vocabulary. Racism and sexism and homophobia are
not in their vocabulary. It is because, as Aquinas analyzes,
they are in a world of their own passion of fear that they pay
no attention to the suffering of others. When I read the Jesus
story, I come to the conclusion that if Jesus redeemed humanity from anything, it is a redemption from fear. The first
thing the angel says to Mary in Luke's Gospel is "Fear not."
And the word *fear* is used 365 times in the Gospels—once
for every day of the year, and it's always about fearing not.
As John's epistle says, "Love drives out fear." Rabbi Heschel
says, "A prophet casts out fear." If Jesus was a prophet, he

was teaching people how to cast out fear—not to build religions on fear and call it Christianity, call it his religion.

The word *courage* in French means a large heart. Ours is a time for magnanimity, for building up our souls, for building up our hearts. The opposite of magnanimity is pusillanimity, which means a puny soul, a timid soul. And most of our institutions today, political, economic, educational, and religious, are suffering deeply from pusillanimity and timidity. Fear is overtaking them, and only the spiritual awakening that begins with the hearts of people can renew this kind of civilization. Our institutions lack spirit. Let me remind you how important it is to build up your hearts; caregivers have to have compassion for themselves. As Eckhart says, compassion begins at home with one's own body and one's own soul. Compassionate caregivers can easily burn out. Their work too is inestimable, and their health too is important in itself. A very high percentage of caregivers run extreme risks of addiction—addiction to their work. It's good work, but it's not enough. Caregivers also have to take time to receive, to breathe, to run, to experience the flowers and the stars and the glorious gifts of being. Unless we are all mystical, we will all become addicted, even to good work—especially to good work.

And so we learn from people with AIDS, from prisoners, from hospice people that ministry is always ministry with—we undergo what they undergo. God suffers when we suffer. It is God who glows and glitters when creation glows and glitters, and God is the person with AIDS suffering; God is the mystic and the prophet waking up, resurrecting. The divine permeates us all. This is the tradition of the Cosmic Christ. What is AIDS? AIDS is another way of living deeply in the universe.

I remember doing a workshop for the Episcopal church in New Jersey for AIDS and AIDS caregivers. We did circle dancing and ritual during the day, and some exchanging of ideas and dreams. At the end of the day a man came up and said, "I have AIDS, I'm not connected with the Episcopal church, but I saw this title, 'Spirituality and AIDS' and was very curious. So I came." And he said, "What most strikes me about this day is that you hardly talked about AIDS at all. We danced circle dances together. We are all players in the universe. That is what I learned: we are all on the same journey. That is what I learned today, and it has given me a lot of energy."

What does it mean to live deeply? Does it mean to live in the fast lane, or to make big money, or fame? It means divine life. We live the divine life. Compassion is happening in the gay community and beyond because of AIDS. Every time compassion births forth, divinity is bursting forth. Meister Eckhart says, "The first act of God, whatever God births, the first outburst is always compassion." Conversions are happening, openings of hearts, discovery of the mystic inside, community building, and celebration.

My advice is that all of us live each day as if it was our first day. That is what a resurrection consciousness is all about. And that is why the Bible begins, as Eckhart says, "in the beginning," because he says, "Wherever God is, God is always in the beginning. God is always new—*novissimus*, the newest thing there is." And we need to live every day as if it was our last day. For the first day and the last day are connected. Our death is a return to our beginning, to our source, to the Godhead from which we all began this journey. Aquinas says, "God is the source without a source." We flow out of the source, we live our days, we do our work, we return to the source. Living deeply is living all Four Paths of Creation Spirituality: the awe and wonder of the Via Positiva, the darkness of the Via Negativa, the breakthrough and creativity of the Via Creativa, and the transformation of the Via Transformativa. We are all supposed to live deeply. That is why AIDS is just one more way to live deeply in the universe. To live out of our inner person and let go of the outer person.

AIDS invites us all to let the outer self go and befriend the true self: the creative person eager to give back to the world our unique gift. In this process we join the mystics of the past and all our ancestors, living and dead. We will come to know what they knew, we will come to taste what they tasted. We will come to grieve at levels at which they grieved. Thomas Aquinas says, "There are times in life when we must roar like a bear out of our grief and lamentation." We all need the heart work that will make us strong mystics and prophets with senses of humor.

I WANT TO end with some practical ways of expanding our hearts and thereby building up courage—"a big heart"—in order to combat fear, so that we may life fully.

I visited the Amazon jungle and met Bishop Casadaliga there, a beautiful mystic, a saint, who works with the Amazon Indians and with the people defending the rain forests, and of course they are the same thing. If the rain forests go, the native people go and vice versa. He's been shot at; he's also been silenced by the Vatican—a beautiful man. And one night, he had eighty church workers there for the week who work for the Indians and the rain-forest defenders, and one night they had a very simple liturgy that was dedicated to our martyrs. Everyone went up and lit a candle and spoke two names they knew of someone who worked personally with them who had been tortured and murdered in the rain forests with the native people. And afterward a man told me, "The hard part was to limit it to two; I know at least ten right off the bat."

The martyrdoms that have gone on in Central America, not only the highly publicized ones of Catholic sisters and

Jesuit priests and their housekeepers, but union leaders and peasants and farmers . . . Just take one of these martyrs into your heart and your heart will grow—just as it did for the early Christians in the first and second centuries. It's part of the resurrection story, that we take in the blood that flows from the big hearts of our brothers and sisters. And what I learned being with these people in Latin America is that they're just like you and me. They're no braver, they're no more saintly, but they have something to teach us. Because in North America, we need courage. We need courage to get at our addictions and to confess them.

A second way to make a heart expand is to breathe. It's very subtle information, especially for Christians, but I do remind you that our hearts are in our bodies and our lungs are in our bodies, and the best way to breathe is to get in touch with our bodies again: to move them in ritual dances, to run, to do yoga, to stretch. Learn to breathe again; don't take breath for granted. Hildegard of Bingen says that prayer is nothing but inhaling and exhaling the one breath of the universe. The one *ruah*, the one Spirit. Let us cease taking breathing for granted. Let us learn to breathe again.

A third way to expand the heart is to drink in awe every day. Drink awe on a daily basis. Awe expands the heart, it expands the mind, it expands the joy. Fear contracts, Aquinas says. Find awe on a daily basis: read the new cosmology. Ernesto Cardenal in Nicaragua has written a six-hundred-page poem, called *Cántico cósmico*, the cosmic song—a celebration of the new cosmology. I went into his library at his home, and all of his books were written in North America, in English—indeed, many of them here in Berkeley—Erich Jansch's *Self-Organizing Universe*, Brian Swimme's and Thomas Berry's *The Universe Story*. The new cosmology has been written in English, and it took a Nicaraguan whose second language, not first language, is English to respond with a great poem about the power of this. Just as we have courage to learn from Latin America, they are learning the new cosmology from us. And they are learning much faster than we're learning courage. Because we ourselves have not been able to take the new cosmology into our hearts and have it expand our forms of worship, for example. And have it wake us up.

A fourth way to expand our hearts is to meditate on the pain. Enter the broken hearts and suffering of our time. Go there, go to an AIDS ward, befriend people with AIDS and who are HIV positive, help out, go to prisons, help out. Stand by, learn the stories of people, help them tell their stories. Honor them by asking them their stories, and all of our hearts will grow.

A fifth way to make your heart grow is to read the mystics. Your heart expands when you read an Eckhart, a Mechtild, or a Hildegard, because these people have done their heart work. You learn to play tennis by playing with someone who knows how to play tennis. So you learn to bring the mystic out of you by playing with the mystics. If you read the mystics with your right brain, with your heart, they will invite the mystic out of us.

A sixth way to expand the heart is through art. All art is heart work. Creating rituals, massage as meditation, painting as meditation, clay as meditation, storytelling, poetry, dream work—we have to let go sometimes of the capitalist definition of art as producing a product and rediscover art as meditation, which is always a process. And remember especially dreams. I have yet to find a person traveling the journey of AIDS who does not have the most amazing dreams to tell. The universe always breaks through with truth in our dreams, and AIDS people are becoming oracles, vehicles with amazing dreams. Invite them to paint their dreams, to tell their dreams, listen to their dreams and to your own dreams. Dreams and liberation, reexperiencing the communion of

saints, the eternal now through our dreams. Entering the
mysteries through our dreams.

A seventh way to expand the heart is to laugh a lot. Paradox is what all struggle is about, all tragedy is about, and all
loving and living are about. To be able to let go through
laughter is a cosmic response to being here. Look for the
irony in things.

Rule number eight for expanding our hearts: let go by
jumping in and doing it. Don't wait for Daddy's permission
to be a mystic, for Daddy's permission to be a prophet, or
for Daddy's permission to create rituals that are effective and
that work. You don't need Daddy's permission for any of
these things. We are all called to be mystics, to be prophets,
and to be ritual makers—to bring about that kind of healing.
A friend of mine who is a Jungian therapist and also a theologian, John Giannini, said that he's convinced that after
years and years of listening to people's stories and dreams
that the addiction behind all addictions is the addiction of
child to parent. And I'm reminded of Jesus' radical words:
unless you leave your father and your mother, you're not
worthy of me. There is no resurrection until we leave our father and our mother in that sense. And that is why we cannot wait around for permission to do what obviously has to
come about. As Eckhart says, we actually assist in the birth of
the Holy Spirit when we break through and realize that we
are sons and daughters of God, because the Son of God
sends the Holy Spirit.

The ninth way to expand the heart is to expand our God
talk. As Eckhart says, "I pray God to rid me of God." To let
God go at times, to let God grow, to let God take on different forms, different colors, different gender from what we
may be used to. To allow our experiences of God to give us
the deeper names of God and to trust those experiences.

And a final way to expand our heart is to work in base
communities. To realize that in the North we have our own

base communities. And they need to be critiqued, they need
to be beefed up with a healthy spirituality. A good example
is Alcoholics Anonymous. AA is a North American invention; it is a base community. The truth is told in AA and
those many spin-offs, Al Anon and so forth. And therefore
community builds. But AA too deserves critique. It needs a
more panentheistic and less theistic theology, a less vertical
patriarchal theology and one that's more rounded. We will
find that all our professions are potential base communities
today. That is to say that all our professions need groups who
are critical and who love the profession—but love it enough
to bring the new paradigm into it, to bring mystical practice
into it.

Let me give you an example. This spring, I was being
driven home from a workshop by a young woman who had
just graduated from Duke med school. She was twenty-four
and a new doctor, and when she was in med school, she and
several of her peers decided that while Western medicine
had something to offer, they wanted to study Eastern medicine along with spirituality. So on their own they would
gather and study Eastern medicine, and they would do mystical practices—read the mystics, etc. Now they're graduat-
ing and they're more than just Western doctors, and they're
going to be leaven in their profession. All of our professions
need these kinds of base communities, groups within them,
because that is what most middle-class people do: prepare
for work by getting educated, then we work, and then we
spend our time recovering from work. Work is where we
give back our blessing. So work deserves to become a place
of base community; we need to bring mysticism and the
new paradigm into our work world, whether it's education
or health work, religion or parenting or any other kind of
work. We need to learn from the base community of
women's groups and now male liberation groups how important it is that we gather to tell our stories.

Finally, two words, one from Peter Russell, the scientist who did the video and book on the *Global Brain*. In an article he says, "The root of our environmental crisis is an inner spiritual aridity. Any truly holistic environmental policy must include this in its approach; we need not only to conduct research in physical and biological sciences, we also need to explore the psychological and more sacred sciences. The true intelligence of our species has yet to shine into this world. We've had glimpses of it from Saint Francis, and Saint Teresa, and all the other saints. But what we've forgotten is that every one of us is a mystic like a Francis or a Teresa. What we need today is a new Manhattan Project. The Manhattan Project was dedicated to breaking open atomic energy. This new Manhattan Project would be dedicated to untapping the enormous potential within human consciousness, the nucleus of our being."

It seems to me that the journey that we will take with AIDS is part of the opening of the nucleus of our being. And when we open to it, as all mystics do, we will learn what Julian of Norwich learned in the fifteenth century: "All will be well, all manner of things will be well." She did not say this from some kind of Pollyanna optimism—she lived through the black death, the most devastating plague of European civilization. Still, out of her broken heart and out of her journey of despair, which included resurrection and hope, she was able to remind us that all will be well, every manner of thing will be well.

CHAPTER 15

Is Creation Spirituality "New Age"?

☾

Intellectually lazy journalists, as well as frightened Christians, often try to dismiss Creation Spirituality as "New Age." The latter use "New Age" as a scapegoat now that there are so few Communists to kick around. But what can be considered "New Age" about a community that is so interested in Thomas Aquinas, Hildegard of Bingen, Meister Eckhart, and others who have been dead for seven hundred to eight hundred years? And in Jesus and the prophets, who are even older? An ecumenical bridge does indeed exist between Creation Spirituality and New Age movements, since both are trying to find their way in a postmodern world. And frankly, I would rather die of New Age than old age and religious sclerosis. But the New Agers that I'm familiar with usually lack the awareness of shadow and injustice that imbues the prophetic tradition of Creation Spirituality and the biblical tradition to which it is heir.

NCREASINGLY, DURING MY recent speaking engagements, people have asked about the relation of Creation Spirituality to New Age. I find the New Age movement—like other human movements—to cover a spectrum that ranges from health to unhealth. In this essay I will attempt an analysis of the differences and likenesses between New Age and Creation Spirituality.

The term New Age is, in fact, derived from Teilhard de Chardin, who said, "We are inevitably approaching a new age in which the world will throw off its chains and at last give itself up to the power of its inner affinities." It is telling that New Agers have paid more attention to this Christian prophet of our century than have most church people. Teilhard in turn gets the idea of a "new age" from Saint Paul. Even the preface for the Eastertime liturgy in the Roman Catholic church uses the term new age.

This origin of the term ought to prove an embarrassment to those who would like to dismiss New Age as some kind of plot of the devil. It also underscores the vast vacuum of eschatology that exists in much contemporary religion and that New Age movements have moved in to fill. "New Age" is apocalyptic, cosmological, and eschatological language. It appeals to the hope for a future. One reason for its success in our time is that the Enlightenment churches and synagogues have lost all sense of the apocalyptic and eschatological. The Quest for the Historical Jesus that has, in historian Jaroslav Pelikan's terminology, "deposed the Cosmic Christ," has denuded the West of apocalyptical, cosmological visions. Creation Spirituality seeks to reestablish the Cosmic Christ movement within the churches and synagogues (for the Cosmic Christ tradition is the preexistent Wisdom tradition of Israel). This awakening would complement and supplement what is called New Age.

A second contribution of New Age has been its insistence on recovering the spirit and energy of body. The awakening to the spiritual power of massage that began in the

1960s at Esalen was no minor breakthrough for white-
dominated Western culture and its centuries-old complex of
body-soul dualisms. Though the West has a tradition—that
of Creation Spirituality—that has insisted on the harmony of
body, soul, and spirit instead of dualism, rarely has that har-
monious tradition been celebrated in mainline Western consciousness. The New Age movement deserves credit for its
celebration both in theory and in practice of body-spirit energies. Creation Spirituality seeks the same. In thirteenth-
century Germany, the creation-centered mystic and social
activist Mechtild of Magdeburg believed likewise when she
wrote,

> Do not disdain your body.
> For the soul
> is just as safe in its body
> as in the Kingdom of Heaven—
> though not so certain.
> Just as daring—
> but not so strong.
> Just as powerful—
> but not so constant.

A third contribution of New Age has been its insistence
on bringing science and religion/spirituality together again.
The New Age seeks a cosmology, and a cosmology cannot
be rediscovered without both a scientific worldview and a
mystical awareness. New Age at its best—as in its appreciation of the work of Gregory Bateson, for example—has
sought both. Creation Spirituality is also committed to recovering a living cosmology and is doing so with the kind
of interaction between scientists and artists and spiritual theologians that takes place in the Institute in Culture and Creation Spirituality, or in the pages of *Creation Spirituality*
magazine.

A fourth effort by New Age that deserves applause from
Creation Spirituality is the effort to reground psychology not
on the fall-redemption motif of "What is your problem?"

but on the basic spiritual motif: "What is your divine power?" What might be called New Age movements in psychology, like Gestalt and transpersonal psychology, were in some regard efforts to celebrate the "Now" of the mystics and to celebrate our capacities for altered states of consciousness. These efforts to reawaken mystical and meditative traditions that honor the presence of the divine in all persons and at all times are laudable. Such efforts at psychic healing and awakening are truer to mystical traditions than previous psychological schools of thought that—in fall-redemption fashion—were problem-oriented instead of power-oriented. Thus, they complement, in part, the movement of Creation Spirituality, which seeks to awaken the mystic in everyone and to draw the divine powers of creativity and compassion from all persons.

Having said these things about certain likenesses between Creation Spirituality and New Age—the New Age that lies at the healthy end of the spectrum—I will now discuss some differences.

1 There is a tendency in some New Agers to cover up the wounds of the Cosmic Christ and to present a Cosmic Christ that has no wounds. This exclusive emphasis on the "light" aspects of the Christ is a flight from the pain of the world, from justice and injustice and the responsibility of everyone to participate in that struggle in some form. It reinforces the comfortable, assuring them that their "heightened state of awareness" somehow legitimizes their refusal to explore the darkness of pain—theirs and others. Many New Agers have a seriously wounded child inside them who is not getting the attention it needs at the level of suffering and mourning and grieving where it is most radically wounded and in need of healing. The result is that light energies, levitations, and spiritual good times banish all lessons learned from the wounds of the Cosmic Christ about serving the *anawim*, or those without a voice.

2 The New Age is sometimes so "new" that it ignores all history and all tradition to its peril. A flight from all tradition—or a quick dash into some foreign one—reinforces the uncritical inheritance of one's past; many a New Ager is an ex-Catholic or an ex-Jew who has not dealt with his or her roots in a critical fashion. The wounds go unattended and the beauty goes unsung. Jung warned that Westerners cannot "pirate wisdom from foreign shores as if our own culture was an error outlived." Our own culture and its religious traditions must be plumbed and challenged to deliver to us the wisdom and mystical heritage that is rightfully ours. Only this deliverance will truly renew our civilization. For a civilization is not changed by the salvation of a few but by reinventing its institutions, including educational ones and religious ones, so that all can participate in renewal.

3 The New Age sometimes appears as a kind of fundamentalism of the rich. It boasts a kind of Gnostic, esoteric, "we are saved and you aren't" mentality that is anything but inclusive. In contrast, the cosmic Wisdom tradition of the Bible is deeply universalist as played with, for example, in the Wisdom literature. It is never elitist. Wisdom, it says, "walks in the streets." Mysticism is everyday and available to all.

4 Some New Agers have been so busy developing their misused right hemispheres that their left hemispheres have been all but forgotten. All the champions of Creation Spirituality celebrate both right and left brains—that is, our capacity for mysticism and our capacity for intellectual work. Hildegard of Bingen said, "All science comes from God," and she insisted that the greatest gift we have all been given is our intellects. She said we should arise every morning and ask ourselves what we are doing today with our intellect to serve the earth and her creatures. The awakening of mysticism and the right brain that Western education and religion have so ignored during the Enlightenment era does not need to take

place at the expense of the left brain or at the expense of a
sense of history and tradition. In fact, as James Hillman
points out, the healthy *senex* or wise person from the older
generations redeems history from being a "statue in the park
for pigeons," to being a place from which we can derive excitement, visions, eschatology, and strength for the contemporary journey that will complement *puer* yearnings to fly
from the earth. Some New Agers are all *puer* and no *senex*,
with an anti-intellectual bias and an ahistorical outlook.
They forget that important test of all authentic mysticism:
the test of paradox and dialectic. Mysticism is not just about
the Now. It is also about the past and the future—that is,
about not-now, or nothing. Healthy mysticism is always
both/and. Creation Spirituality resists all efforts at loboto-
mizing our left brains, our sense of history, or our sense of
responsibility.

5 New Agers love to talk about reincarnation and often ask
if the West has a tradition of reincarnation. Actually, I would
recommend two areas of religious doctrine in the West as
bridge builders in an ecumenical attitude toward reincarnation. One is the doctrine of purgatory. When this doctrine is
divorced from an exclusively fall-redemption mind-set, it is
seen to say the following: we are here to learn love, and if
we don't learn it this time around we are going to learn it
someplace, some time around. The second set of doctrines
that has much in common with reincarnation is that of the
communion of saints and the resurrection of the body. These
doctrines teach that no beauty is lost, that the power of our
ancestors is with us very much at this time, that the form
resurrection takes is complete mystery but that the *fact* of
resurrection is undeniable.

Having pointed out some common ground between
New Age and Creation Spirituality around the topic of rein-

carnation, it is also necessary to underscore an important difference. Certain New Age teachers would have us believe that persons living in oppressive situations—for example, South Africans living in apartheid—actually *chose to be born in such situations*. It is difficult to imagine a more sinister teaching than this one to support movements that are unjust. How thoroughly it reinforces and legitimizes the privileges of the few while the many suffer. Here is New Age at its worst. Here is New Age that has not only lost its left brain but its heart as well. Here, indeed, Creation Spirituality and New Age part ways. As Meister Eckhart put it, "compassion means justice." Justice is the test of all authentic mysticism, and the heaping of riches on comfortable gurus and the ignoring of the cries of Mother Earth and her youth who suffer world over today are no substitute for a living spirituality. I praise New Age for its accomplishments, and I challenge it with the justice demands of age-old Wisdom traditions.

New Age ideas of reincarnation are often built on a laissez-faire view of time, a sense of cyclical complacency that is too self-satisfied for a creation-centered person. Gandhi encountered this in trying to reform his own religion, Hinduism, among those who did not want the caste system questioned and who used as their excuse the fact that the untouchables would be born into a better situation the next time around. But it was Gandhi who confessed that he "learned to say no from the West." It was the Western prophets—Jesus and the others—who insist that this time around *is* the time for the kingdom and queendom of God to happen and for justice to flow like a river. I agree with Gandhi and the Western prophets. As Eckhart put it, "earth must become heaven so that God can find a home here." And as Mechtild of Magdeburg said, "who is the Holy Spirit? The Holy Spirit is a compassionate outpouring of the Creator and the Son. This is why when we on earth pour out compassion and mercy from the depths of our hearts and give to the poor and dedicate our bodies to the service of the broken, to that very extent do we resemble the Holy Spirit." This is the New Age I believe in. It deserves to be reclaimed—both within the churches and without.

On Desentimentalizing Spirituality

☾

Creation Spirituality is a nonsentimental spirituality, committed as it is to ecological and social justice and to both an intellectual and a feeling life. The media as well as fundamentalist religion, on the contrary, often link hands in sentimentalizing both culture and religion. Given the power of this alliance in American culture today, it seems fitting to conclude a collection of essays on Creation Spirituality in everyday life with this essay on Desentimentalizing Spirituality.

Mass culture and especially the mass media thrive on titillation and sentimentalism. More and more of "mainstream media" news demonstrates a National Enquirer sort of appeal. But sentimentalism and violence go hand in hand. If we are looking for origins of violence in our culture, we ought to take a close look at sentimental religion and media for the illusory values they promote. Raising our consciousness about *sentimentalism can help convert us from religion to spiritual-ity, from childishness to childlikeness, from fear to love and justice—even from violence to nonviolence.*

L ECTURING A FEW years ago to a convention of campus min-isters, I inserted into my talk a reference to C. J. Jung's remark that violence and sentimentalism go hand in hand, the one being merely the obverse side of the other. Afterward a Lutheran pastor approached me and asked where he could go to pursue the subject of sentimentality more thoroughly. I told him I simply did not know; sentimentalism was itself a re-pressed topic in America and even in theological scholarship.

Now I know. If the gentleman is reading this essay, or for anyone else who is tempted to investigate sentimentalism and its origins in American culture, go to Ann Douglas's book *The Feminization of American Culture*, subtitled: "How the Victorian al-liance between women and the clergy, and the popular litera-ture to which that alliance gave birth, fostered a sentimental society and the beginnings of modern mass culture" (New York: Knopf, 1977). Ann Douglas teaches American literature and culture at Columbia University and has published in those fields. This, her first book, has already received numer-ous and well-earned complimentary reviews—but none, as far as I know, from any spiritual theologian. Because the im-plications of her study are so pertinent to spirituality, I would like to interact with her book in this essay.

WHAT IS SENTIMENTALISM?

Webster's New Collegiate Dictionary defines sentimentalism rather innocuously as "the disposition to favor or indulge in sentimentality," and it defines sentimentality as "resulting from feeling rather than reason or thought." Ann Douglas is much more thorough in her examination of sentimentalism. Refusing to define it out of the head or a priori, she postpones a definition until two-thirds of the way through her book. The journey leading up to her definition takes the reader through the loss of power and status among clergy and women in the nineteenth century, when the Industrial Revolution removed the authentic moral issues and decision making of the day from church and home into factory and marketplace. The reader journeys into some of the emotional consequences for both these groups when the important energies of culture (such as economic ones) suddenly left the sphere of their interest. Ann Douglas teaches sentimentalism by example for 254 pages, by reporting the new sphere of influence that clergy and women sought—namely, harmless pulpit preaching by the one group and journals and magazine articles dedicated to cultivating general sweetness by the other. It is not a pleasant journey.

The Industrial Revolution meant, insists Douglas, that women were no longer producers in the economy but consumers. "Middle-class women in the Northeast after 1830 were far more interested in the purchase of clothing than in the making of cloth," she observes (p. 51). Women lost both their right to vote and their right to participate in the specialized professions of a medical corps, even though they had worked as midwives for centuries. "Women no longer marry to help their husbands get a living, but to help them spend their income" (52). As the marketplace became more and more thoroughly male and competitive, "the lady's preoccupation is to be with herself: her clothes, her manners, her feelings, her family" (57). The cultivation of domestic piety was to be the woman's full-time occupation and that of the clergy as well.

The compensation for this loss of real power was a pedestal piety that put both women and clergy "above" the everyday world of work and economics. "Indulgence," observed English radical Harriet Martineau, "is given as a substitute for justice." The German visitor Charles Follen commented that in America "women and clergymen are most honored," while lawyers and businessmen have "the greatest influence."[1] What did middle-class women do in addition to buying clothes (often ones that flattered at a price of considerable discomfort)? They wrote and read "domestic novels" that were "themselves courses in the shopping mentality" (62). The novel was the mass medium of the middle classes of the nineteenth century and served the purpose of "uncritical self-confirmation and instantaneous satisfaction of their appetites" admirably (63).

And what about clergymen? Orville Dewey, a Unitarian minister from New York, felt that as a minister he was "not fairly thrown into the field of life . . . [but rather] hedged around with artificial barriers . . . a sort of moral eunuch." He complained of his treatment in a large American city: "People say, while turning a corner, 'How do you do, Doctor?' Which is very much as if they said, 'How do you do, Abstraction?' " (22). While seventeenth- and eighteenth-century clergy had often farmed and been financially independent, those of the nineteenth century grew more and more dependent on parishioners who were making a living in the capitalist marketplace. The previous generations of clergy had participated in hot political debates, but the dependent nineteenth-century clergy offered "a fundamentally passive" position to the most intense issue of that era, slavery (33). The result was a "trivialized piety" (41) and a cultural isolation that was rivaled only by that of the American lady. The minister's place "was increasingly in the Sunday school, the parlor, and the library, among women and those who flattered and resembled them" (43).

So much for some examples of sentimentalism from women and clergy. What is Douglas's definition of it? On page 254 she finally lays it out for us: "Sentimentalism might be defined as the political sense obfuscated or gone rancid. Sentimentalism, unlike the modes of genuine sensibility, never exists except in tandem with failed political consciousness." A recent phenomenon whose appearance is linked with capitalist development, sentimentalism presents distractions of sheer publicity. "Sentimentalism is a cluster of ostensibly private feelings which always attain public and conspicuous expression. Privacy functions in the rituals of sentimentalism only for the sake of titillation, as a convention to be violated. Involved as it is with the exhibition and commercialization of the self, sentimentalism cannot exist without an audience." Thus Douglas lays bare the poisons of what she calls the "heresy of sentimentalism" or what she also labels "feminization"—a heresy of rancid political consciousness, of distraction from life's deeper mysteries, of privatization, of titillation, and, finally, of commercialization by way of publicity.

SEVEN SINS OF SENTIMENTALISM

How sentimental is the spirituality of the nineteenth century? Very, very sentimental. This is the judgment not only of the American Protestant scene that Douglas investigates so thoroughly, but of much of nineteenth-century European Roman Catholicism as well. One need only consider the hagiographic abuses heaped on a person like Thérèse of Lisieux or visit European cathedrals to see how nineteenth-century piety tried to cover up with emotive offerings and plaques of piety what was once beautifully simple. One might also consult scholars of the period, one of whom, for example, frankly confesses that "sentimentality was à la mode in the spirituality" of nineteenth-century France.[2] Although Douglas's study does not treat this subject, I strongly suspect that a serious investigation of Roman Catholic spirituality in America of the past century would find it much less sentimental than either its European counterpart or its native Protestant counterpart, for the simple reason that being a church of the immigrant poor, it simply could not afford the middle-class preoccupations that sentimentalism presumed.

The strength of Douglas's analysis is to point out how essentially a sentimental culture depends on a sentimental piety and spirituality. Confessing a "belief in the centrality of religion in the American experience," Douglas leaves the believer with no doubt whatsoever about her or his primary challenge: "to understand, resist, and vivify our culture" (ix). In other words, to remove sentimentalism from spirituality is to remove its most radical legitimization from our culture. It is to cause an authentic kind of cultural revolution.

What would be the result of this revolution? A society sans the sins of sentimentalism. And what might some of these sins be?

1 *Materialism.* The subject-object relations that are so central to a consumer-oriented society derive their sick energies from sentimentalism, according to Douglas. Advertising, "the only faith of a secularized consumer society" (68), came into its own in America from 1860–1890. Nathaniel Fowler, the pope of American advertising, declared that all advertisements, even those for male shoppers, were to be directed toward women since the woman "buys, or directs the buying of . . . everything from shoes to shingles." Thus, "the feminine occupation of shopping," comments Douglas, "would constitute the dream-life of the nation" (67).

2 *Anti-intellectualism.* A sentimentalized and materialistic society depends on the loss of critical concern or caring. It de-

mands "the death of the critical instinct" that eventually involves the preparation of the individual for the role of consumer. For the consumer is by definition the person with no interest in theorizing, the person possessed of only the haziest powers of discernment (189). Ideas count, insists Douglas. Without them there will be no communal values, goals, or thinking. There will be only emotional supportiveness lacking all structure and theorizing. Without ideas, ideology reigns and public relations substitute for thinking. A religion without ideas will become mere "window dressing for the forces which control . . . society" (166).

In fact, anti-intellectualism found its way into the basic symbols and theology of American religion. On the cover of the *Christian Parlor Magazine* of June 1846 is an engraving of "The Good Shepherd" that pictures Christ in a fashion that resembles "nothing so much as Little Bo Peep" (234). The Scriptures are also victims of this sentimentalizing; one heroine comments on her preference for the biblical creation story over Darwin's with the following argument: "I think it is a good deal easier to believe the Garden of Eden story, especially as that's pretty and poetical, and is in the dear old Book that is so sweet and comfortable to us" (251). Theology gives way to smiles, kissing of babies, and public relations.

3 *Anti-aestheticism.* In sentimentalized culture, art lacks any intellectual dimension as a search for truth. It becomes mere entertainment—and elitist entertainment at that. Douglas is witty and brilliant in laying bare the roots of American philistinism and prejudice against the arts—what has been referred to as our collective Andy Hardy syndrome. Materialism and the insecurities it generates in the artist account for many of the mass-produced objects that lack any pretensions to art. This lack of art only makes the object more attractive to the consumer for "it can be read casually, then forgotten.

Its very insignificance frees the consumer from guilt" (238). Art and artist fall victim to consumerism, anti-intellectualism, and elitism. Taste, not creativity, bolsters a separate world called art.

4 *Anti-body.* Sentimentalism was the sure underfooting for a Victorian attitude that wanted to pretend that people were not bodily. Sentimentalized religion was only too eager to oblige. Sarah Hale comments that in a true Christian civilization, "the men must become more like women, and the women more like angels" (108). In numerous journals women are idealized to the point of having no body, no personality. "Physicality itself is painfully absent. The constant reiteration of feminine 'purity' . . . was not only a denial of patriarchal values, but of matriarchal ones" (46). In the *Ladies Magazine* of 1830 we read about the proper female:

> See, she sits, she walks, she speaks, she looks—unutterable things! Inspiration springs up in her very paths—it follows her foot-steps. A halo of glory encircles her, and illumines her whole orbit. With her, man not only feels safe but is actually renovated. For he approaches her with an awe, a reverence, and an affection which before he knew not he possessed. (46)

As Douglas observes, the opening line in particular sounds strikingly similar to an advertisement for a doll.

Included in the anti-body attitudes and the flight from healthy pleasure lies an implicit though very prominent masochism. Sentimentalism is masochistic in its pleasure energies. Many clergy, Douglas points out, suffered so much self-doubt that "the only viable role" they could envision for themselves was "that of victim" (20). The pious heroine of the novels of the period learned to consent to pain and play the role of "the immolated one" (194).

The masochist needs a sadist, and it would seem that the compulsion toward combative competition that is so prevalent in American mass culture (for example, its professional sports and its male-female relationships) is a working out of that basic pleasure energy: who will control whom? Masochism and sadism reign as the substitutes for love in a violent—that is, sentimental—society.

5 *Prodeath.* One might rightly inquire where the energies of a person and a culture go if not into thinking, bodily sharing, and the arts—in other words, if they do not go toward living. The answer is that they go toward death. A sentimentalized worldview is one that glorifies death and extols the afterlife rather than the present life.

No one could accuse the nineteenth century of being silent on the subject of death. The memoirs of women and clergy in this period, observes Douglas, were nothing if not "exercises in necrophilia" (200). The children of many popular stories were notable "less for their lives which were usually short, than for their deaths which were often protracted" (201). The nineteenth century gave us the Sunday school movement and the elaborate cemetery. It also gave us the undertaking business, which specializes in making the dead over into dolls and thus obfuscates the reality of death. Victorian graves resembled "enlarged victory trophies" (202), as if what the dead failed to win in life they could now claim in death.

Consolation literature abounded with the most elaborate explanations of what the afterlife consisted of. In fact, heaven proved to be a projection of middle-class hopes of the period. Finally, ministers and women have a sphere of influence: it is heaven, where they "become at last the only genuine authorities" (203). As if to prolong this spirituality's flight from the earth, coffins were invented that would only slowly disintegrate. According to the tombstone engravings, people did not die; they were "asleep in Jesus." Visits to elaborately decorated cemeteries were commonplace holiday

excursions. The cemetery "functioned as a Disney World for
the mortuary imagination of Victorian America" (210).

Novels—as well as hymns, sermons, and treatises—were
written about heaven. It was a place where families were re-
united and where nurseries were available for children who
died before their parents. Day-care centers after life if not
before death! But it was by no means an attractive place.
Nathaniel Emmons preached, "The truth is there is nothing
which God requires men to do in this life in order to go to
heaven that is harder to be done, than to be willing to be in
heaven" (222). Heaven becomes a "celestial retirement village"—the ultimate fulfillment of the pleasures of a consumer society.

6 *Ageism*. Sentimental piety treats both children and old persons as objects—objects of pity and feeling, of course, but
objects nonetheless. An *ecclesia* with no adult interests in politics, body, art, or thinking becomes in fact a nursery. Clergy
begin to feel that they have to smile continually and even
like all children. Family becomes an idol and a refuge. "Domestic life," wrote one minister, is "that life in which now
almost all our joys or sorrows are centered" (113). In the
literature of the period, children often play a narcissistic role
for the parent who is busy "multiplying her image by creating little domesticated replicas of her life" (252). In this
process of sentimentalizing children, what is most significant is that adults never grow up.

Ministers speak of the elderly as "fossilized, weakened,
sentimentalized. The emotions they arouse in us are more
important than the emotions they feel; they have been de-
flected precisely through their gray hairs and silvered piety
from subjects to objects" (196). The reason for ageism, according to Douglas, is that "the aged are by definition close
to the feminine ideal: they are pious creatures of the Sabbath
destined to embody the virtues of debility, pensioners of

memory unfit for competition with the world" (370, n. 105).

7 *Injustice.* The final sin of sentimentalism is that injustice remains uncriticized and the claims of the violent and powerful are perpetuated over the claims of the powerless and the authentic sufferer. In a spirituality of self-immolation, as Douglas comments, "morality is strangely irrelevant" (73). For a justice-based morality presumes intellectual decision making no less than bodily awareness. It presumes a world beyond the home. Justice, being an affair not merely of the heart, would have no place in an anti-intellectual, anti-body worldview. Harriet Beecher Stowe commented on the lack of a "sense of justice" in her time. She rebukes the "utter deadness to the sense of justice" that prevails in religion and culture and which is itself promulgated "as a special grace and virtue" among women (380, n. 76). Ignorance is spiritual bliss.

Without any community of value derived from a thinking out of common goals, what would be worth getting angry about, except one's property or other objects (for example, one's slaves or women)? History is not conceived as a challenge to redo or recreate society so much as a nostalgic trip, a reinforcing of society's only agreed-upon value: that of material possessions. Women and clergy became preoccupied with "what he or she owns, with what in an almost biological sense belongs to her or him, whether family, home, job, or even the sense of self" (199). It was this anal need to cling to objects rather than a commitment to what people might become that offered the sole substratum for morals. Little wonder that the word *morality* came to mean private, especially homebound, concerns. Little wonder that in place of justice the religion of clergy and women sought to exert influence, which meant "totally consensus and conformist thought" (198). To be everything to everyone is to stand for nothing important.

Douglas is by no means suggesting that there were no politically conscious persons or prophets in the nineteenth century. She affirms only that as a rule, they were hardly honored by the sentimentalized mass culture—which, it seems, might be a general rule of thumb for all the prophets from the ancient Hebrews on. But she makes a careful and significant distinction between the romantics who *did* have a political awareness and who therefore were not sentimental, and the sentimentalists. Among the former she would put, for example, Margaret Fuller and Herman Melville. Precisely what distinguishes them is that they fall into none of the seven sins of sentimentalism that I have presented.

SENTIMENTALISM AND CONTEMPORARY CULTURE

Ann Douglas has studied American sentimentalism in the nineteenth century. How about our own times? It seems that the sentimentalism detected by Douglas in the novels, sermons, and journals—the mass media—of the past century has returned with a vengeance in the media today. The difference is the overriding presence of the new media, especially, of course, television, which ensures that sentimentalism need not await a capacity or decision to read but may begin as soon as a child can see images. The signs that Douglas detects for sentimentalism, such as publicity, titillation, public relations, and advertising, are not things of the past: they are only better organized, funded, and sold.

Have you ever wondered, for example, why it is that fires—or plane crashes—occupy so many of the headlines, whereas the daily deaths of unemployment, underfed children, schools that do not teach, and inhuman prisons make the news only when a titillating subject accompanies them?

In a recent issue of a major American newspaper, the headlines and front pages covered such subjects as a murder, a rape, and a plane crash, while on page fifty-six we read an article about how more poor people live in America today than at any time in the past decade.

Tellingly, America's largest news digest empire, Time Incorporated, in giving birth to its two recent offspring, gave us one magazine called *Money* and another called *People*, which seems to be a slick gossip sheet, sort of a movie-star magazine for adults (or adult look-alikes). ABC Television Network boasted as head of its News Division a man named Roone Arledge, who also doubles as president of ABC Sports. He has been described as a "manipulative showman" who "doesn't even try" to differentiate between news and sport.[3] News is now entertainment, and entertainment is stimulating gossip, as in the sadistic coverage of the Son of Sam murder case by many major newspapers and television networks, and as is clear in the excessive press coverage of the O. J. Simpson murder trial. As one commentator has put it, "the new 'ABC Evening News' under Arledge has taken a turn toward 'tabloid journalism,' a sort of 'pop news' being perpetrated by publisher Rupert Murdoch's trashy *New York Post*."[4] One journalist, especially notorious for his sensational treatment of this same murder case, put his "morality" bluntly: "If the reader buys it, it's moral."[5] So much for sentimental sins one and seven.

What are the motives behind all this gossip-as-news and sadism-as-entertainment? Ratings. And money. And greed. Can we look for some relief soon? It seems highly unlikely, since today chains control 71 percent of newspaper circulation and this proportion is rising monthly—a fact that might help to explain why more and more large-circulation newspapers are beginning to look either like *Ladies Home Journal* in their contents or like *National Enquirer* in their headlines. It would be the height of naïveté to expect from news chains any news of those who suffer in our society. Their boards of trustees hardly got where they are through the exercise of compassion. This might explain why only recently the *Detroit News* promoted an editor who recommended turning the paper's back on urban problems in favor of "sex, comedy, and tragedy."

Sex is being exploited in the media more than ever. A legitimate place exists for the bodily and sexual in our lives and media, certainly. To repress the sensual would be to reproduce sentimental sin four. But media exploitation of sex is not the same as an appreciation of bodily truth, as one writer comments.

"Most television producers use sex to titillate, not to form; sex is becoming the functional equivalent of violence. The fact that violence is going off the air and the networks are in a ratings battle means that sex will be the next subject to be dealt with in an extensive manner," says Michael Lepner of Benton and Bowles. Adds adman Joel Segal: "With the trend away from violence, what do you do for excitement? Sex."[6]

We have a revelation here: the trend is toward excitement rather than ecstasy; toward titillation, rather than deeply felt experience—in other words, toward . . . sentimentalism. Sex used in this way then becomes one more abuse of our bodies and their wonderful and beautiful possibilities for expressing love, truth, and intimacy.

Given the current state of much of the media, we need to ask whether the "dream life of the nation" has not reached, through television's commercial industry that offers "instantaneous satisfaction of appetites" to all comers, that zenith which Douglas called the "feminine occupation of shopping." As the producers and advertisers of America's sentimental and violent Sunday Super Bowl ceremonies

demonstrate, there are those in America who have a great
stake in keeping the rest of us sentimentalized. They wield
great power in the media industry.

DESENTIMENTALIZING:
THE TASK FOR SPIRITUALITY

A people's primary worldview—and therefore the basis for
their spirituality—is the culture in which they live. Culture
provides individuals and groups with their language, symbols, and values and the projection of same onto institutions
of all kinds, from family to media to education and com-
merce. No Christian or incarnational spirituality can be
without a critical look at culture. Since the media play so
significant a role in social education today, a living spirituality will address the media for their sentimental suppositions
and offer alternative ways of life. It will take the seven sins of
sentimentalism and put the hard questions they suggest to
media and culture.

Yet to offer authentic alternatives to sentimentalized living, spirituality needs first to critique itself. As Douglas has
demonstrated, nineteenth-century religion was part of the
problem, not the solution, of sentimentalism. What can we
say of twentieth-century religious spiritualities? On the negative side, there seems still to be no lack of sentimentalized
spiritualities—gatherings of folks as well as academic programs that offer no integration of body and spirit, of arts
and the intellectual life, of sociopolitical realities of the body
politic, of injustice and skills to cope with it. In short, many
spiritualities are perpetuating the violent sentimentalism of a
century ago, and this is especially true in American Catholicism, which has recently become so comfortably middle
class. There is a materialistic curiosity, for example, about

cures (which is not at all the same as an interest in the broader and deeper movements of healing). There are public churchmen who wallow in the masochistic spirituality of their seminary training by referring to themselves as immolated victims, à la the pious heroines of nineteenth-century novels. A trivialized piety still haunts parochial life, where so much energy is expended over issues such as communion in the hand rather than, for example, hands working in communion to rebuild neighborhoods and broken people and to create humanizing working conditions and jobs. There is violence masquerading as religion in the often fascistically inclined movements to sentimentalize family life, no less than in certain quarters of the antiabortion movement that so often sentimentalizes fetal life while ignoring the rights of those already born to decent work, housing, education, and health care. And there persists the responsibility that religion holds for anti-intellectualism in America—a picture painted by Hofstader and repeated by Douglas: "To the extent that it becomes accepted in any culture that religion is largely an affair of the heart or of the intuitive qualities of the mind and that the rational mind is irrelevant or worse," to that extent will ideas be considered dangerous or unimportant.[7]

On the cheerier side, some religious spiritualities are rediscovering their nonsentimentalized origins. For example, biblical exegetes such as Jose Miranda are asking more public and less domesticated questions of Scripture. The results are powerful and long range in their potential impact for de-sentimentalizing society, as, for example, Miranda's critique of what the West has done to the biblical notion of love. He writes, "One of the most disastrous errors in the history of Christianity is to have tried—under the influence of Greek definitions—to differentiate between love and justice."[8] The bringing together of love and justice will prove a giant exorcising of sentimental sin seven. Theologians are insisting that religion's own institutions are proper places to begin critical analysis and social reconstruction.[9] A return to biblical spirituality will mean a bypassing of the overly introverted and privatized "God and me" spirituality that the West has been locked into under the overriding influence of Augustine.

The desentimentalizing of death is being accomplished by persons like Elizabeth Kübler-Ross and Ernest Becker. The latter has wisely pointed out how it is ultimately the fear of life, ecstasy, and letting go that is responsible for the fear of death. This capacity to let go of life implies a trust of self and body that is being learned by persons through a myriad of methods, including Eastern practices of yoga, tai chi, and the experiencing of sexuality as mysticism. The recovery of our authentic heroes or saints as rooted in political-bodily-imaginative lives and cultural periods—in other words, the critical understanding of hagiography as distinguished from a sentimentalizing of saints—is a hopeful sign. The development of crafts such as potting and carpentry and photography as authentic spiritual disciplines—these too announce the beginning of the end of sin three, the elitism of art.

The refusal of women—married, single, and celibate—to be pampered children or objects of "little nun" or "good sister" stereotypes—this marks the end of masochism and the beginning of the end of sadism in a society. Christian movements for the rights of gay persons such as Dignity (the Roman Catholic organization) and Integrity (the Episcopalian organization) also mark the beginning of integrating sexuality, politics, and spirituality, and at the same time show the mainstream heterosexual society how to renew itself along similar moral principles instead of with emotional panegyrics to "family."

These are just a few examples of hope in the spiritual renewal of our culture—hope that desentimentalizing has begun and with it, perhaps, some authentic and adult spirituality might be born. Archbishop Helder Camera, in a brief but powerful book called *Spiral of Violence*, insists that the first stage of violence is not the confrontations the media show us between rebels and police but is in fact the injustice that creates rebels in the first place. Here we see the intimate connection between violence and sentimentalism—that kind of exaggerated feeling that ignores injustice and thereby perpetuates it. To desentimentalize self, society, and spirituality is to begin to build a people where violence finds no home.

Testing the spirits against the seven sins of sentimentalism offered in this essay can only be a beginning to spiritual education. Significantly, in the spiritual process of desentimentalizing, we have authentic Via Negativa, a true dismantling of the symbols, structures, and self-images that we now have. There is implied in this, as in any Via Negativa, a dying—a dying to the violence and sentimentalism that so adeptly covers up violence in our society; a dying to the titillation and consumerist preoccupations of a violent culture; a dying to the introverted spiritualities that pit body against spirit, others against self, artists and idea people against everybody, thereby creating violence within ourselves and among ourselves. It means a dying to ersatz ecstasies that offer highs without bodies, history, politics, art, economics, work—domesticated and sissy highs that are based on repression, not expression. Thanks to Ann Douglas's hard work and insightful questioning, we have a map for taking personal and institutional stock of spirituality's primary task today: to desentimentalize itself and by this process to contribute boldly to desentimentalizing American culture.

NOTE

1. For example, Willie Lee Rose, "American Women in Their Place," *New York Review of Books*, 14 July 1977, 3, and 15 September 1967, 19.

2. Charles Berthlot du Chesnay, "Direction spirituelle en Occident du 17 siècle à nos jours," *Dictionnaire de spiritualité*, vol. 3 (Paris: Beauchesne, 1957), 1135.

3. Gary Deeb, "ABC News Fumbles Its Credibility," *Chicago Tribune*, 14 October 1977, 11.

4. Ibid.

5. Tony Schwartz, "Mr. Blood-and-Guts," *Newsweek*, 17 October 1977, 67.

6. Arthur Lubow, "Soap Hits the Fan," *New York Times*, 2 September 1977, 67.

7. Richard Hofstader, *Anti-Intellectualism in American Life* (New York: Knopf, 1963), 47.

8. Jose Miranda, *Marx and the Bible* (Maryknoll, N.Y.: Orbis Books, 1974), 61.

9. For example, Marie Augusta Neal, *A Socio-Theology of Letting Go* (New York: Paulist Press, 1977); Gregory Baum, *Religion and Alienation* (New York: Paulist Press, 1975); Eulalio Baltazar, *The Dark Center* (New York: Paulist Press, 1973).

SOURCES FOR ESSAYS
that Appear in *Wrestling with the Prophets*

1 "A Mystical Cosmology: Toward a Postmodern Spirituality," in *Sacred Interconnections*, David Ray Griffen, ed., State University of New York Press, 1990, 15–33.

2 "Religion As If Creation Mattered," in *Resurgence* no. 154, (September–October 1992), 24–28.

3 "Creation Mysticism and the Return of a Trinitarian Christianity: Theology in Ecological Perspective," Address to the National Association of College Teachers, New Orleans, La., 1990.

4 "Creation-Centered Spirituality from Hildegard to Julian: Three Hundred Years of an Ecological Spirituality in the West," in *Cry of the Environment: Rebuilding the Christian Creation Tradition*, Philip N. Joranson and Ken Butigan, eds., Santa Fe, N.M.: Bear and Co., 1984, 85–106.

5 "Thomas Aquinas: Mystic and Prophet of the Environment," in *Creation Spirituality* vol. 8, no. 4 (July–August 1992), 33–35.

6 "Native Teachings: Spirituality with Power," in *Creation Spirituality* vol. 2, no. 6 (January–February 1987), 10 ff.

7 "Howard Thurman: Creation-Centered Mystic from the African-American Tradition," in *Creation Spirituality* vol. 7, no. 2 (March–April 1991), 8 ff.

8 "Creation Spirituality and the Dreamtime," in *Creation Spirituality and the Dreamtime*, edited by Catherine Hammond, Newtown, Australia: Millennium Books, 1991, 1–19.

9 "Liberation Theology and Creation Spirituality," in *Creation Spirituality* vol. 2, no. 2 (May–June 1986), 28 ff.

10 "Meister Eckhart and Karl Marx: The Mystic as Political Theologian," in *Understanding Mysticism*, Richard Woods, O.P., ed., Garden City, N.Y.: Doubleday, 1980, 541–63.

11 "Otto Rank on the Artistic Journey as a Spiritual Journey," in *Spirituality Today* vol. 31, no. 1 (March 1979), 73–83.

12 "Deep Ecumenism, Ecojustice, and Art as Meditation." To be published in the German theological journal, *Ökumenische Rundschau*.

13 "The Spiritual Journey of the Homosexual . . . and Just About Everyone Else," in *A Challenge to Love: Gay and Lesbian Catholics in the Church*, Robert Nugent, ed., New York: Crossroad, 1987, 189–204.

14 "AIDS and the Quest for an Authentic Spirituality," Address to Catholic Charities, Diocese of Oakland, California, October 1990.

15 "Is Creation Spirituality 'New Age'?" in *Creation Spirituality* vol. 4, no. 3 (July–August 1988), 10 ff.

Conclusion

"On Desentimentalizing Spirituality," in *Spirituality Today* vol. 30, no. 1 (March 1978), 64–76.